TORCH BIBLE COMMENTARIES

General Editors

THE REV. JOHN MARSH, D.PHIL.
Principal of Mansfield College, Oxford

THE VERY REV. ALAN RICHARDSON, D.D.
Dean of York

FOREWORD TO SERIES

The aim of this series of commentaries on books of the Bible is to provide the general reader with the soundest possible assistance in understanding the message of each book considered as a whole and as a part of the Bible.

The findings and views of modern critical scholarship on the text of the Bible have been taken fully into account; but we have asked the writers to remember that the Bible is more than a quarry for the practice of erudition; that it contains the message of the living God.

We hope that intelligent people of varying interests will find that these commentaries, while not ignoring the surface difficulties, are able to concentrate the mind on the essential Gospel contained in the various books of the Bible.

Volumes in the series include

EZEKIEL

Introduction and Commentary
by

D. M. G. STALKER

SCM PRESS LTD
BLOOMSBURY STREET LONDON

S B N 334 00435 7

First published 1968

© SCM Press Ltd 1968

Printed in Great Britain by
Northumberland Press Limited
Gateshead

CONTENTS

II

ORACLES AGAINST FOREIGN NATIONS

25.1–32.32

III

ISRAEL'S RESTORATION

33.1–39.29

A*

IV

THE FUTURE TEMPLE AND COMMUNITY

40.1–48.35

DIAGRAMS

BIBLIOGRAPHY

There is no up-to-date commentary in English. The best is:

G. A. COOKE, *Ezekiel* (ICC), 1936.

Useful material is also to be found in:

A. B. DAVIDSON, *Ezekiel* (Cambridge Bible), 1892.
W. F. LOFTHOUSE, *Ezekiel* (Century Bible), Edinburgh, 1907.
Israel after the Exile (Clarendon Bible, Old Testament, 4), 1928.
H. WHEELER ROBINSON, *Two Hebrew Prophets*, London, 1948 (the chapters on Ezekiel).

A thorough review of the present-day discussion is given in H. H. Rowley, 'The Book of Ezekiel in Modern Study', *BJRL* 36, 1953, pp. 146-90.

The main German commentaries are:

A. BERTHOLET, *Hezekiel* (HAT 13), 1936.
G. FOHRER, *Ezechiel* (HAT 13), 1955.
W. EICHRODT, *Der Prophet Hesekiel* (Das Alte Testament Deutsch), Göttingen, vol. I, 1959; vol. II, 1966; ET in preparation.
W. ZIMMERLI, *Ezechiel* (Biblischer Kommentar), Neukirchen, 1955 ff.

Other books cited, often by author's name only, are as follows (when there are two entries under one author, subsequent references are to his commentary unless otherwise stated):

P. AUVRAY, *Ezéchiel* (commentary), Paris, 1947.
Ezéchiel (La Sainte Bible de Jérusalem), Paris, 1957.

A. BERTHOLET, *Das Buch Hesekiel* (Kurzer Hand-Commentar zum Alten Testament 12), Freiburg im Breisgau, 1897.

H. BRANDENBURG, *Hezekiel*, Giessen and Basle, 1965.

L. E. BROWNE, *Ezekiel and Alexander*, London, 1952.

R. BRUNNER, *Ezechiel* (Prophezei 8, 9), Zürich, 1944.

A. BRUNO, *Ezechiel: eine rhythmische und textkritische Untersuchung*, Stockholm, 1959.

C. H. CORNILL, *Das Buch des Propheten Ezechiel*, Leipzig, 1886.

A. B. EHRLICH, *Randglossen zur hebräischen Bibel* V, *Ezechiel*, Leipzig, 1912.

S. FISCH, *Ezekiel* (The Soncino Bible), London, 1950.

G. FOHRER, *Die Hauptprobleme des Buches Ezechiel* (BZAW 72), 1952.

V. HERNTRICH, *Ezechielprobleme* (BZAW 61), 1932.

J. HERRMANN, *Ezechiel* (KAT), Leipzig, 1924.

G. HÖLSCHER, *Hesekiel, der Dichter und das Buch* (BZAW 39), 1924.

C. G. HOWIE, *The Date and Composition of Ezekiel* (*JBL* Monograph Series IV), Philadelphia, 1950.
Ezekiel, Daniel (LBC), 1961.

W. A. IRWIN, *The Problem of Ezekiel*, Chicago, 1942.

R. KRAETZSCHMAR, *Das Buch Ezechiel* (Hand-Commentar zum Alten Testament III 3. i), Göttingen, 1900.

H. G. MAY, 'The Book of Ezekiel', *The Interpreter's Bible 6*, New York and Nashville, 1956.

N. MESSEL, *Ezechielfragen* (Skrifter utgitt av Det Norske Videnskaps-Akademi i Oslo II, Hist.-Filos. Klasse), 1945, No. 1.

J. MUILENBURG, 'Ezekiel' in *Peake's Commentary on the Bible*, new ed. by M. Black, London and Edinburgh, 1962, pp. 568-90.

K. VON RABENAU, 'Die Entstehung des Buches Ezechiel in formgeschichtlicher Sicht', *Wissenschaftliche Zeitschrift der Martin-Luther-Universität Halle-Wittemberg*, Gesellschafts-und sprachwissenschaftliche Reihe, Heft 4 (1955/56), pp. 659-94.

H. GRAF REVENTLOW, *Wächter über Israel* (BZAW 82), 1962.

J. W. ROTHSTEIN, 'Das Buch Ezechiel' in E. Kautzsch, *Die Heilige Schrift des Alten Testaments* I, Tübingen, 1922, pp. 868-1000.

H. SCHMIDT, *Die Grossen Propheten* (Die Schriften des Alten Testaments in Auswahl II 2), Göttingen, 1923.

M. SCHUMPP, *Das Buch Ezechiel* (Die Heilige Schrift für das Leben erklart), Freiburg, 1942.

J. SKINNER, *The Book of Ezekiel* (The Expositor's Bible), London, 1895.

R. SMEND, *Der Prophet Ezechiel* (Kurzgefasstes exegetisches Handbuch zum Alten Testament 8), Leipzig, 1880.

J. SMITH, *The Book of the Prophet Ezekiel*, London, 1931.

F. SPADAFORA, *Ezechiele*, Turin and Rome, 1951.

J. STEINMANN, *Le prophète Ezéchiel et les débuts de l'exil* (Lectio divina 13), Paris, 1953.

C. C. TORREY, *Pseudo-Ezekiel and the Original Prophecy*, New Haven, 1930.

C. H. TOY, *Ezekiel* (Sacred Books of the Old Testament 12), London, 1899.

J. ZIEGLER, *Ezechiel* (Echten Bibel 6), Würzburg, 1953.

W. ZIMMERLI, *Erkenntnis Gottes nach dem Buche Ezechiel* (Abhandlungen zur Theologie des Alten und Neuen Testaments 27), Zürich, 1954.

ABBREVIATIONS

AV	Authorized Version of the Bible
BA	*Biblical Archaeologist*, New Haven
BASOR	*Bulletin of the American Schools of Oriental Research*, Baltimore
BJRL	*Bulletin of the John Rylands Library*, Manchester
BZAW	Beiheft zur *Zeitschrift für die alttestamentliche Wissenschaft*, Giessen and Berlin
ET	English translation
EVV	English Versions of the Bible
HAT	Handbuch zum Alten Testament, Tübingen
ICC	International Critical Commentary, Edinburgh
JBL	*Journal of Biblical Literature*, Philadelphia
KAT	Kommentar zum Alten Testament, Leipzig
LBC	Layman's Bible Commentaries, London
LXX	The Septuagint, the Greek translation of the Old Testament
MT	The Masoretic Text of the Hebrew Bible
NF	Neue Folge (=New Series)
NT	New Testament
OT	Old Testament
PEFQS	*Palestine Exploration Fund Quarterly Statement*, London
PEQ	*Palestine Exploration Quarterly*, London
RSV	Revised Standard Version of the Bible
SBT	Studies in Biblical Theology, London
TLZ	*Theologische Literaturzeitung*, Leipzig
TR	*Theologische Rundschau*, Tübingen
TWNT	*Theologisches Wörterbuch zum Neuen Testament*, Stuttgart
VT	*Vetus Testamentum*, Leiden
ZAW	*Zeitschrift für die alttestamentliche Wissenschaft*, Giessen and Berlin
ZTK	*Zeitschrift für Theologie und Kirche*, Freiburg im Breisgau, Leipzig and Tübingen

INTRODUCTION

A SUMMARY OF CRITICISM

No other book, perhaps, of the Old Testament has undergone such drastic criticism as the Book of Ezekiel, and this all within the past forty years. Ezekiel was the last prophet to have the traditional view of his writings called in question. As late as 1913 Driver could say that 'no critical question arises in connection with the authorship of the book, the whole from beginning to end bearing the stamp of a single mind',[1] and in the same year Buchanan Gray wrote that 'no other book of the Old Testament is distinguished by such decisive marks of unity of authorship and integrity as this'.[2] This view, however, was soon to be challenged. First, the work of Herrmann and Hölscher (both 1924) made it apparent that the book had been composed in much the same way as those of Isaiah and Jeremiah. Then, with the studies by Torrey (1930), Smith (1931) and Herntrich (1932), came a radical reappraisal, of which Torrey himself wrote in 1939: 'Quite recently, the long-standing picture of unity and harmony has been violently disturbed. It is as though a bomb had been exploded in the Book of Ezekiel, scattering the fragments in all directions. One scholar gathers them up and arranges them in one way, another makes a different combination.'[3] During this period almost everything was called in question: there was 'a

[1] S. R. Driver, *Introduction to the Literature of the Old Testament*, 9th ed., 1913, p. 279.
[2] G. Buchanan Gray, *A Critical Introduction to the Old Testament*, 1913, p. 198.
[3] Notes on Ezekiel', *JBL* 58, 1939, p. 78.

plethora of divergencies: unity or composite, genuine or pseudepigraph, poet or writer, prophet or pastor, genuine prophecy or fictitious, Babylon or Palestine, Samaria or Jerusalem'.[4]

Today, however, a more sober view is beginning to prevail. The major studies which have appeared since 1950, those of Fohrer (1952 and 1955), Zimmerli (1955 onwards), von Rabenau (1956) and Graf von Reventlow (1962) from the Continent, as well as the smaller works by the American Howie (1950 and 1961), suggest a more conventional picture, and the present period is witnessing a return to something like the position before 1930. For example, von Rabenau writes (p. 681): 'The Book of Ezekiel is, however, to be understood, like the older prophetic books, as oracles actually delivered and later collected. The prophet doubtless drew up the various units and gave them their shape: in particular, he gave the whole collection a form by means of putting it all in the first person.' Or, from a different angle, Graf von Reventlow can say (p. 165): 'In Ezekiel we meet with a prophet who stands right at the end of a developing series, but who still beyond any doubt belongs to the classical period of prophecy.'

THE PROBLEMS IN EZEKIEL

During the course of recent critical investigation, four main problems have been discussed: (a) the unity of the book; (b) the time of Ezekiel's activity; (c) the place of Ezekiel's activity; and (d) the prophet's personality and office. Because they are so closely interrelated they will be treated together here.

[4] C. Kuhl, 'Zur Geschichte der Hesekiel-Forschung', *TR*, NF 5, 1933, p. 115.

The chief reasons why the book was for so long regarded as a unity are these. (i) It seems to have been carefully planned and logically arranged. Chs. 1-24 (a small part excepted) are oracles of doom against Jerusalem and Judah, prefaced by the prophet's call; chs. 25-32 contain oracles directed against foreign nations; chs. 33-39 are prophecies of restoration, and chs. 40-48 describe the new temple and the ordering of Israel's life after the return. There appear to be no breaks in continuity such as we find in Amos, Isaiah and Jeremiah. (ii) The book is written in an uniform style marked by the continuous appearance of certain stock expressions, terms—particularly introductory and concluding formulae— and ideas. It gives the impression of having been written down 'at one sitting'. (iii) It is throughout an account in the first person. (iv) It is furnished with a system of dates in more or less chronological order. (v) It appears to bear in all its parts the imprint of a somewhat strange personality.

The strongest statement on the unity of the book was that of Smend (pp. xxi ff.): 'The whole book is the logical development of a series of ideas according to a well-considered and to some extent schematic plan: no part could be taken away without destroying the whole ensemble. Just observe the correspondence between ch. 1 and chs. 8-11 . . . as well as the strict logical connection and advance in the several divisions of the book . . . which, moreover, is also characterized by the recurrence and fuller exposition of the same images . . . and the same significant turns of phrase. Thus it is highly probable that the whole book was written down all of a piece.'

The first to attempt a critical analysis was Kraetzschmar, who discovered 33 doublets. Following him, Herrmann in his 1924 Commentary broke further with the concept of the unity of the book by admitting a certain amount of redactorial work, though his inclination was, as Hölscher said (p. 3), 'to deny as little as possible to Ezekiel himself'. It was Hölscher

himself who first put a serious question-mark to the essential
unity, and thus became the fountain-head of the modern study
of the prophet. Starting from the same assumption as Duhm
had made for Jeremiah,[5] that prophets were in all essentials
poets and messengers of doom, Hölscher regarded as genuine
Ezekiel only sixteen brief oracles (and five prose passages)—
some 150 verses out of a total of about 1,270. The rest was
due to fifth-century redactors, who added promises of hope to
give the ancient prophecies of doom significance for a later
generation.[6]

In principle Hölscher's method was no different from
Herrmann's. Both men agreed that the book contains genuine
sixth-century prophecy, the only divergence being on the
amount of the redactorial activity. The early nineteen-thirties
were to see a quite new approach.

Working independently, C. C. Torrey in the USA (1930)
and James Smith in Scotland (1931) arrived at not dissimilar
conclusions. Both argued that the prophecies were addressed,
not to the exiles in Babylon, but to men in the homeland of
Palestine. They further agreed in dating these the reign of
Manasseh (687-642), the Babylonian setting and date being
due to a later hand. Both also believed that, in spite of
editorial work, the book was substantially a unity. They were,
however, in disagreement on the question of genuineness. For
Torrey, the book was a pseudepigraph, and 'Ezekiel' a fictitious name. Its author, who lived in the Greek period, wrote
such a book as might have been written in the idolatrous days
of Manasseh by a prophet denouncing that idolatry (cf. the
methods of apocalyptic). About 230 it was given its Babylonian setting as part of Jewish propaganda vindicating the

---

[5] B. Duhm, *Das Buch Jeremia*, Tübingen, 1901.
[6] A similar result was reached by Irwin in 1943 in *The Problem of
Ezekiel*. He complained of the lack of objective criteria for the study
of Ezekiel. These he found in ch. 15, and on their basis left only
some 250 verses genuine.

claims of Judaism against the Samaritans.[7] For Smith, however, Ezekiel was a real person. He lived in the northern kingdom in Manasseh's reign, worked from about 722 to about 669, and delivered two sets of oracles, one in Palestine and one in the exile, which were artificially united by a redactor.

The reason why both Torrey and Smith thought of the reign of Manasseh was their belief that Josiah's reform made such idolatries as are depicted in Ezek. 8 impossible in the reigns of Jehoiachin and Zedekiah. A further ground for Torrey's questioning of the traditional view was the audience whom the prophet is said to address. 'More attentive readers will agree that the bulk of the prophecy . . . is directly addressed to the people of Judah and Jerusalem,'[8] and not to the Babylonian exiles. And Torrey gives an impressive list of data which might seem more natural on the hypothesis that the prophet was confronting hearers in Palestine in person.

'These two scholars were therefore primarily concerned with the date of the prophet, either fictitious or real, and with the sphere in which he worked, rather than with the breaking down of the unity of the book. Both, however, detected the hand of a later editor, who had radically transformed the whole book. . . . Shortly afterwards Herntrich combined the two approaches.'[9]

Herntrich's monograph took its rise from the question of Ezekiel's audience, and his answer largely determined the direction that research was to take during the next decade or so—as Herntrich himself said (p. 129), this problem put the

---

[7] Nils Messel in *Ezechielfragen*, 1945, reached a view similar to Torrey's. The prophet worked about 430 BC, the exiles are the Golah who have returned to Palestine, and the purpose of the book is to promote their monotheistic faith directed exclusively to Yahweh as against the syncretism of the population which had never been in exile.

[8] *Pseudo-Ezekiel*, p. 24.

[9] H. H. Rowley, 'The Book of Ezekiel in Modern Study', *BJRL* 36, 1953, p. 154.

whole estimation of Ezekiel in a new light. Unlike Smith and
Torrey, he kept the traditional exilic date, that given in the
book itself, but discarded the exilic setting: Ezekiel was a
prophet who worked in the homeland, and his oracles in chs.
4-24, directed against Jerusalem and Judah, were delivered
by him there, face to face with his audience. The ecstatic
visions and the oracles of salvation inserted in a Babylonian
context are the work of a redactor in the exile who wished
not only to ensure that the deportees of 597 should have the
spiritual leadership of exilic Israel, but also to bear evidence
for Yahweh that should be effective even in the conditions
obtaining in Babylonia.

Herntrich's view had obvious attractions. The symbolic
actions in chs. 4, 5 and 12 receive a new urgency if they were
performed before the eyes of those actually to be affected by
the terrors they represent. It also explained the prophet's intimate knowledge of what was going on and being said in Jerusalem (8.5ff.; 22.2ff.; cf. 24.6, 9). Above all, it seemed to offer a
reasonable solution of some at any rate of the problems of
Ezekiel's personality. Connected with the prophet is a series
of what have been called 'weird phenomena'.[10] He falls upon
his face (1.28; 3.23; 9.8; 11.13; 43.3; 44.4); he is 'overwhelmed'
for seven days as he begins his mission (3.14-15); 'the hand
of Yahweh was (strong)' upon him or 'came upon' him (1.3;
3.14, 22; 8.1; 33.22; 37.1; 40.1), both phrases meaning the condition of ecstasy; he is apparently bound with cords and
unable to go amongst people (3.24f.); he lies for two long
periods upon first the one side and then the other (4.4ff.); a
mysterious dumbness comes upon him (3.26; 24.25-27;
33.21f.); he trembles and quakes as he takes food (12.17); for
one living in Babylon, he has a very detailed knowledge of
the course of events in Jerusalem (8.5-16; 24.2) and of what
people were saying there (8.12; 12.22, 27; 18.2; 33.10);

---

[10] A. C. Welch, *Post-Exilic Judaism*, Edinburgh and London, 1935,
p. 59.

apparently as the result of a word which he utters in Babylonia, a man in Jerusalem falls down dead (11.13). Before Herntrich—and indeed since—various attempts were made to explain these phenomena along the lines of an abnormal personality. Ezekiel has been called a cataleptic, a neurotic, a victim of hysteria, a psychopath, and even a definite paranoid schizophrenic, as well as being credited with powers of clairvoyance or levitation. But these phenomena, Herntrich argued, are easy to explain either when it is remembered that Ezekiel was in fact ín Jerusalem, or when some of them are seen as the device of the redactor to transfer an originally Palestinian prophecy to a new environment in Babylonia.

This thesis—represented sometimes in the form of a synthesis, a ministry in Jerusalem followed by one in the exile—for a time won quite wide acceptance, for example by Oesterley and Robinson,[11] Bertholet (in 1936), Wheeler Robinson, Pfeiffer,[12] Auvray (in 1947) and Steinmann. More recently, however, as was said, it has been fairly largely abandoned (as for instance by Fohrer, Zimmerli, Howie and others). The truth of Cooke's comment on Herntrich's views (p. xxiii) has been increasingly accepted: 'And after all, what relief do they give us? It is just as hard to believe in the highly imaginative redactor as to accept the statements in the text.' Cf. the statement of Weiser: 'All these attempts [to make Ezekiel a prophet in the homeland as well as in Babylon] suffer from the objection that the dates and places assigned to Ezekiel's oracles are regarded as the inventions of redactors without a really convincing reason being brought forward for this assertion (cf. now also Howie and Fohrer). Besides no explanation is offered as to how a redactor, especially perhaps in chapters 8-11, could be thought to have made

[11] W. O. E. Oesterley and T. H. Robinson, *Hebrew Religion: its Origin and Development*, London, 1930.
[12] R. H. Pfeiffer, *Introduction to the Old Testament*, New York and London, 1941.

alterations and invented trances and things heard and seen
from afar merely in order to stamp Ezekiel as an exilic prophet. By tracing the para-psychological phenomena back to
the editor, the problem is only transferred, but its difficulty is
not thereby reduced, still less solved.'[13] As will be shown in
the commentary, most of the 'weird phenomena' can be explained without recourse to a ministry in Palestine.

Most recent criticism sees the book as formed in much the
same way as those of Isaiah and Jeremiah. It is the deposit
of the ministry of a genuine prophet exercised among the
exiles in Babylon just before the fall of Jerusalem and for
some time after it. Not all of its content is in its original form.
Parts of what he said the prophet himself seems to have
worked over and elaborated, and to have left parallel versions
of the same oracle behind, e.g. the divine chariot twice described, in chs. 1 and 10; the prophet's office as 'watcher' is
given in similar terms in 3.16-21 and 33.1-9; the treatment of
sin and punishment in 18.21-32 is closely related to that in
33.10-20. Often it is quite impossible to decide what derives
from Ezekiel himself and what from a later date. Subsequently, disciples who, with conspicuous success, copied their
master's diction and style and so gave the book the impression
of unity which it undoubtedly has, as well as including these
doublets, altered and expanded original oracles to make them
speak to a later situation, and also inserted sermons of their
own based on the prophet's words. The process is comparable
with the Deuteronomic sections in Jeremiah, and some at least
of the disciples may have been members of the Zadokite
priesthood in Jerusalem. Much, especially in the last section
dealing with the new temple, is considerably later than
Ezekiel himself. There is also a good deal of redactional expansion and glossing, most of which is generally absent in
the LXX. The text of Ezekiel is one of the worst preserved

[13] A. Weiser, *Introduction to the Old Testament*, trs. D. M. Barton,
London, 1961, p. 226.

in the OT, and frequently even the LXX shows that it was at
a loss. The RSV represents a great advance on the AV, but
still leaves much to be desired.

THE PROPHET HIMSELF

Something more must be said about Ezekiel's personality.

Fohrer in his commentary (p. xxv) has spoken of 'the
polarity and the wide range of tensions' within his person.
Auvray expands this: 'Ecstatic and man of reason, utopian
and realist, a poet with an unrestrained imagination and the
most precise of jurists, priest and prophet, a prolix, coarse
and popular writer, yet sometimes also obscure, recherché
and difficult to grasp.'[14] To this may be added what was
noticed by Hölscher: because of the magnificence of some
of his poetry, for example, parts of the oracles against Tyre,
chs. 26-29, Ezekiel has been called the Aeschylus of the Old
Testament; yet side by side with this, sometimes in the very
next oracle, we can come upon some of the most wearisome,
repetitive and pedestrian prose and ideas to be met with
anywhere.

However we seek to resolve the dichotomies of our
prophet's personality, the basic fact from which we must start
is that he was a priest (1.3), and that, even after he was called
to be a prophet, he never parted with this inheritance. What
stands almost always in the forefront of his thought is the
temple. The most serious thing about the exile is not the suffering it brings to human beings, but that the sin for which it
was the punishment caused the glory of Yahweh to quit the
temple (ch. 10). Again, the goal of the restoration is a community gathered round a carefully planned temple (chs. 40-42),
to which the glory of Yahweh returns (ch. 43). He also gives
detailed regulations for the temple's servants, its services and

[14] *Ezéchiel*, 1947, p. 9.

its calendar of festivals (chs. 44-46). The sins, too, which he condemns are in the main cultic. The temple is 'defiled' by idolatry or by the presence of foreigners or by Yahweh himself (5.11; 7.22, 24; 23.38, 39; 24.21); Yahweh's name is 'profaned' (20.39; 36.20-23; 39.7; 43.7f.); the sabbaths are profaned (20.13, 16, 21, 24; 22.8; 23.38); the people 'defile' themselves because of their sins (14.11; 20.30, 43; 37.23), particularly the sins of idolatry (20.7, 18, 31; 22.3, 4; 23.7, 30; 37.23) and child-sacrifice (20.26, 31; 23.29); the land is 'defiled' because of sin (36.17). The priestly categories of 'clean' and 'unclean' also play a large part in his thinking (22.26; 44.23); he has a horror of ritual impurity (4.14; 44.7f.); he makes careful separation between the sacred and the secular (45.1-6; 48.9f.). As a jurist he gives regulations for cases of right and wrong (ch. 18). He shows very close affinities in thought and language with the Holiness Code (Lev. 17-26). The rationalizing and schematizing element in his thought is, too, typical of the priestly mind, and it may be also to the leisure of a priestly class that he owed his wide knowledge—he shows himself well acquainted, for example, with legend and mythology (ch. 16, the foundling child; 28.11ff., the primeval man; ch. 31, the marvellous tree), and with conditions and procedures in Tyre, etc.

At the same time, this priest-theologian, with his urge to think things through, is also a true prophet. Not only do we find a call, visions, symbolic actions and parables, and denunciations of false prophets, all of which are elaborated more in his work than in the earlier prophets;—we also find Ezekiel denouncing moral and social sins in the old manner: oppression of the poor (18.7, 16; 22.29), oppression of widows and orphans (22.7, 25), contempt of parents (22.7), robbery and lending at interest (18.7f.; 22.12), murder (18.10; 22.2-4, 6, 9, 12, 27; 33.25; 36.18), inchastity and adultery (18.6; 22.10f.). And, as will be shown below, he paints a far darker picture of his nation's past than any of his predecessors did, denouncing its sins with an even more pointed and unrestrained invective than theirs.

In certain respects, however, there is a falling off. Like the prophets before him, Ezekiel delivered oracles in poetic form. The parable of the vine (ch. 15), those of the twig and the two eagles (ch. 17), and of the lioness and her whelps (ch. 19), the allegory of Jerusalem as the faithless adulteress (ch. 16) and of Samaria and Jerusalem as two shameless harlot sisters (ch. 23), Judah-Jerusalem as the forest which is to be burned (20.45ff.), Tyre as the gallant ship which founders (ch. 27), Pharaoh as the crocodile which is captured (chs. 29, 32) and the cedar which is felled (ch. 31), all show power of imagination. But there is little of invention or originality. Perhaps every one of these figures were already in circulation. Again, when he is a poet, he is a poet of the head and not of the heart: he is much more at home with reason than with emotion. The only feelings he greatly shows are zeal, zeal for God's glory, and fury, loathing and disgust at whatever profanes this. The lyric tenderness of Jeremiah is completely absent.

Ezekiel's medium is really prose, even if some of it is rhythmic prose—perhaps yet another sign of the priestly mind. Yet even as a prose writer, he is not great. However much we excise as due to the expansions of disciples and redactors, he is diffuse and repetitive, full of stock phrases and standard terms. Doubtless it was no easy task to convey the impression of the sublime transcendence of God, as he wished to do in the inaugural vision. Yet, the reader is left with little idea of the Almighty, and—even allowing for much working-over by redactors—with only a vague idea of the heavenly chariot. Perhaps only in the vision of the valley of dry bones (37.1-14) does imagination kindle his prose style to near-sublimity. Elsewhere little stands out in relief to break the monotony.

We must, however, bear in mind that part of the monotony in chs. 4-24 is due to the prophet's subject. As will be shown, in these chapters there is in fact only a single theme, the demonstration that the fall of Jerusalem was both inevitable and deserved. This had to be hammered home to men who were unwilling to envisage the possibility. And if the doom of Jerusalem is already firmly decreed by Yahweh, there can be no call to repentance. Part of the attraction of Jeremiah is the alternation of 'chaos come again' (4.23-26) and 'Return' (3.12-14), and the division of Jeremiah's heart between the two messages. For Ezekiel such variety was of necessity ruled out.

The visions, too, more frequent in Ezekiel than in his predecessors, represent a falling off. Their elaboration, their grandiose character, and the bizarre and recondite elements they contain mark the transition from genuine prophecy to apocalyptic. This is especially true of the Gog vision (chs. 38f.), where the course of the struggle of the world-powers against God's people is 'revealed' to the prophet in the fashion of apocalyptic. But neither chs. 38-39 nor chs. 40-48 are apocalyptic proper. There is no rise and fall of world-empires, no calculation of times and seasons, no revelation of the secrets of heaven, Israel's sufferings are no problem, nothing is said of the delay of redemption—and in Ezekiel redemption is most certainly not the reward for the merits of the saints. Ezekiel does no more than point the way to apocalyptic. If he is sometimes called its 'father', it is questionable whether the designation is appropriate.

In one respect, however, the prophetic office advances in Ezekiel. Ezekiel is appointed a 'watchman' for the house of Israel (3.17; 33.7), and he feels himself responsible for the salvation of individual men (3.16-21; 33.1-20). 'If I [Yahweh] say to the wicked, "O wicked man, you shall surely die", and you [Ezekiel] do not speak to warn the wicked to turn from his way, that wicked man shall die in his iniquity, but his blood I will require at your hand' (33.8). This involvement of man and office, much closer and more potentially perilous than it was even with Jeremiah, also comes to expression in the denunciation of the false prophets, where by implication the office of the true prophet is 'to go up into the breaches' (13.5), a position of danger. Again, the fact that person and office are now less and less separable is also seen in that the reception of revelation seems to have had even a physical effect upon the prophet. 'Sigh, therefore, son of man; sigh with breaking heart and bitter grief before their eyes' (21.6). Further, if Ezekiel was to be 'a sign for the house of Israel' (12.6), the symbolic action in which he lay for a considerable time first on one side and then on the other (4.4-8) must have had an effect not only on those who witnessed it, but on the prophet himself. Jeremiah suffered both at the hands of enemies and in his inner life with Yahweh. There is, however, no hint that he regarded his sufferings as in any way mediatorial. Isaiah's Servant 'was wounded for our transgressions, he was bruised for our iniquities' (Isa. 53.5). Ezekiel stands midway between the two. Falling away is far from being the whole story.

Ezekiel's work, begun in 593, continued till at least 570, the last date in the series (29.17). He was married, and his wife died suddenly before the fall of Jerusalem (24.2, 15-18). We know nothing of his end, though later Jewish tradition says that he was put to death by his fellow Israelites because of his preaching.

THE HISTORICAL BACKGROUND

Two events dominate the first section of the book (chs. 1-24), the first exile of 597, and the fall of Jerusalem in 586. Between these two Ezekiel received his call to be a prophet (593).

After the death of Josiah, who had been the dominant figure in religion and politics in the second half of the seventh century (640-609), Judah fell under the domination of Egypt; then, after Egypt's decisive defeat by Nebuchadnezzar at Carchemish in 605 (Jer. 46.2ff.), she was subject to Babylonia. She was not however content to be a vassal. Taking advantage of a reverse suffered by her new overlord at the hands of Egypt, King Jehoiakim, the nominee of the Pharaoh, who had deposed Josiah's son and successor Jehoahaz (II Kings 23.31-35), rebelled by refusing to pay tribute (II Kings 24.1). Nebuchadnezzar sent Babylonian troops against him, along with armed bands from the neighbouring Syrians, Moabites and Ammonites (II Kings 24.2; Jer. 35.11). The result of this attack it not known. But in December 598 the Babylonian army itself marched west and laid siege to Jerusalem. Before this, however, Jehoiakim had died, whether by natural death or by assassination at the hands of opponents of his rebellion is uncertain (II Kings 24.6; Jer. 22.18f.; 36.29ff.). He had been succeeded by his eighteen-year-old son Jehoiachin (II Kings 24.6, 8), who had to suffer the consequences of his father's revolt. After the capitulation of the city, he, the queen mother, the chief officials and leading citizens, among them Ezekiel himself, and the craftsmen, were deported to Babylon, along with the temple treasures and much spoil (II Kings 24.10-16). This, in 597, is the first deportation. While the state was not destroyed, it was very much diminished and impoverished—it lost Josiah's recently won conquests in the north. Had it been willing to submit, it might have remained as a vassal under the protection of the Babylonians. As things turned out, 597 was the beginning of the end.

In Jehoiachin's place Nebuchadnezzar installed his uncle, Mattaniah, to whom he gave the throne-name of Zedekiah (II Kings 24.17). Zedekiah was to be the last of the Davidic line to sit on the throne. According to Jeremiah, he was weak —afraid of his court (Jer. 38.5), and fearful of public opinion (Jer. 38.19). It also seems clear that a certain section regarded

him as an usurper, and continued to hold Jehoiachin as the
rightful monarch. Again, there were those who looked to
Egypt for deliverance from Babylon. Others, in addition,
asserted that the exiles of 597 would soon return home and
the temple treasures be restored (Jer. 28.1-4). A rebellion in
Babylon led to talks in Jerusalem about revolt among the
smaller Palestinian vassal states (594/3). Nothing came of the
conversations. But five years after, for reasons which we do
not know, Zedekiah renounced his allegiance to Babylon (II
Kings 24.20; Jer. 52.3). Nebuchadnezzar acted at once. By
January 588 (II Kings 25.1; Jer. 52.4) a Babylonian army had
appeared in Palestine. Ezekiel tells of the way by which the
Babylonian king decided whether to strike first at the
Ammonites or at Jerusalem (21.18-23). He quickly overran
the country and laid siege to Jerusalem (Jer. 34.1-7; 21.3-7).
Though the advance of an Egyptian army compelled the raising of the siege, it was only a temporary relief, and in July
or August 587 a breach was made in the walls of the famine-
ridden city, and Jerusalem fell. Zedekiah and some of his
entourage fled by night eastwards, but he was taken prisoner
near Jericho and brought to Nebuchadnezzar's headquarters
at Riblah, where, after seeing his sons put to death, he himself
was blinded and taken in chains to Babylon, where he died
(II Kings 25.6f.; Jer. 52.9-11; cf. Ezek. 17.20, and note on
6.14). The city itself, with the temple and the royal palace, was
plundered and set on fire, and the walls razed. Some of the
leading officials and citizens were taken to Nebuchadnezzar
at Riblah and executed (II Kings 25.18-21; Jer. 52.24-27), and
those who had still remained in Jerusalem after the deportation of 597 were themselves now deported. The terrible sufferings caused by the siege are vividly and pitifully pictured in
Lamentations.

The physical conditions under which the deportees lived
were not so terrible as they have often been depicted. They
were placed in settlements by themselves, one of which was

Tel-Abib (3.15), and were under the local jurisdiction of their elders (8.1; 14.1; 20.1, 3). The Babylonians made use of their labour on the land, for building, and as artisans (Bertholet). Many soon became comfortably off. They could not, of course, practise sacrificial worship, for this could only be offered at the Jerusalem temple, and Babylon was an unclean land. As far as concerns the deportees of 597, they regarded their exile as only temporary (see next section), an expectation which was fostered by prophets among them (Jer. 29.15ff., cf. 28.1ff.). But with the fall of Jerusalem a new mood set in, which resulted in a change of tone in Ezekiel's message.

Ezekiel tells of the attitude of those who were not deported in 597. That they had been allowed to remain in Yahweh's land they regarded as a sign of his favour—the deportees had 'gone far from the Lord' (11.15). They themselves were there-fore the true heirs of Abraham. Hence they laid claim to the land and property of the exiles ('To us this land is given for a possession,' 11.15; cf. 33.24). Ezekiel's attitude towards them was the same as Jeremiah's: the future lay with the exiles (Jer. 24).

THE MESSAGE OF EZEKIEL

After the introduction (chs. 1-3) telling of the prophet's call, the book falls into four distinct sections.

1. Oracles concerning Judah and Jerusalem delivered before the city's fall (chs. 4-24).

2. Oracles against foreign nations (chs. 25-32).

3. Oracles of restoration, including the final destruction of Israel's enemies (chs. 33-39).

4. The future organization of the restored community and especially of the temple and its worship (chs. 40-48).

As has already been said (p. 22), it has often been felt that the first section (4-24) involves a certain lack of realism. What point is there on harping on the coming fall of Jerusalem to men in Babylonia who have already been driven from it, and to whom the sufferings of the fresh calamity would mean little? Therefore Ezekiel has been thought of as a theorist of the study, or a play-actor, not really a prophet, but using the forms of prophecy for his lucubrations, and quite unlike his contemporary Jeremiah, who played so active a role in the events of 586 and those leading up to them. This, however, is to ignore certain factors. As is shown in the notes on chs. 4-5, a prophet's word, and his symbolic actions, were charged with power. They were regarded as in some sense bringing into being, or setting in motion, that which they foretold, so that what the prophet said or represented could not fail to come to pass. Now, Ezekiel's first task had to do with inevitability. As was noted, in the ten years between the first deportation in 597 and the final collapse of the Judean state in 586, hopes were cherished, both in the homeland and in the exile, that the present position would soon be reversed: the threat from the Babylonian empire would shortly cease, probably by intervention from Egypt, and the exiles of 597 return home. These hopes Ezekiel had to destroy among the exiles. This gives the two main propositions enunciated in the first section of the book: first, the people of Judah and Jerusalem are steeped in guilt before Yahweh, and, secondly, Yahweh is a just God, and must therefore punish them. Thus chs. 4-24 are described as a scroll on which were written 'words of lamentation and mourning and woe' (2.10).

'The way of the Lord is not just,' people were saying (33.17, 20). Ezekiel also quotes another current proverb, given as well in Jeremiah, 'the fathers have eaten sour grapes, and (it is) the children's teeth (that) are set on edge' (Ezek. 18.2; Jer. 31.29). Had there not been a reformation under Josiah? Yet, since then, so far from improving, things had gone steadily from bad to worse (cf. Jer. 44.15-19). Men were not only bewildered, but impugning the fairness of the divine action.

B

Ezekiel took various ways of demonstrating God's absolute justice. In three of his best-known allegories (chs. 16, 20 and 23) he reviewed the nation's history, to prove that Israel had been a 'rebellious house'—his favourite designation—rebelling against God not only, as other prophets also admitted, after it had entered into Canaan and been seduced by the ideas it found there, but even at its very election. Jerusalem itself was pagan in origin and heathen in behaviour, much worse than Samaria, more sinful than the Gentiles: even Sodom had more justification than she. Again, she is a rusty pot whose filth can only be purged by re-melting (24.1-14).

In particular, Ezekiel attempts to show the absolute justice of God by asserting that God deals with individuals (3.17ff.; ch. 18; 33.10-20). Israel had for long worked with the concept of solidarity. The unit with which Yahweh was supposed to deal was the nation or, at best, the family. But by the time of Jeremiah and Ezekiel, the individual was beginning to assert himself in his own right. Deuteronomy (published in 621) had already condemned the concept that fathers should be put to death for their children's sins and *vice versa* (Deut. 24.16), and Jeremiah echoes this (12.1; 31.29f.). Ezekiel carries the process forward. The unit with which Yahweh deals is the individual. A good man is not involved in the guilt of his ancestors: 'If a man is righteous and does what is lawful and right . . . he shall live' (i.e. survive the coming calamity) (18.5-9). But if a man does 'abominable things, he shall surely die' (18.13). This is put in another way where it is stated that even paragons of righteousness will deliver only themselves, and not their (presumably wicked) children in the disaster to come (14.12-20). Thus, the ancient principle of solidarity, which led to the complaint that God's way was not just—in II Kings 21.10ff. the fall of Jerusalem is represented as punishment for the sins of King Manasseh—is here repudiated by Ezekiel. This leads to one of the greatest evangelical utterances of the Old Testament: 'Behold, all souls are mine; the soul of the father as well as the soul of the son is mine; the soul that sins shall die' (18.4), with which we may compare 'As I live, says the Lord God, I have no pleasure in the death of the wicked, but that the wicked turn from his way and live; turn back, turn back from your evil ways; for why will you die, O house of Israel?' (33.11; cf. 18.23).

One criticism of this doctrine of rigorous individualism is that it is not consistently applied by the prophet himself. Indeed, the only other hint of it, apart from chs. 18 and 33, is in the vision of chs. 8-11, where certain men 'who sigh and groan over all the abominations that are committed in it' [Jerusalem] are exempted from the otherwise total destruction of the inhabitants of the city (9.4). Yet even there, little children and women are not spared: 'collective and individual retribution are spoken of in the same breath.'[15] And elsewhere throughout, as for example in the wholesale condemnations in the historical excursuses of chs. 16, 20 and 23, the subject is the nation.

A further criticism, also arising from the book itself, is that considerations of merit are among the last things we look for in Ezekiel. God's action towards Israel is always 'for the sake of his name' and not primarily for the good of Israel or motivated by love for her (see below pp. 38f.). 'It is not for your sake, O house of Israel, that I am about to act, but for the sake of my holy name, which you have profaned among the nations to which you came' (36.22). Here preservation and restoration are not due to any desert.

Ezekiel's individualism has also been criticized as theoretic and atomistic, untrue to the facts of heredity and environment, a *tour de force* to maintain the justice of God. This must be admitted. It is a one-sided doctrine. Three things, however, ought to be borne in mind:

(a) Much of Israel's thought in the post-exilic period was

---

[15] Yehezkel Kaufmann, *The Religion of Israel*, translated and abridged by Moshe Greenberg, London, 1961, p. 439.

devoted precisely to this question of the place of the individual, and to the related question of undeserved, or apparently undeserved, suffering. They are the subject of some of the Psalms, they occur in Proverbs, and are the theme of Ecclesiastes and Job. But no really satisfactory solution was arrived at until the time of the Maccabees, when the doctrine of a life beyond the grave began to emerge (Dan. 12.1f.). (Hitherto, the Hebrews had believed that good and bad alike went down to a ghost-like, bloodless existence in the underworld of Sheol, cf. Job 10.20-22.) Ezekiel takes one of the first steps, and a very important one, along this road.

(*b*) Ezekiel did not intend the principles set out in chs. 18 and 33 to be taken as valid universally, as a general truth. What he means is that this was the principle on which Yahweh was acting *in this period of calamity*. Solidarity, the normal principle, was being temporarily suspended in favour of a different one. See the notes on ch. 18.

(*c*) As a preacher, Ezekiel was not only denouncing sin, but was also calling his fellow-exiles to repentance. That is, his task was practical, and not an exercise in logic. He had thus first to show that repentance was necessary. This he did by way of the doctrine of solidarity—the whole nation was utterly bad. But his denunciations in chs. 4-24 could hardly have helped but confirm the already prevalent feelings of fatalistic hopelessness and inability to take any step towards salvation. Even before 586 men must have felt that 'Our bones are dried up, and our hope is lost; we are clean cut off' (37.11). Thus, for his call to repentance to have any effect, he had to break with the former doctrine, and offer hope along a different road, that of the responsibility of the individual. His doctrine is therefore the opening of a door to repentance.

Ezekiel went even further than saying that a man is not the prisoner of his heredity: he is not even the prisoner of his own past. When a wicked man turns from his wickedness, his past is no longer reckoned against him. 'But if a wicked man turns away from all his sins which he has committed . . . none of the transgressions which he has committed shall be remembered against him; for the righteousness which he has done he shall live' (18.21f.). In this connection, however, Ezekiel is more logical than evangelical. God's justice demands the punishment of sinners. But what of a righteous man who has fallen away to wickedness at the time when God requires his soul of him? 'None of the righteous deeds which he has done shall be remembered; for the treachery of which he is guilty and the sin he has committed, he shall die' (18.24).

There is, therefore, nothing to hinder a man's turning to God in order to escape the coming calamity and continue to 'live'. Ezekiel is not attempting a fully rounded doctrine of the individual and society, but in face of an urgent practical pastoral need is asserting the truth that God does make it possible for men to break with both their heredity and their own guilty past.

Apart however from these few 'individualistic' passages, the main tenor of Ezekiel's message in chs. 4-24 is that the doom of Jerusalem and all its inhabitants is inevitable, and that the time for repentance is past. Ezekiel nowhere explains why it was on his own generation, and not on an earlier or a later one, that the stroke of God's anger was to fall, why God no longer acted for the sake of his name and, as in the past, desisted from pouring out his wrath upon them and spending his anger against them (ch. 20). Certainly, the Deuteronomic editors of the Books of Kings had the same idea (cf. II Kings 22.14-17), and Jeremiah too became increasingly convinced of the inevitability. There is no suggestion that the men of Ezekiel's own age were more sinful than previous generations, nor does he mention Manasseh (II Kings 21.10-15). He simply states that the cup is now full. For centuries Yahweh has been on the point of destroying his

people (ch. 20). Now he is about to act, and nothing remains
but destruction, punishment and exile. Only in that way is
salvation possible—though indeed there is little hint of salvation in chs. 4-24. 'Because I would have cleansed you and
you were not cleansed from your filthiness, you shall not be
cleansed any more till I have satisfied my fury upon you. I
the Lord have spoken; it shall come to pass, I will do it; I
will not go back, I will not spare, I will not repent; according
to your ways and your doings I will judge you, says the Lord
God' (24.13f.). 'When this comes—and come it will!—then
they will know that a prophet has been among them' (33.33).

Before leaving the subject of God's justice, we may note
that Ezekiel's attempt to establish it was important not only
as explaining the present but also as giving confidence for
the future. In exile Israel lost all upon which she had previously relied. She had been driven forth from the land
promised to Abraham and his seed in perpetuity. The Davidic
line had ceased, in spite of Nathan's prophecy to David,
'your house and your kingdom shall be made sure for ever
before me; your throne shall be established for ever' (II
Sam. 7.16). Gone, too, was the temple, of whose inviolability
the people were convinced (Jer. 7.1-15), and in Babylon there
was no possibility of the accustomed worship by sacrifice. But
if Ezekiel could convince the exiles that God was nevertheless
just, they had something still to cling to, and also something
to look forward to. They had survived the calamity: surely
justice would not admit of perpetual punishment?

In Ezekiel's eyes Yahweh has another motive of action
over and above the demonstration of his justice. He also acts
'for the sake of his name', that is, out of regard for his own
honour and reputation. 'It is not for your sake that I am
about to act, but for the sake of my holy name' (36.22, cf.
v. 32; cf. also 20.9, 14, 22, 39). There is nothing here of
Amos' Yahweh who relents from the evil he proposed because of the nation's smallness (Amos 7.1-6), nothing of

Hosea's 'How can I give you up, O Ephraim! How can I hand you over, O Israel!' (Hos. 11.8), nothing of Jeremiah's profound sympathy with the people whom he denounced with a fierceness the equal of Ezekiel's—'O that my head were waters, and my eyes a fountain of tears, that I might weep day and night for the slain of the daughter of my people!' (Jer. 9.1). This is not to say that there is no tenderness at all in Ezekiel's God. In 34.11-16, 'I myself will be the shepherd of my sheep. . . . I will seek the lost, and I will bring back the strayed, and I will bind up the crippled . . .', we come to the very threshold of the Christian gospel. But in general, the prophet's own hardness is reflected in his conception of God. The regular reason given for some act of chastisement, or it may be of mercy, is 'and they shall know that I am Yahweh', or some equivalent formula. To Ezekiel Yahweh is so awesome—think of the inaugural vision—that his holiness hardly allows any glimmering of his love for his people to shine through. In this respect, it must be confessed, Ezekiel falls far short of his predecessors. In his typical and constantly recurring 'They shall know that I am Yahweh', there is nothing of what Hosea meant by 'knowledge of God', an intimate relationship with him. One should, however, remember Lofthouse's words: after saying that Ezekiel was too deeply impressed by the outraged majesty of Yahweh to understand his love, he goes on, 'It must be remembered that for Ezekiel a deliverance which was grounded on Jahveh's reverence for his own name supplied a firmer assurance than anything which could have sprung from Israel's own conduct.'[16]

This no doubt is again due to his training as a priest. For in Ezekiel holiness is conceived, as in the Priestly Code, in almost physical terms. This is perhaps most clearly seen in the plan for the restored community, where the Holy of Holies is separated from the secular world by various courts whose

[16] *Israel after the Exile*, p. 85.

sanctity—i.e., withdrawal from the contamination of the secular—increases the nearer they approach the Holy of Holies, or in the prescription that, after serving at the altar, the priests must lay up their garments in the holy chambers, 'lest they communicate holiness to the people with their garments' (44.19). And when the glory of Yahweh, which had departed from the temple before its destruction, returns to the new temple by the east gate, this gate remains thereafter shut (44.2). One can appreciate Ezekiel's desire to safeguard against 'pollution', and even the logical, almost clinical, means by which he sought to effect this, but at the same time one can hardly help feeling that he opened the way to what was to lead to the denunciation of the scribes and Pharisees in Matt. 23.27f.

As has been said, Ezekiel is the great prophet of the grace of God. The God whose transcendent majesty is almost ineffable yet condescends to his utterly undeserving people. Ezekiel's teaching that Yahweh will give the exiles 'a new heart and a new spirit' (36.25-32) is in essence Jeremiah's doctrine of the new covenant (Jer. 31.31-34), and may have been taken over from the latter, since, as the notes will show, Ezekiel too conceives of the new relationship as covenantal in form. Here again there is no thought of merit on Israel's part, or that the sufferings of the exile had brought her to repentance, for she had continued to profane Yahweh's holy name among the nations (36.23). Her heart remained apparently as stony as it had always been. The initiative is wholly with God, and, as we have seen, the motive of his action is regard for his name. Indeed, repentance and conversion seem to come only after God's action (36.31). This is not the full Pauline or Christian theology of God's grace, but, along with Jeremiah's, it is the nearest to these in the Old Testament.

As to the future of the restored nation: a purified, covenanted and now obedient people is to dwell in holiness, plenty

and security (34.25-31; 37.24-28). True, the hordes of Gog
will make a great assault, but Yahweh will annihilate them,
and so establish his universal supremacy (38f.). Not only are
the exiles of the southern kingdom to be restored, but also
those of 722 (37.15ff.). The reunited flock is to have one
shepherd, David, that is, a line of Davidic rulers (34.23f.;
37.24f.). David however is not called king, but prince and
servant. He lives in the midst of his people, and is not a
tyrant or a warrior, but a shepherd who is to protect the weak
(34.23ff.), and to contribute to the maintenance of the temple
worship (45.21-25). Thus, one can hardly speak of direct
messianic teaching in Ezekiel, though passages like 34.25-30
take up traditional messianic themes, such as one finds in
Amos 9.13-15. The focus of the people's life is the temple and
its services, which are in their turn designed to give God his
proper glory.

Except in the Book of Revelation, which does draw very
greatly upon Ezekiel, there is hardly an echo of our prophet
in the New Testament, apart from his adumbration of the
doctrine of God's grace. The Good Shepherd of John 10 can
hardly be attributed to his influence, for the designation of a
ruler as shepherd was common in Israel, and indeed throughout the ancient Near East. (The present writer does believe
however that Jesus' title Son of man owes something to
Ezekiel as well as to Daniel and Enoch, but this is contrary
to the generally accepted view.)

But for Judaism he had a profound importance. He did
not remain 'like one who sings love songs with a beautiful
voice and plays well on an instrument, for they hear what
you say, but they will not do it' (33.32). His teaching that the
holy people should be separate led no doubt to results which
he himself would have deplored, but it furnished Jewry with
a *modus vivendi* which has enabled it to survive centuries of
persecution and the danger of assimilation. Internally too,
his subordination of the civil ruler to ecclesiastical authority

B*

persisted. Again, if his programme in chs. 40-48 was far from being completely realized—and parts of it, such as the division of the land among the tribes and the stream which was to issue from the temple can never have been expected to be literally fulfilled—still, enough was put into operation to determine the main lines of Jewish worship down to the destruction of the temple in AD 70. The present writer also believes that, in attempts to solve the vexed question of the prophets' attitude to the cult, not enough account is taken of Ezekiel. If Amos 5.21-24, Hos. 6.6, Isa. 1.12-17, Micah 6.6-8, Ps. 51.16-17 (cf. Amos 5.25, Jer. 7.21-23) are correctly interpreted as meaning that the pre-exilic prophets were totally opposed to the sacrificial system and wished for its abolition, then it may have been the priestly outlook and teaching of our prophet which led the post-exilic age to turn its back upon them. Finally, the notes on 11.16 will suggest that Ezekiel may have had some connection with the origin of the synagogue. (His relationship to apocalyptic has already been noticed, p. 28 above; see also p. 103 below.)

I

JUDGMENT ON JUDAH AND JERUSALEM

1.1–24.27

THE CALL OF EZEKIEL

1.1–3.27

THE VISION OF THE CHARIOT

1.1-28

INTRODUCTION

1.1-3

The Book of Ezekiel is furnished with a system of fourteen dates (1.1f.; 3.16; 8.1; 20.1; 24.1; 26.1; 29.1, 17; 30.20; 31.1; 32.1, 17; 33.21; 40.1). These reckon from the year of the deportation of King Jehoiachin, 598. (Recent discoveries have shown that in Babylonia Jehoiachin retained the title 'King of Judah'; this may explain why Ezekiel takes his reign and not that of Zedekiah, whom he may not have regarded as a legitimate monarch, as the basis of his chronology.) Ezekiel thus received

his call to be a prophet in the year 593 (v. 2). But what of THE
THIRTIETH YEAR in v. 1? No completely satisfactory solution
has yet been found. It may refer to Ezekiel's own age (so, e.g.
Origen); Albright and Howie suggest that it means the thirtieth year of Jehoiachin's exile, and that this was the time
when the prophet first dictated the book to a disciple. Since,
however, the answer makes no difference to the substance of
the prophecy, the many various conjectures need not be discussed here. The change of persons in 1-3 shows the Introduction to be composite. Verse 1, which links with v. 4, goes back
to the prophet himself, v. 2 is a disciple's or scribe's attempt
to make THE THIRTIETH YEAR precise, while v. 3 is the common
superscription to a prophetic book. The river Chebar was a
canal constructed for the purpose of irrigating the land between the Tigris and the Euphrates. It started from the latter
above the city of Babylon, passed through Nippur, and re-
joined the Euphrates near Ur. Acts 16.13, as well as other
evidence, shows that Jews often worshipped beside running
water. Thus, when Ezekiel received his call, he was probably,
like Isaiah (Isa. 6), engaged in some act of worship. THE HAND
OF THE LORD WAS UPON HIM THERE (v. 3, cf. 3.22; 8.1; 33.22;
37.1; 40.1) means that some ecstatic experience suddenly overcame the prophet.

THE APPEARANCE OF THE GLORY OF YAHWEH

1.4-28

4. As I looked   The call of Ezekiel took the form of a vision
of Yahweh seated upon his throne. In I Kings 22.19 Micaiah
ben Imlah saw Yahweh sitting on his throne in heaven, while
Isaiah (6.1) saw him enthroned in the Temple. But Ezekiel
sees the throne appearing in a foreign land. A land other than
Palestine was technically not Yahweh's land, and was there-

fore unclean, so Ezekiel would not expect a throne vision in Babylon. But one of the prophet's main purposes is to convince the exiles that Yahweh had not abandoned them when he drove them forth from the homeland. His presence was still with them. And this is what is to be conveyed by the chariot on which the divine throne rests, and which has wheels. Yahweh is not localized in the temple at Jerusalem, but may move in all directions. His advent to Babylon is accompanied by storm and wind, a common feature of older theophanies, cf. Ex. 19f.; Judg. 5.4f.; Pss. 18.7-12; 68.7f. But why OUT OF THE NORTH (v. 4), for the references just given picture Yahweh as appearing from Sinai, which is to the south of Palestine? Babylonian mythology spoke of a mountain in the north as the dwelling place of the gods, and there are survivals of this idea in the OT, especially in Ps. 48.2, where Zion, on which the Temple stood, is described as 'in the far north' (RSV). Thus, geographical considerations do not here enter in, and the words are equivalent to 'from Yahweh's dwelling-place'. Yahweh was generally conceived as dwelling in heaven, but also as specially present in the Jerusalem Temple, see I Kings 8.

Verse 4 has probably been expanded. From the cloud manifestation issued the LIKENESS OF FOUR LIVING CREATURES (v. 5). (All through this inaugural vision the prophet displays the greatest reserve in describing the divine, and 'likeness' and 'appearance' and 'as it were' are used repeatedly. This may reflect the influence of Ezekiel's training as a priest.)

5-14. *The living creatures*

The description of the four living beings, which in ch. 10 are said to be cherubim, is not clear in detail, and Zimmerli may be correct in regarding vv. 6a, 7-11a, as a later expansion. Taking the text as it is, they had human form (v. 5), which, in view of what follows, may mean no more than that they stood upright like a man. Each one had four faces—here the pro-

phet has been influenced by Babylonian and Egyptian art—
THE FACE OF A MAN IN FRONT, . . . OF A LION ON THE RIGHT
SIDE, . . . OF AN OX ON THE LEFT SIDE, AND . . . OF AN
EAGLE AT THE BACK (v. 10), cf. Rev. 4.7. 'Thus four different
faces were presented in each direction, so that in whatever
direction the whole moved, while a man's face was presented
first, those of a lion, an ox and an eagle were also encountered'
(Davidson). 'The symbolism of the faces is well explained by
the Rabbis: "man is exalted among creatures; the eagle
is exalted among birds; the ox is exalted among domestic
animals; the lion is exalted among wild beasts; and all of
them have received dominion, and greatness have been given
them, yet they are stationed below the chariot of the Holy
One," Midrash Rabba *Shemoth* § 23 (on Ex. 15.1)' (Cooke).
Four is a figure symbolizing completeness. R. H. Charles,
following Zimmern and Gunkel, believes that the four living
creatures are to be traced back to the four chief constella-
tions of the zodiac, the Ox, the Lion, the Scorpion, and
Aquarius.[1] 'The relation of the lion and the ox to the con-
stellations of the lion and ox is obvious. The man corresponds
to the scorpion-man, while the eagle is taken not from
Aquarius, but from the constellation of the eagle in its neigh-
bourhood, probably because the former had no particularly
bright stars.'

6. Four wings Cf. the six wings of the seraphim in Isa. 6.2.

7. Their legs were straight That is, without joints. These
were not necessary, since the living creatures, who bore the
throne, did not require to lie down (Rashi). CALF'S FOOT: 'i.e.
rounded, for turning smoothly in every direction. Yahweh
must be entirely unimpeded in his own movements' (Lofthouse).

8-9. The meaning is uncertain. For 8b-9 LXX reads simply:

[1] *The Revelation of St John* (ICC), 1920, vol. I, pp. 121-3.

'the faces of the four did not turn round as they went; each went straight forward.' 'Each creature having a face on each side, it had no need to turn round when it desired to alter its course; the face towards the intended course moved forward in that direction' (Fisch, p. 4).

10. See above on v. 5.

11. Their wings Each creature had four wings. TWO WINGS, EACH OF WHICH TOUCHED THE WING OF ANOTHER, i.e. of the living creature on the right and the left, were outstretched ABOVE when they were in flight; the other two COVERED THEIR BODIES, cf. Isa. 6.2.

12. Cf. v. 9. THE SPIRIT: Yahweh's intention.

13. In the centre of the square formed by the living creatures there was a fire (cf. 10.2, 6). LIKE TORCHES MOVING TO AND FRO AMONG THE LIVING CREATURES is probably a gloss from Gen. 15.17 (so Zimmerli). The fire is an altar-fire, cf. Isa. 6, but with it has been combined the idea of the 'coals of fire' in the theophany of Yahweh in Ps. 18.13.

14. Omit with LXX.

15-21. *The four wheels*

A new element now comes in. Ezekiel sees a wheel beside each of the living creatures. They are the wheels of the divine chariot. It is possible that such a chariot, regarded as a vacant throne, stood in the holy of holies of Solomon's temple (Schmidt). Later, in Enoch 61.10; 71.7, the wheels are personified as Ophannim and represented as angels attending with the cherubim and seraphim upon God. Here, however, their function is connected with the motion of the chariot.

16. chrysolite AV 'beryl'; lit. 'the eye of Tarshish'.
a wheel within a wheel Davidson's explanation remains the

most convincing—'each of the four wheels looked like two wheels, cutting each other at right angles. In this way each of the four wheels had a rim or circumference facing each of the four directions, just as the living creatures had a face looking in each direction, so that towards whatever quarter the chariot moved *four* wheels seemed to be running in that direction.'

18. The text is uncertain, but the meaning seems to be that they had felloes or rims full of eyes. The eyes may symbolize life and intelligence (Kraetzschmar), cf. 10.12, or 'the divine omniscience' (Toy). Steinmann, however, suggests that the Hebrew word, lit. eye, should be taken in the secondary sense of *éclats* (perhaps 'gleams,' 'sparkling') and this may well be correct.

19-21. The wheels only moved as the living creatures moved, and these moved 'as intended by the Divine Presence in the *Merkabah*' (i.e. the Throne Chariot).[2]
'It is obvious that the idea of the Living Creatures and the wheels supporting the throne are syncretistic. It rested originally either on the living creatures or on the wheels. Both ideas were prevalent in the ancient world.'[3]

22-28. *The throne and the glory of Yahweh*
Above THE LIVING CREATURES was what looked like A FIRMAMENT (22-25), which proved to be the base of Yahweh's throne, and on the throne what looked like a man (26), surrounded by what looked like FIRE and BRIGHTNESS. SUCH WAS THE APPEARANCE OF THE LIKENESS OF THE GLORY OF THE LORD (28b). 'In speaking of supernatural realities the prophet can only suggest a *likeness* to familiar things' (Cooke).

22. The FIRMAMENT above the heads of the living creatures was a platform. CRYSTAL may mean ice. Verse 23 points back to v. 11. Two of each creature's wings were outstretched under

[2] Rashi, quoted by Fisch, p. 6.
[3] Charles, *op. cit.*, p. 123.

the platform to touch its neighbours', the other two wings covered the creature's body. But the verse is secondary, as are also vv. 24-25, for the interest is now no longer upon the living creatures, but on what is above the firmament. The verses have come in from 10.5.

24. The Almighty Shaddai, perhaps derived from Akkadian *šadū*, mountain, occurs as a designation for God chiefly in the poetical books.

26. The THRONE which rested on the platform looked LIKE SAPPHIRE, cf. Ex. 24.10. 'In his insistence on "likeness" in the vision of God, Ezekiel comes midway between the earlier narratives in the Pentateuch, where God is seen as clearly as a man, and the later ones where God Himself is not seen at all' (Lofthouse). (Omit AS THE APPEARANCE OF FIRE ENCLOSED ROUND ABOUT from v. 27.) This brightly shining figure is enclosed in light which resembled the colours of the rainbow. 'Just as the colours of the rainbow are not real but merely the effect of sunlight, so the likeness of the glory of the Lord as visualized by the prophet was only the reflection of the Divine light.'[4] This 'glory of God', which 'probably refers to the particular glory of the appearance sitting on the throne and the rainbow colours around him, not to the whole manifestation embracing the cherubim and wheels' (Davidson), is Ezekiel's way of indicating the divine presence. In ch. 10 the glory leaves the temple and, it is implied, departs to Babylon to dwell with the exiles there.

In this inaugural vision, which is composed of elements of various kinds and has been elaborated both by the prophet himself and by disciples, two things stand out, the splendour and incomparable power of God, and God's ability to work as he wishes. He is not bound to the holy land. This was an almost revolutionary idea.

[4] M. L. Malbim, quoted by Fisch, p. 8.

THE VISION OF THE ROLL
OF THE BOOK

2.1–3.9

THE CHARACTER OF EZEKIEL'S AUDIENCE

2.1-7

The Israelites had a long history of rebellion against God, but the prophet must speak to them without fear, whatever may be their attitude to him.

1. Son of man This form of God's address to Ezekiel occurs some ninety times in the book. According to Hebrew idiom 'son of' denotes membership of a class, e.g. II Kings 2.3, 'the sons of the prophets', Amos 7.14, 'son of a prophet'; while 'man' (Heb. *'ādām*) is collective. The complete phrase could be rendered 'man'. The title conveys at once the distance at which Ezekiel feels himself to stand before Yahweh, and the lack of claim which man has upon God, cf. Ps. 8.4; Job 25.6. There is no messianic sense here, as in the later Book of Enoch (46.2; 48.2). Steinmann may be correct when he says: 'In the expression itself there is something like a savour of anonymity and an evidence of universalism. Yahweh calls anyone at all to prophesy, without limits of caste, race or country.'

Stand upon your feet 'Those whom he (God) calls to his service are his fellow-workers, who may look upon his face. It is man erect, man in his manhood, with whom God will have fellowship and with whom he will speak—stand upon thy feet "that I may speak with thee"' (Davidson). On the other hand Lofthouse sees the prophet 'rather as a slave before his master'.

2. The Spirit Better 'spirit', the energizing power of God.

3. I send you The prophet's authorization.

The people of Israel In 3.4 the prophet is told, 'Get you to the house of Israel' (the normal phrase), and in 3.11 'Get you to the exiles'. But Ezekiel's mission included the whole nation, and embraced even the previous exiles of 722 (37.15ff.). A NATION OF REBELS: Ezekiel is not thinking simply of the worsening situation in his own day, but of Israel's whole history. Even at her election itself, she was rebellious, and had continued so ever since, see chs. 20, 23. Hosea also implies early rebelliousness (Hos. 11.1ff.), and Isaiah uses the adjective (Isa. 1.23; 30.9); cf. also Jer. 2.4ff.

4. Omit the first clause with LXX.

5. They will know This is the first occurrence of Ezekiel's most characteristic phrase, THEY WILL KNOW. Broadly speaking, the purpose of all God's actions, and of the prophet's, is that Israel and the rest of the nations may know Yahweh and his power. THEN THEY WILL KNOW THAT I AM YAHWEH is one of the most frequent conclusions of an Ezekiel oracle. To some extent (THEY) WILL KNOW THAT THERE HAS BEEN A PROPHET AMONGST THEM means the same thing, since a prophet is Yahweh's ambassador and spokesman; cf. 'He who hears you (the seventy) hears me (Jesus)' (Luke 10.16). But the words, implying as they do Ezekiel's eventual vindication—Deuteronomy's test of the true prophet is that his prophecies should be fulfilled (Deut. 18.20ff.)—are intended both to strengthen him for the public discharge of his office and to comfort him in personal trials such the scorn expressed in 33.32. BRIERS

AND THORNS among which SCORPIONS lurk, is an expressive way of describing dangerous opponents. Ezekiel is exhorted to convey his message to the people without fear for his personal safety (Fisch). There is here no promise of divine protection such as was given to the young Jeremiah at his call, Jer. 1.8, 17ff. Did the hard streak that is apparent in Ezekiel's personality render this unnecessary?

THE MANNER OF EZEKIEL'S INSPIRATION

2.8–3.3

A prophet is above all a speaker, a spokesman for Yahweh, and the most characteristic opening of an oracle is the 'messenger formula', 'Thus says the Lord'. Correspondingly, at Isaiah's inaugural vision his lips are touched with glowing coals taken from the altar (Isa. 6.7), while in the case of Jeremiah, Yahweh put forth his hand and touched the prophet's mouth, and said to him 'Behold, I have put my words in your mouth' (Jer. 1.9). Ezekiel advances on the latter conception, and sees A HAND—Yahweh's, though this is not stated—holding a SCROLL, which he is to eat, and then go and speak to the house of Israel. (The whole experience is, of course, visionary.) There is thus a difference between Ezekiel's inspiration and that of Isaiah and Jeremiah. When the two latter were to speak, Yahweh spoke directly to them. But Ezekiel's communion is with a written book: the whole content of chs. 4-24 (see below) is given here at one time for him to reproduce, as it were, from time to time. (In contrast, the Suffering Servant's inspiration is a daily thing: 'Morning by morning he wakens, he wakens my ear to hear as those who are taught' [Isa. 50.4].) This change may have been due in part at least to the publication of Deuteronomy, which gathered together various legal words of Yahweh spoken on different occasions and made of them the authoritative written 'word' of Yahweh. But Steinmann is surely right when he says that 'it bears a hypertrophy of literature', as is also Grether: 'It is a coarsening of the concept of the reception of relevation when Ezekiel (2.8ff.) is in a moment given a scroll to eat, this is to say, is right away given a whole store of "words" to last for years.'[5] Another cause of the change may be the greater need felt by the exilic and post-exilic prophets to have their authorization recognized, a need reflected in Ezekiel in the greater frequency of abnormal physical and psychical conditions accompanying revelation.

10. Writing on the front and on the back That is, on both sides of the parchment. Normally a roll was written on one side only. This may be meant to suggest the great load and burden of LAMENTATION AND MOURNING AND WOE that the prophet was to speak. This description applies only to chs. 4-24 (or 4-32): thereafter there are oracles of hope.

3.3. It was in my mouth as sweet as honey Not because of its content, or because the prophet rejoiced in the delivery of such a terrible message (see also on 6.11), but because it was the word of Yahweh, cf. Ps. 119.103.

A WARNING AGAINST DISAPPOINTMENT

3.4-9

The prophet's instant obedience to Yahweh's command (3.2f.) is in the sharpest contrast to the attitude he will find in his hearers, the house of Israel. Their obstinate refusal to listen is then compared with the reception that God's emissary

[5] O. Grether, *Name und Wort Gottes im Alten Testament* (BZAW 64), 1934, p. 144.

might have found among foreigners, had he been sent to them. This is a new note in prophecy: while Isaiah speaks of the Assyrians as Yahweh's tool (Isa. 10.5), and Jeremiah makes him call Nebuchadnezzar his servant (Jer. 27.6), neither of these had any idea that 'barbarians' might be more open to Yahweh than his chosen people. This is then the germ of universalism. The idea is taken up again in the Gospels, e.g. Matt. 11.21-24; Luke 11.32.

8. I have made your face hard God gives the prophet the strength to endure and persist.

9. Adamant harder than flint Cf. the Servant, Isa. 50.7. Yahweh here puns on the prophet's name, for Ezekiel means 'he makes strong, hard'.

EZEKIEL ENTERS UPON HIS WORK

3.10-15

After a further and final commission (10, 11), in which Ezekiel's mission to the house of Israel (3.4-6) is more clearly defined as directed to the exiles, the vision ceases, though the prophet remains under the effects of the ecstasy (THE SPIRIT, 12, 14), and still hears, though no longer seeing, the divine chariot throne (12f.). Grieved with the message he has to deliver, Ezekiel comes to the exiles at TELABIB, which was probably their main settlement. Telabib, which in Heb. means 'hill of corn ears', represents the Babylonian Til-abûbi, 'the hill of storms', a sandhill thrown up by storms.

15. It took the prophet some considerable time (SEVEN DAYS is a round number) to recover from the effects of the vision.

TWO LATER INSERTIONS

3.16b-21, 22-27

16a. And at the end of seven days These words are to be connected directly with 4.1. 16b-21 are a later insertion, as the Hebrew text makes clear. They anticipate ch. 18 and 33.7-9, and are put here as a kind of programme that there are to be other aspects of the prophet's message than sheer doom. See on ch. 18 and 33.7-9.

Verses 22-27 depend on 4.4, 5, 8, and also link up with 24.26f.; 33.22f.

24. shut yourself within your house Ezekiel is not to exercise a public ministry, but the exiles are to come to him, cf. 8.1; 11.25; 14.1, etc.

25. cords will be placed upon you Cf. 4.4-8, from which the idea is derived.

26. The dumbness is probably not any physical condition such as intermittent aphasia, but merely a figure denoting absence of public activity, which only begins again after tidings come of the fall of Jerusalem (33.22; cf. 24.27), that is, when the prophecies contained in chs. 4-24 have been fulfilled.

JERUSALEM MUST BE DESTROYED

4.1–24.27

'With the fourth chapter we enter on the exposition of the first great division of Ezekiel's prophecies.' Chapters 4 to 24 'cover a period of about four and a half years, extending from the time of the prophet's call to the commencement of the siege of Jerusalem' (Skinner, p. 59).

SYMBOLIC ACTIONS

4.1–5.17

As the first part of his work among the exiles, Ezekiel is commanded not to speak prophetic words, but to perform certain acts. Such action had been part of Yahweh's revelation through the prophets from the beginning. Ahijah of Shiloh (c. 925) tore his mantle in twelve pieces to symbolize the division of the kingdom in the time of Rehoboam (I Kings 11.29-30), while in the reign of Ahab (c. 873-852), Zedekiah made himself horns of iron to represent the destruction of the Syrians (I Kings 22.11). Similar symbolic acts were continued by the later classical prophets (Hos. 1.3; Isa. 8.1-4; 20.1-6), and became particularly frequent with those of the exilic period, Jeremiah (Jer. 13.1-11; 16.1-4, 5-7, 8-9; 19.1-2a, 10-11a; etc.) and Ezekiel. Current scholarship regards them as more than simply vivid visual representations of a truth proclaimed also in words—as it were, a calling in of the eye to reinforce the ear. Like the prophet's word, they were thought to have power. Their roots lie in magic. When early

57

man performed a symbolic action, he believed he was com-
pelling the gods to give effect to what was represented. With
Ezekiel and his strong insistence on the absolute sovereignty
of Yahweh, such primitive and mechanical ideas have of
course been left behind. Nevertheless, the element of effective-
ness remains. As William A. Irwin says: 'Ezekiel's drama of
the captured city (4.1–5.3; 24.1-11) and his numerous similar
performances, although regarded by the populace as merely
good entertainment, had, for the prophet . . . some positive
worth in accomplishing the ends he predicted.'[1] (When he
speaks of entertainment, he has in mind Ezek. 33.30-33.)

Shortly after Ezekiel's time, the Second Isaiah was to say
of the word of Yahweh spoken by a prophet: 'It shall not
return to me empty, but it shall accomplish that which I
purpose, and prosper in the thing for which I sent it' (Isa.
55.11). Again, and perhaps contemporaneously with Ezekiel,
the Deuteronomistic school of historians edited the history of
the monarchy from the point of view that 'there exists . . .
an inter-relationship between the words of Jahweh and history
in the sense that Jahweh's word, once uttered, reaches its goal
under all circumstances in history by virtue of the power
inherent in it'.[2] It is exactly the same with symbolic actions—
they are, in fact, 'prophecies in act' (Cooke), 'in miniature,
the purpose of Yahweh' (H. Wheeler Robinson).[3] What is
represented, as for example here the destruction of Jerusalem
and the exile, will inevitably come about; indeed, one might
even say that the prophet's action, which properly speaking
is not his but Yahweh's, sets the train of events in motion. Or,
putting it in another way, we may say that these actions are
anticipations of the historical fulfilment of what the prophet

[1] In *The Intellectual Adventure of Ancient Man* by H. Frankfort
and others, Cambridge, 1947, p. 298.
[2] G. von Rad, *Studies in Deuteronomy*, ET (SBT 9), 1953, p. 78.
[3] In his essay 'Prophetic Symbolism' in *Old Testament Essays*, ed.
D. C. Simpson, London, 1927, p. 14.

declared in his preaching. (The siege of Jerusalem did not begin until four years after Ezekiel's call, cf. 1.2 and 24.1f.) Word and act have therefore parallel functions, the only difference being that the latter would perhaps strike home more vividly. Word and deed are much more closely connected in Hebrew thought than in ours. '*Dabhar* means not only "word" but also "deed".'[4] It has long been noted that, as they now stand, some of the symbolic actions recorded in Ezek. 4–5 refer to the siege of Jerusalem (4.1–3; 4.7; 4.9a, 12, 14–15 with secondary additions 10–11, 16–17; 5.1–2 with secondary additions 3–4), while others refer to the exile (4.4–6, 8; 4.9b, 13). Almost certainly only the first set is original: the latter were added after the fall of the city, as the disorders in the text make clear (e.g. 4.7 is an awkward attempt to connect vv. 4–6 with 1–3, while 4.16–17 connect with vv. 10–11, on which see below). The addition of the exilic symbolism and the verses connecting it with the original siege passage may have been the work of the prophet himself. Much more probably, however, is it due to his disciples, who desired to bring their master's teaching up to date so that it would still have something to say to later altered conditions. In the ancient world there was no such thing as copyright: later ages freely added to, adapted, and even gave a new turn to, earlier matter (cf. the growth of the Pentateuch, or the commonly accepted view of the Pastoral Epistles). In the prophets some of these 'redactions' are of great value as showing the way in which

[4] T. Boman, *Hebrew Thought Compared with Greek*, trs. J. L. Moreau, London, 1960, p. 65, Cf. J. A. Lindblom: 'The effect of the prophetic symbolic actions upon the onlookers was consequently not only to present visibly what the prophet had to say, but also to convince them that the events predicted by the prophet would really take place. They were also intended to arouse the motions of fear or hope, according to circumstances. Thus what was done powerfully reinforced the word' (*Prophecy in Ancient Israel*, Oxord, 1962, p. 172). 'Its [the sign's] intention is to attest to the speech in the hour which it was delivered (C. Westermann, *Basic Forms of Prophetic Speech*, trs H. C. White, London, 1967, p. 159).

the tradition connected with a particular prophet continued as a living force after he himself fell silent.

FIRST SYMBOLIC ACT: THE SIEGE PORTRAYED

4.1-3

While we may think Ezekiel's action strange, and even childish, it accurately represents the various means used to besiege an ancient city, and the terms are the proper technical terms. This has been shown by excavations. The siege of a fortified city has been described as 'that crowning horror of ancient warfare' (Skinner); cf. II Kings 6.24-31.

1. Bricks, dried in the sun, were the common building material of Babylonia, and architects also drew their plans upon them. (This is one of the arguments against a Palestinian location for chs. 1-24: in Palestine the material commonly used was stone.) EVEN JERUSALEM is a gloss: Ezekiel's audience was not to know right away what city was meant. It might have been Babylon itself—see on 5.5.

2. The SIEGE WALL is a rampart encircling the city, to cut it off from its food supplies. The other works were designed to facilitate its capture.

3. The verse may describe another, originally independent, siege symbol. The prophet takes an IRON PLATE, such as was commonly used for baking, and places it between himself and the city. The meaning of the action is not altogether clear. (A similar image occurs, though with a different implication, in Jer. 1.18.) IRON and PRESS might suggest that the power of the Babylonians was irresistible. Yet SET YOUR FACE against (not TOWARD as RSV) IT suggests that the actor whom the

prophet represents is rather Yahweh. The symbol may therefore signify 'the inexorable grasp which the judgment of God
has taken of the city' (Davidson). This is in keeping with the
rest of the first twenty-four chapters, and Ezekiel may also
have had in mind Isa. 29.3, where the speaker is Yahweh
and the city Jerusalem : 'And I will encamp against you round
about, and will besiege you with towers, and I will raise
siegeworks against you.'

set your face Cf. vv. 2, 7; 13.17; 20.46 etc. 'Possibly the formula had originally a magical significance; cf. Fohrer in HAT.
The same phrase is frequently utilized in the Ugaritic texts
to indicate the person to whom a speech or a message is
addressed, someone to whom a visit is to be paid, etc.'[5] The
real adversary with whom the once chosen people have to
deal is not a foreign invader but Yahweh himself. (For a vivid
illustration of the way in which the prophets regarded Israel's
enemies as instruments of Yahweh whom he uses to punish
her, see Isa. 10.5-15; cf. also the designation by Jeremiah of
Nebuchadnezzar as 'my servant', Jer. 25.9; 27.6; and by II
Isaiah of Cyrus as his [Yahweh's] 'anointed', Isa. 45.1.) The
IRON PLATE placed between the prophet, representing Yahweh,
and the city, could also suggest the divorce which there now
was between God and his people (Bertholet).

That the whole nation, and not simply the capital city
itself, is to be involved in the judgment is implied in the words
THIS IS A SIGN FOR THE HOUSE OF ISRAEL; for in Ezek. 1-24
THE HOUSE OF ISRAEL generally means the whole people still
in the homeland (see further notes on 4.4-8).

[5] Lindblom, *op. cit.*, p. 154, n. 74. He refers to examples in G. R.
Driver, *Canaanite Myths and Legends*, Edinburgh, 1956, pp. 89, 91,
103, 105, 107.

SECOND SYMBOLIC ACT: THE PROPHET
BEARS SIN

4.4-8

[Verses 4-6, 8: exile; v. 7: siege.]

There may be an unexpressed connection between this act
and the foregoing, for without saying so, the latter gives the
reason why Yahweh had become the opponent and destroyer
of his people. After the calamity of 586, the question was
inevitable: *Why* has this befallen us? What has caused the
failure of the promises made to our forefathers, particularly
that of a land in which we were to dwell for ever? Cf. Gen.
12.1; 13.15 etc. For now we are in the same plight as the ten
tribes of the northern kingdom, and, as for 'Mount Zion which
lies desolate, jackals prowl over it' (Lam. 5.18). Is the reason
that the gods of Babylon are stronger than Yahweh, and he
shares in the defeat of his people; or has he for some cause
tired of us and cast us off? In Ezek. 4.4-6, 8, the responsibility
is, on the contrary, placed fairly and squarely on the shoulders
of the nation itself. It is her own sin that has brought her to this
pass. Once more to quote Lamentations, which was probably
composed shortly after 586: 'Her foes have become the head,
her enemies prosper, because the Lord has made her suffer
for the multitude of her transgressions; her children have
gone away, captives before the foe' (Lam. 1.5). This had been,
of course, the burden of the prophets ever since the time of
Amos (Amos 4). But evidently in the intervening century and
a half the lesson of the fall of Samaria had been largely forgotten (see notes on Ezek. 16.44ff. and 23.11ff.), and Ezekiel
—like Jeremiah—had to make the old teaching once more
alive.

As it now stands, the symbolic action has two parts. In the

first (vv. 4-6), the prophet is to lie for a hundred and ninety days (taking the Septuagint reading instead of the MT) upon his left side, bearing the punishment of the house of Israel, which here (exceptionally in chs. 1-24, though cf. 37.16) means the former northern kingdom, and not, as in 4.3 and usually, the whole nation. Thereafter, for forty days he is to lie on his right side, doing the same thing for the southern kingdom of Judah. (In Hebrew the left signifies the north and the right the south.) The PUNISHMENT is, of course, for the northern kingdom, the exile of 722, and for the southern, that of 586. In the second part of the action (v. 8), the prophet is to have cords put upon him.

The verses are full of difficulties. (a) Symbolic actions were normally performed, but even taking the shorter period of a hundred and ninety days, how are we to conceive of the prophet lying, presumably motionless (v. 8), for such a length of time? He may, of course, have lain for only a short period each day. The impossibility of carrying out the act has led some to think of cataleptic or similar abnormal conditions; parallels—rather unsatisfying—have also been drawn between the prophet and Indian fakirs and Yogi. Perhaps the text represents an experience which Ezekiel only had in vision, and which he recounted to his audience without actually carrying out the symbol.

(b) It is not easy to understand the numbers, certainly not the MT's three hundred and ninety. A hundred and ninety days and forty days are meant to represent the length of the exile of the northern and the southern kingdoms respectively. The natural starting point for the exile of Samaria would be 722. If Ezekiel were writing in 593, then Israel had been roughly a hundred and thirty years in exile. If the prophet expected her to be restored along with Judah (cf. 37.15ff.), then the forty years of the Judean exile brings the total up to a hundred and seventy years. But forty years looks like a schematic figure for a generation. Again, v. 9 suggests that a hundred and ninety days (LXX: MT again gives 390) was the total period, which, deducting the forty years for Judah, would leave a hundred and fifty for Israel. There is really no satisfactory explanation.

(c) Verse 8, the second part of the action, introduces a new element: Yahweh is to bind the prophet so that he cannot move. This seems to have some connection with, and perhaps to presuppose, 3.25. But unless the words mean no more than that he cannot move during the hundred and ninety days and again during the forty, they are hardly consistent with v. 7. The use of the word siege in connection with Ezekiel himself is also suspicious. In itself, v. 8 has a fairly plain meaning: 'the consequent discomfort symbolized the rigours of the siege' (Fisch). If, however, the symbol is read as referring to the exile, it alludes to the restriction of movement there.

It is probable that the text as we have it represents the expansion of a relatively simple symbolic act in which Ezekiel lay for some time, perhaps originally unspecified, on his side or sides, signifying some aspect of the siege of Jerusalem. Later, after the exile had already taken place, this was worked over. The idea of 'punishment', which refers to the exile, was then brought in, but at the same time a further connection with the siege was made by the introduction of v. 7.

7. With your arm bared The baring of the arm is preparation for battle, cf. Isa. 52.10.

Two points of perhaps greater interest to ourselves in the second symbolic act are:

(a) As we have already noticed (see on 3.16-21), and shall have to deal with more fully again in connection with chs. 18 and 33, one of the questions which occupied the exilic and post-exilic ages was that of the correspondence between guilt and punishment. Was a man's suffering in exact proportion to his guilt? Verse 5 seems to suggest the answer given by the earlier orthodoxy in the OT tradition, as for example Deuteronomy and Job's friends, namely that the correspondence is exact—*one* day for *one* year, neither more nor less. However, since part of the answer given by Ezekiel himself (see chs. 18 and 33) is different, v. 5 is probably a gloss.

(b) As Zimmerli has shown,[6] the phrase BEAR THE PUNISH-MENT (guilt) is used in connection with ideas of representa-tion and substitution: e.g. in Lev. 16.22 the scapegoat bears the people's iniquities into the wilderness as their representa-tive, and in Lev. 10.17 the goat of the sin offering is appointed 'to bear the iniquity of the congregation, to make atonement'.

When Ezekiel is commanded to BEAR THE PUNISHMENT of Israel and Judah, a new note enters into the preaching of the prophets (though we do find a somewhat similar development in Ezekiel's contemporary Jeremiah). To a larger extent earlier spokesmen of Yahweh stood as it were outside Israel. They addressed her, in terms of reprimand and threats, or with words of appeal. But they never gave the impression of being one with her. They were, so to speak, wholly on Yahweh's side. Now, no prophet is more harsh to his contemporaries than Ezekiel. He sees in Israel no good at all: she is a rebellious house (2.3ff., etc.), and had been so from the very beginning (ch. 20). Indeed, the passion of his denunciations of his own people, and the coarseness of his language towards them, e.g. in ch. 16, repel us. Yet, here this same prophet is commanded to BEAR their PUNISHMENT. And this is more than simply identification with his people—while still remaining the spokesman of Yahweh, he is also, as never before among the prophets, a member of the house of Israel. The phrase therefore means that his own experience is now caught up in theirs, and that to some extent he embodies and represents them. The prophetic office is no longer a thing apart, but the bearer of it and those for whose benefit it had been instituted were 'bound up in the bundle' together. This is no doubt still

---

[6] *ZAW* 66, 1954, pp. 9-12; cf. his commentary, p. 116.

C

far from the vicarious atonement which Christianity sees in
the sufferings and death of Jesus Christ, but it is a first, and
momentous, step along this road.

Further, Zimmerli asks whether it is an accident that not
only the words 'bear their iniquities', but also 'yet he opened
not his mouth . . . like a sheep that is dumb, so he opened
not his mouth' (cf. Ezek. 3.26f.; 24.27; 33.32), occur in connection with the Suffering Servant of II Isaiah (Isa. 53.12, 7).
'The Ezekiel tradition, too, seems to have made its contribu-
tion to the shaping of the picture of the Suffering Servant
of Yahweh who bore the sins of many' (p. 117 of his commentary).

THIRD SYMBOLIC ACT: HARDSHIP

4.9-17

[Verses 9a, 12, 14-15: siege, with secondary additions, 10-11,
16-17; vv. 9b, 13: exile.]

Here it is much more difficult to be certain what part comes
from Ezekiel himself, and what is later addition.

What these verses emphasize are the straits which the continuing siege will bring with it, the necessity of, as it were,
scraping every barrel for anything, of however poor quality,
that might lessen the pangs of hunger and help to eke out
what meagre stores of food, water and cooking material
still remain in the city; for, of course, in conditions of siege
nothing can be brought in from the country districts.

9. spelt   A kind of grain like wheat (*triticum satirum*, Köhler-
Baumgartner, *Lexikon; triticum spelta, OED*). In spite of
Lev. 19.19 and Deut. 22.9-11, the mixture of grain in v. 9 was
not ritually unclean and so was lawful.

12. you shall eat it as a barley cake The point is probably that, in the normal course of events, each of the kinds of food mentioned would have been prepared in a different way; but now, perhaps because of shortage of fuel, they were to be baked as barley cakes are (Ehrlich).

But, if the food itself was not unclean, its method of cooking, BAKING IT . . . ON HUMAN DUNG, rendered it so. The usual way of baking barley cakes was on hot stones (I Kings 19.6). Where stones were not available, animal dung mixed with straw was used—as among the Bedouin to this day. 'The hot ashes remaining from it are perfectly clean, and retaining their glow for a considerable time were used for firing cakes upon or under' (Davidson). But human excrement caused defilement (see Deut. 23.12ff.), and therefore the food now became ritually unclean.

14. Ezekiel is appalled by Yahweh's command—the more so since, as a priest, he has been obliged most scrupulously to shun all contact with uncleanness. He therefore protests—the one occasion in the whole book. (In this matter of protesting, Ezekiel shows himself very different from Jeremiah—see e.g. Jer. 20.7ff. Compared with the latter, Ezekiel is the passionate, willing instrument of Yahweh's commands.) WHAT DIED OF ITSELF: on the various kinds of flesh here mentioned see Ex. 22.31; Deut. 14.21; Lev. 17.15 (Ezek. 44.31); Lev. 7.18; 19.7. While a cake baked on human excrement does not, of course, fall into the category of forbidden flesh, the fact that this last immediately came into Ezekiel's mind in connection with the BARLEY CAKE shows how revolting Yahweh's command was to one brought up in priestly scrupulosity. As the result of his protestation, a concession is made.

We may remember that the OT division of foods into clean and unclean (see especially Lev. 11 and Deut. 14.3-21) made a problem for the early Church once it entered a non-Jewish environment, which knew nothing of such food laws (Acts 10.9-16).

Verses 10-11 and 16-17 are to be taken as secondary additions, for while still dealing with the siege of Jerusalem, they introduce a new hardship motif: it is not now the uncleanness of the food, but the scarcity of it.

10. twenty shekels a day About eight ounces.

11. the sixth part of a hin About two pints. Jerusalem's water-supply has always been a problem. In Ezekiel's time it depended on one or two springs, and on cisterns which stored the water which fell in the rainy seasons. For an attempt by Hezekiah to improve the supply, see II Kings 20.20.

16-17. There is a close parallel to these verses in 12.17-19, and they may be a duplicate recension. They have also close connections with Lev. 26.26, 39. They intensify the terrors of the siege as described in vv. 10-11. But there is a new element as compared with vv. 10-11. Verses 16-17 are not a command to the prophet to do something, but the interpretation, to himself, of the symbolic action he is to perform.

9b, 13. These verses have been added to the siege symbolism, in order to make a connection with the exile. Those deported are to eat unclean food (v. 13). The point is that any land except Yahweh's own land of Palestine was unclean (cf. Amos' words to Amaziah, the priest of Bethel, when he threatened the latter with banishment: 'you yourself shall die in an unclean land', Amos 7.17), and the produce of its soil was also unclean (Hos. 9.3, where the foreign land is Assyria). The reason for this uncleanness was the belief held in the earlier pre-exilic period that lands other than Palestine belonged to other deities (I Sam. 26.19), and that therefore there could be no contact with Yahweh in them. (As we have already seen (pp. 44f.), one of Ezekiel's main tasks was to destroy this idea.)

We today do not realize how dire a threat v. 13 involved for Ezekiel's contemporaries. 'The idea is that all food which has not been consecrated by being presented to Jehovah in the sanctuary is necessarily unclean, and those who eat of it contract ceremonial defilement. In the very act of satisfying his natural appetite a man forfeits his religious standing. This was the peculiar hardship of the state of exile, that a man must become unclean, he must eat unconsecrated food unless he renounced his religion and served the gods of the land in which he dwelt. . . . The whole life of Israel was to become unclean' (Skinner).

On a question of unclean food in a foreign land, see also Dan. 1. For another aspect of the dietary question, see I Cor. 8.

FOURTH SYMBOLIC ACT: THE DIVINE ANSWER

5.1-2, expanded by 3-4 (siege)

1-2. Taking over what had already been used by Isaiah (Isa. 7.20) as an image and turning it into a symbolic action, the prophet shaves the hair of his head. 'The word spoken a hundred and forty years previously [by Isaiah] is now authoritatively brought into a new situation and actualized.'[7] Shaving could signify disgrace (II Sam. 10.4f.) or mourning (Isa. 15.2; Jer. 41.5), but Fohrer may be right when he says that 'the hair was taken as the part of the body in which life and force resided, or it symbolized the whole man from whom it had been taken, so that he experienced the same thing as the hair did. Accordingly, the shaving which followed the

[7] Zimmerli, *Das Alte Testament als Anrede*, Munich, 1956, p. 50.

sword of war meant the severance of the inhabitants of a city
or country from the basis of its life' (HAT, p. 34). The SWORD
represents the Babylonians; the BALANCES suggest 'the
inerrancy of the divine judgment: cf. Isa. 28.17' (Lofthouse).
Zimmerli points out that dividing, counting and weighing are
also judicial procedures, cf. Dan. 5.26ff.

2. The phrases IN THE MIDST OF THE CITY, WHEN THE DAYS OF
THE SIEGE ARE COMPLETED, and ROUND ABOUT THE CITY may
not be original. Some take THE CITY to mean the model of the
first symbolic act (4.1-3). The last clause, with its abrupt
change to the first person, is also secondary: its purpose was
to show that even those who escaped would still be punished;
this is in keeping with Ezekiel's own thought, as later
expressed in 20.33-38.

By the first of the three parts into which the hair is divided
are meant those who perish during the course of the siege,
by the second those who are killed in battle, in skirmishes
near the city or, like Zedekiah, in attempts to escape (II
Kings 25.4ff.), or else in the general carnage which would
accompany the capture; the last part means those who survive
and are deported. It has however been maintained (Ziegler)
that there is a difference in meaning between SCATTER TO THE
WIND and the phrase 'scatter among the countries' (11.16,
etc.): the former signifies the complete dissolution of the
community, the latter exile in the sense of Diaspora, removal
from Palestine, with (presumably) the possibility of continuance of some form of community life. Verses 3-4 are a later
expansion, and their exact meaning is not clear. (The last
clause in 4 is quite unintelligible.) The general idea seems to
be that even among the exiles there is to be a further act of
judgment, a winnowing, cf. 20.33-38.

We have thus had four symbolic acts. These are followed
by an interpretation.

INTERPRETATION

5.5-17

The commentary falls into two parts. The first (vv. 5-10, 14-15) gives the reason for the fate which was to overtake Jerusalem, and may therefore be said to connect most closely with the first symbolic act, the second (vv. 11-13, 16-17) deals rather with the nature of the punishment, and is therefore particularly related to the last symbolic act. Probably no more than vv. 5-6a (down to ROUND ABOUT HER), 8-9 and 14-15 derive from Ezekiel himself.

5-10, 14-15. *Jerusalem's failure*

The general thought is that Jerusalem fell because she paid no regard to the high dignity conferred upon her, the honour of having been set IN THE CENTRE OF THE NATIONS (5).

In Babylon and Assyria the world was thought of as the microcosm: things on the earth here correspond to things in the heavenly sphere. 'Such unity . . . necessitates the creation of a symbol that will express the point of physical connection between the two separate parts, the point at which the stream of being flows from the cosmos into the empire. . . . The symbol . . . may be called by the Greek name *omphalos*, meaning the navel of the world, at which transcendent forces of being flow into the social order.'[8] The idea is also found in China, Greece (Delphi, cf. Pindar, *Pythians*, 4.13f.) and Rome. In 38.12 Palestine is called the navel (RSV: 'centre') of the earth, and here Jerusalem is regarded as the *omphalos*. 'The people of the omphalos were under a special obligation to abide by the order of the Lord. What was pardonable in the outlying parts of the world was an unpardonable

[8] E. Voegelin, *Israel and Revelation*, Louisiana, 1956, p. 27.

offense if committed by the people of the center. If the people of the omphalos imitated the ways of the outlying neighbors, they could be visited with severe punishment' (5.7-17).[9]

5. I have set her   This is another way of expressing Israel's election. Since he belonged to the Jerusalem priesthood and was at home in the traditions of that city, what Ezekiel probably had in mind was Yahweh's choice of David and Zion (II Sam. 7; II Chron. 6.6). We also find the idea of the glory of Jerusalem in Isaiah (Isa. 29.5ff.; 31.5, 9).

6. But Jerusalem was not equal to her privileged position. Because of her election, 'she should have been distinguished above the nations in righteousness, but (v. 6) her corruption was become deeper than theirs' (Davidson). The ORDINANCES and STATUTES, a favourite collocation of terms in Ezekiel, cf. 11.20, etc., mean the Law, which was from the very beginning connected with the election at Sinai. Ezekiel's complaint that Israel had acted according to the ordinances of the surrounding nations is echoed by Jeremiah (Jer. 2.10, 11), who adds that these nations have been faithful to their gods. What the ORDINANCES OF THE NATIONS are (v. 7), the prophet does not say, but Toy is certainly correct: 'all moral and religious precepts and rules, even those known to other nations, are here considered as enacted by the God of Israel.' (While v. 8 does not expressly state that the Law was superior to the ordinances of the nations, and that therefore Israel's rebellion was all the more culpable, cf. Amos 2.11, this is no doubt implied.)

This brief and rather colourless historical retrospect given in vv. 5-7 is the justification of the action of Yahweh which follows in vv. 8-9, introduced by the typical THEREFORE. These verses, too, are in general terms—all that is said is that

[9] Voegelin, *op. cit.*, p. 28.

Yahweh's action is to be unparalleled in its severity. Verse
10, which adds details, is later. Lam. 4.10 says that children
were actually eaten for food during the siege.

8. In the sight of the nations 'The prophet insists repeatedly
that the divine judgments on Israel are to take place IN THE
SIGHT OF THE NATIONS both as an example, and to vindicate
Jahveh's Godhead and essential Nature before the world:
20.9, 14, 22, 41; 22.16; 28.25; 38.23; 39.27' (Cooke). The
nations will thereby learn both the justice and the power of
Yahweh. As we shall see later (pp. 253), this is one of the
main motives of Yahweh's action on Israel.

Verses 14-15 should be taken here, since with 5-6a, 8-9
they form the original oracle. The thought is that the nation
is to suffer more than dire physical calamity: she who perhaps
boasted of her election to 'unclean' foreigners—is not
merely to be placed dishonoured among them, but also to
have to endure their mockery as having forfeited her
privileges.

5.11-13, 16-17. *Terrors of punishment*

Verse 11 brings another justification of Yahweh's action,
the profanation of the temple, which is also the subject of
ch. 8. DETESTABLE THINGS and ABOMINATIONS are synonyms,
and refer to idolatry. Verse 12 resumes v. 2, though in a
slightly different way: the FIRE in v. 2 is now more nearly
defined as PESTILENCE and FAMINE. Pestilence, famine and
sword form a frequent triad in Ezekiel as instruments of the
divine punishment (e.g. 7.15; 14.13, 17, 19), and are taken
over from Jeremiah (e.g. Jer. 15.2).

13. Jealousy 'The word . . . expresses the *heat* of any
passion, here resentment, ch. 16.38, 42; 23.25; 36.5, 6; 38.19'
(Davidson). 'Yahweh's . . . jealousy is a strong emotion for
what is right, especially with regard to the exclusive covenant-
c*

relationship of Israel with Himself alone (Ezek. 8.3). He cannot brook any rivals in Israel's affections, and must punish Israel's defections from the covenant-relationship, and also those who seek to destroy that relationship from without (Nahum 1.2).'[10] On the last clause see the oracles against foreign nations, chs. 25-32, 38-39. On jealousy and the marriage bond, see ch. 16.

Howie writes: 'Verses 13-17 introduce a dominant theme of Ezekiel's prophecy. God's actions in history, whether for judgment or for redemption, are all designed that the nations may know that he is the Lord, the only God, and that they may see his true nature.'[11]

Verses 16-17, which are composed of stock phrases, may be regarded as giving concreteness to v. 13.

This section 5.5-17 thus offers the justification for the threats made in Ezekiel's symbolic acts. The way in which the exiles would receive the idea that Jerusalem must be destroyed may be inferred from Jeremiah's letter to them (Jer. 29, cf. also Jer. 27.16). Incited by nationalist prophets, they were hoping for a speedy return to the homeland and the continuance of normal life there. Thus, the words in Ezek. 3.7, 'The house of Israel will not listen to you', probably now received their first fulfilment.

Mention of Jeremiah suggests a significant difference between him and Ezekiel. Right up to the time when the Babylonians captured Jerusalem, and in spite of moods when he was overtaken by despair and so seemed to speak with a different voice, Jeremiah believed that the doom might still be averted, if there were real repentance (cf. Jer. 7.5-7). Ezekiel has no such comfort. In his unrelieved gloom he appears to have jumped back more than a century to Amos.

[10] S. B. Frost, article 'Jealousy' in Hastings' one-volume *Dictionary of the Bible*, 2nd ed., 1965, p. 460.
[11] *Ezekiel, Daniel* (LBC), pp. 26f.

No doubt distance—his exilic situation—made it clear to him
that the position in Jerusalem was already hopeless. Therefore, until tidings reached him that the city had actually fallen
(33.21), his message continued to be that the real adversary
of the nation was Yahweh himself (cf. Jer. 21.5), and that
Yahweh would certainly perform the word which he was
speaking by the mouth of his prophet.

THE NATION'S SIN AND ITS PUNISHMENT

6.1–7.27

THE MOUNTAINS OF ISRAEL

6.1-7

After having represented by means of symbolic actions, and in some sense set in train, the destruction of the capital city, which included the Temple, Ezekiel now has recourse to the other form of prophetic activity, proclamation by word, and with it extends the disaster so as to make it overtake the whole land and all the sanctuaries. Ch. 6 is later to have a 'logical counterpoise and balance' (Irwin) in ch. 36, a prophecy of restoration which is also addressed to 'the mountains of Israel'. There are many parallels to ch. 6 in Lev. 26.14-39.

1. The mountains of Israel They are not simply mentioned as being a characteristic feature of the land—'the land of Israel consists of a central mountain-range sloping down to narrow plains by the Mediterranean and the Jordan' (Toy)—but stand rather for a main cause of the calamity now proclaimed, the idolatrous worship, for it was often upon hills that such worship was offered. The shrines there found, the HIGH PLACES of v. 3, had originally been Canaanite, and after they were taken over by Yahwism, the ideas of deity and the cult practices, especially the fertility rites, formerly connected with them, remained alive, to the extent that by the time of the first two canonical prophets Amos and Hosea (c. 750-725), the distinctive features of the Mosaic revelation had been

76

almost choked out of existence. Instead of being the God
who expressed his will in law and who demanded right conduct of his people, Yahweh had come to be thought of as
little different from a nature-god, satisfied with ritual and
sacrifice. The Canaanization of Yahwism also brought about
a change in the idea of the Sinai covenant: this was now
regarded as the guarantee of the chosen people's necessary
and continual occupation of the promised land. Of course,
between the time of Amos and Hosea and that of Ezekiel,
the reform undertaken by King Josiah in 621 (see II Kings
22f., cf. Deut. 12) had abolished the high places and made
the temple in Jerusalem the one legitimate sanctuary. But
few things are less readily abandoned than places of worship
and time-hallowed religious usages and forms, and after
Josiah's death there was apparently a reaction, when the old
cults came once more into use (Ezek. 8; cf. also Jer. 44).

In condemning the worship of the high places (see also
18.6, 11, 15; 22.9; 33-25, and especially chs. 16, 20, 23),
Ezekiel set himself in line with the prophetic tradition as it
had been from the time of Amos (Amos 7.9; Hos. 4.12f.;
Jer. 2.20; 3.6, etc.). In this chapter the worship on the high
places throughout the land is parallel to the profanation of
the sanctuary in Jerusalem in 5.11, and it is so widespread
and deeply rooted, Ezekiel means, that it can only be cured
by the devastation of the land and the extermination of its
inhabitants.

In prophesying against the mountains, Ezekiel was also
prophesying against the people. 'Old Testament religion is
concerned with Yahweh, Israel and Israel's land. People and
land are essentially one.'[1]

The basic meaning of the Hebrew word for HIGH PLACE,
bāmāh, is 'projecting mass of rock, mountain ridge, stone
burial cairn'; as well as sanctuaries, the bāmōth were funerary

[1] S. A. Cook, *The Old Testament: a Reinterpretation*, Cambridge,
1936, p. 119.

shrines. The most important elements in a typical *bāmāh* were the commemorative stelae of important deceased persons (or of 'heroes' who may never have lived on earth at all) and the sacred trees of the mother goddess (or goddesses).[2]

2. As well as prophesying against the mountains, Ezekiel is to set his face towards them. The phrase means more than simply 'look towards', 'direct you attention to' them. See on 4.3.

3. By Ezekiel's time the term 'high place' had lost its original literal significance, and could equally be applied to shrines situated in RAVINES (*wadis*) and VALLEYS. In mentioning the last of these, Ezekiel may have been thinking of child-sacrifice, a custom found among the Phoenicians and occasionally resorted to in Israel (II Kings 23.10; Jer. 19.2ff.; and see on Ezek. 20.25 below), for these took place in the Valley of Hinnom in Jerusalem. The SWORD means war, enemy invasion, which corresponds with the symbolic actions in chs. 4-5.

4. incense altars Altars on which incense was burnt. IDOLS: the whole cult at the high places was regarded as idolatrous. The word here used is almost wholly confined to Ezekiel (he has 39 out of the 47 instances in the OT), and is contemptuous, meaning block-idols or dung-idols. YOUR SLAIN signifies those slain on the mountains. Fisch aptly comments: 'The scene of guilt will be the scene of judgment.' Is there perhaps in the second part of v. 4 some idea, such as we have in Jer. 2.28 and Isa. 46.1f., of the powerlessness of a false religion to protect its devotees?

5-7. The verses are probably due to editorial expansion—

[2] W. F. Albright, 'The High Places in Ancient Palestine', in *VT*, Supplement IV, 1956, pp. 242ff.

notice the change of person in 5a—THEIR—which suggests
that the YOU and YOUR which follow now refer no longer to
the mountains, but to the people of Israel. Verse 5a is also
omitted by LXX. The verses bring the additional thought of
the desecration of shrines, for the presence of dead bodies
would render them unclean. Fisch's comment on the last clause
of 5 is again apt: 'Where once were found the remains of
animal sacrifices will now be found the skeletons of the men
who had brought the offerings.' But there is more to it than
simply irony: 'When the body is laid down into the grave
together with the fathers, the soul is at rest there . . . If it is
not laid in the grave, it is anxious and rushes about restlessly.'[3]

6. Cities No more than villages, settlements, which would
as a rule be close by the high places. WORKS means idols, the
works of their hands.

PUNISHMENT WILL EFFECT SHAME

6.8-10

These verses have no necessary connection with the preceding oracle and are later in date. They revert to the idea of
survivors already expressed in 5.10, 12; from the country
districts as well as from Jerusalem, some will escape death
and be deported. In exile they will REMEMBER Yahweh. The
word 'remember' does not mean 'recollect about the past',
but 'bring to mind in the present' (cf. 'Do this in remembrance
of me', I Cor. 11.24), 'be open to the action of God'. When
this comes about, they will draw the proper conclusions, and
see in what has befallen them the working of his hand. As
always in Ezekiel, the author of this insight, and also of the

[3] J. Pedersen, *Israel* I-II, London and Copenhagen, 1926, p. 181.

nation's penitence (THEY WILL BE LOATHSOME IN THEIR OWN
SIGHT, cf. 20.43; 36.31) is God himself. The breaking of their
wanton heart suggests the 'one heart' and the 'new spirit' and
the 'heart of flesh' in passages of restoration from exile such
as 11.14-21 and 36.26f.

9. The terms WANTON and WANTONLY carry on a metaphor
to which, it would appear, Hosea first gave currency (e.g.
Hos. 4.13ff.), whereby the Canaanized syncretistic worship of
Yahweh was designated as 'whoredom'. Ezekiel is to develop
the idea in chs. 16 and 23. Once again the motive of God's
action is that the exiles should be brought to recognize his
power. The final words of the passage remind us of Lam.
2.17: 'The Lord has done what he purposed, has carried out
his threat; as he ordained long ago. . . .' During the exile
there must have been deep ponderings of the sayings of pre-
exilic prophets who warned of the calamity that had now
come to pass.

AN EXPRESSIVE ACTION

6.11-12

The verses stand apart from the context and remind us
more of chs. 4-5. Cooke calls CLAP YOUR HANDS, AND STAMP
YOUR FOOT 'gestures of malignant satisfaction', and ALAS!
which he renders Aha!) 'an exclamation of joy rather
than of pain'. If this is so, Ezekiel's attitude towards the
tragedy of his fellow-countrymen is very different from that
of Jeremiah: 'O that my head were waters, and my eyes a
fountain of tears, that I might weep day and night for the
slain of the daughter of my people!' (Jer. 9.1.) Undoubtedly,
there is a streak of hardness and even harshness in Ezekiel
that is absent in Jeremiah. But it is not necessary to assume

that the gestures and the exclamations represent the feelings
of the prophet himself. Ezekiel is the agent of Yahweh, and as
such he 'expresses agreement with the divine decisions'
(Ziegler). Yahweh has become the enemy of his people, or
rather, they are in rebellion against him (2.3, 7). 'He (Ezekiel)
has therefore to speak as if he belonged to a foreign people
who jeers at the downfall of Judah . . . as representative of
a foreign power he gives vent to jeering and scorn at Judah's
imminent downfall' (Fohrer).

Another interpretation, too, is possible. The gestures may
express *any* strong emotion, sorrow and dismay as well as
joy and exultation at another's misfortune. In this case (and
keeping the rendering, ALAS!), v. 11 could represent the
prophet's sorrow for his people's fate, however fully justified
the latter was. On the other hand, Toy may be correct in saying
that 'the Prophet rejoices in the condemnation of the sin which
he abhors'.

12. preserved I.e. spared from pestilence and the sword, cf.
Isa. 49.6. FAR OFF and NEAR : that is, from the point of view
of the scene of battle.

THE THREAT REITERATED

6.13-14

The two verses bring little that is new. Certain trees were
regarded as sacred, and sacrifice was offered at them. This is
a further example of the pervasive influence of the cult of
Baal, and Jeremiah also complains of such worship (Jer.
2.20). The PLEASING ODOUR is the smell given off by animal
sacrifices as they were cooked or burnt whole. In early times
the odour was regarded as the means by which the deity
shared in the sacrifice (cf. Gen. 8.21, 'The Lord smelled a

sweet savour', and Amos 5.21, 'and I take no delight in your
solemn assemblies', where, as AV shows, the verb means
literally 'smell'). The deity was thereby propitiated. Later, as
for example in the Priestly Code, the phrase came to mean
simply a pleasing or acceptable offering.

14. the wilderness This, the modern Negeb, here stands for
the southern boundary of the land. The northern boundary
is usually given as Hamath, but RIBLAH, on the Orontes,
would have a topical significance after 586, in that it was the
headquarters of Nebuchadnezzar, and the last Judean king,
Zedekiah, was taken there when he was captured on his flight
from Jerusalem. The Babylonians slew his sons in his
presence, and then, after blinding him, deported him to Babylon (II Kings 25.4ff.; cf. Jer. 39.5ff.; 52.9ff.).

In calamity and through calamity the remnant of the chosen
people was to experience Yahweh, and feel and recognize his
power.

THE END

7.1-27

'Ch. 7 is one of those singled out by Ewald as preserving most faithfully the spirit and language of Ezekiel's earlier utterances. Both in thought and expression it exhibits a freedom and animation seldom attained in Ezekiel's writings, and it is evident that it must have been composed under keen emotion. . . . In its present position it forms a fitting conclusion to the opening section of the book. All the elements of the judgment which have just been foretold are gathered up in one burst of emotion, producing a song of triumph in which the prophet seems to stand in the uproar of the final catastrophe and exult amid the crash and wreck of the old order which is passing away' (Skinner).

We first meet with the concept of 'the end' in Amos: 'the end has come upon my people Israel' (Amos 8.2). It is also in Amos that we first find mention of 'the Day', or, to give it its full title, 'the Day of Yahweh' (Amos 5.18-20, cf. Isa. 2.12ff.). Ezekiel, however, is the only prophet to connect the two ideas.

The concept of the 'Day' probably originated in the times of the Amphictyony, before the monarchy, and in the ideology of the holy war,[4] in which Yahweh took action on behalf of his people, and by his miraculous intervention effected the panic defeat of her foes. But, as Amos shows, the prophets no longer conceived the divine action in terms of the nation's deliverance, but of its punishment—the Day 'is darkness, and not light' (Amos 5.18). Few, if any, would survive it (cf. Amos 3.12). If Yahweh 'visited' a people such as Israel had now become, this could only be in order to chastise

[4] G. von Rad, *Old Testament Theology* II, trs. D. M. G. Stalker, Edinburgh and London, 1965, pp. 119ff.

it. When the two concepts are fused together as in Ezekiel, the 'Day' and the 'end' are equivalent to final destruction. As Zimmerli points out (p. 170), the accent is on the destruction itself rather than on the time of its coming. Once again Ezekiel carries on the traditions of his predecessors, and the fact that the two concepts were common property of the prophets and had fairly fixed forms and terminology attached to them explains the many linguistic affinities of this chapter with other parts of the prophetic writings.

THE ANNOUNCEMENT OF THE END

7.1-4

2-3. There was a close, almost sacramental, union between the people of Israel and its land, as indeed is shown by the use of YOU and YOUR in 3f., referring to the inhabitants of the land, cf. note on 6.2. Right at the beginning the promise to Abraham had contained the promise of a land (Gen. 12.1), and when later in his career Ezekiel speaks comfort to the exiles, one element in his hope is restoration to the land (34.13-14, 25-31; 36.8ff., and especially the important passage 36.24-28; cf. Jer. 32.36-41; 33; also 31.27f.). Thus, the threat of an end to the LAND OF ISRAEL, a phrase peculiar to Ezekiel, is tantamount to the cancellation of Israel's election at Sinai.

2. has come The perfect tense is the perfect of certainty— the prophet is so sure of what he foretells that he thinks and speaks of it as already accomplished; cf. Amos 5.1f. Whatever Yahweh purposes is inevitably fulfilled. The FOUR CORNERS stand for all that is within the LAND, but the exact meaning of this second LAND is not certain. Some (e.g. Fohrer) take it as equivalent to the preceding LAND OF ISRAEL (i.e. Judah), but others (e.g. Eichrodt) think of the catastrophe as cosmic; in which case 'land' means 'world'. The former idea seems the most natural here, but the latter is more in keeping with tradition (cf. Isa. 2.9ff., Zeph. 1f.). In either case the END means destruction for Israel, as with Amos.

3. The end is not unmotivated and Yahweh's anger is not arbitrary: the calamity is due and condign punishment—I . . . WILL JUDGE YOU ACCORDING TO YOUR WAYS. The sin the prophet has in mind is idolatry and apostasy (ABOMINATIONS). Eichrodt points out that the earlier idea that sin of necessity and mechanically brings punishment on its perpetrator is here—as elsewhere in the prophets—personalized: it is Yahweh himself who effects judgment.

4. The purpose of the END is, again, that Israel may KNOW Yahweh (cf. 6.9).

A REPETITION OF THE THREAT

7.5-9

The oracle is largely parallel to the preceding, and the text is not certain. It is probably editorial comment. If, however, the end envisaged in 1-4 is cosmic, here it would seem rather to bear more directly on the events of 586, cf. SOON (v. 8), which makes more explicit the perfect of certainty in v. 2.

6. An end has come, the end has come The definite article denotes the final end. The Hebrew of this verse contains a paronomasia, a kind of pun: THE END is *haqqēṣ*, AWAKENED is *hēqêṣ*. (Amos in the same way plays upon *qeṣ* [end] and *qayiṣ* ['autumn fruit', or, to use the American term, 'fall fruit'], Amos 8.2.)

7. the mountains As the word ABOMINATIONS in vv. 8f. makes clear, this is a reference back to ch. 6. Worship at the high places was accompanied by cultic jubilation.[5]

9. who smite   Notice this addition to the recognition formula, YOU WILL KNOW THAT I AM THE LORD.[6]

A REASON FOR THE DAY

7.10-11

The LXX here explicitly identifies the end with the Day of Yahweh: it introduces v. 10 with the words: 'For thus saith the Lord: behold, the end has come, behold, the day of Yahweh.' Verse 10 is a short poem, but the text of the second half of the verse is uncertain. Zimmerli's comment is: 'The day of Yahweh is the day in which men's "perversion of justice" and their "pride" blossom out into their full development, and men finally come to grief because of them.' However, for INJUSTICE a slight change in pointing gives 'rod' (so AV), that is, 'branch', which well suits BLOSSOMED and BUDDED, though it is not so apt as a parallel to the abstract PRIDE. 'Rod' is used in Jer. 48.17 and Ps. 110.2 to signify the ruler's sceptre. The reference here may then be to the pride and insolence of the court and the ruling classes. This is more likely than an interpretation which has been current from rabbinic times, that the rod is Nebuchadnezzar, an interpretation which derives from Isa. 10.5, where the Assyrian is called 'the rod of my (Yahweh's) anger'. Verse 11 supports the rendering 'rod', but is a commentator's explanation and not original. In the last two clauses both the text and the meaning are quite uncertain.

[5] See F. F. Hvidberg, *Weeping and Laughter in the Old Testament*, Leyden and Copenhagen, 1962.
[6] On this and other variations see W. Zimmerli, *Erkenntnis Gottes nach dem Buche Ezechiel*.

UPHEAVAL OF SOCIAL RELATIONSHIPS

7.12-13

It is 'probable that the prophet is thinking of the forced
sales by the expatriated nobles of their estates in Palestine,
and to their deeply cherished resolve to right themselves when
the time of their exile is over' (Skinner). (The reference is of
course to those already deported in 597 [II Kings 24.10-16],
among whom was Ezekiel himself.) Owners mourn because
they have to sell at buyers' prices. But, the prophet says, those
who have thus become quickly rich need not rejoice, for in the
general destruction of the Day, they will not remain in possession. On the basis of Isa. 24.2, however, Zimmerli thinks that
the reference is general: buying and selling was one of the
stock concepts connected with the Day, symbolizing 'life in all
its many facets of activity': the meaning is then that all normal life comes to an end with the Day. Zimmerli also thinks
that rejoicing/mourning is another stock motif of the Day
(Isa. 24.7, cf. Eccles. 3.4). In 12 and 13 the text is extremely
corrupt, and 12b and 13a are probably a commentator's gloss.
Verse 13b should possibly read something like: 'For wrath
comes upon all their riches, and because of his iniquity none
shall preserve his life.'

12-13. multitude   Read 'riches'.

ARMED RESISTANCE IS USELESS

7.14-18

14. 'Blow the trumpet and prepare the weapons of war' (so
read for RSV; the verbs should certainly be taken as impera-

tives, cf. Jer. 4.5; 6.1). For the idea cf. Jer. 4.19. War was a
further stock topic of the Day: Ezekiel uses it to give a nearer
definition of the form the Day will take; there is no thought
of *Israel's* blowing the trumpet, etc., in order to take counter-
measures against the Babylonians, who were Yahweh's instruments in the Day. MULTITUDE: render 'riches' as in the
preceding verses.

15a. Resistance is unavailing, both inside and outside the city,
since the destruction of the Day is that of Yahweh. Verse 15b
is a commentator's addition, and the same is probably true
of v. 16, where, in addition, the text is uncertain—perhaps
'they will be on the mountains as moaning doves. Yet they
shall all die [so Syriac], everyone because of his iniquity.'

17-18. If v. 16 is not original, these verses, which begin a
closer description of the Day and its panic effects on those
whom it overtakes, refer to the people in Jerusalem, not to the
survivors, and in particular to the condition of the former before they die: they are powerless, and show that death stares
them in the face (with v. 17 cf. Isa. 13.6-8). Girding with sackcloth and plucking out the hair were signs both of humiliation
and of mourning, cf. 27.31; Isa. 15.2f.; Jer. 48.37.

horror covers them That is, 'shuddering clothes them', cf.
v. 27. For the metaphor, cf. Isa. 59.17.

THE USELESSNESS OF MONEY

7.19-21

As the text stands, the last sentence of 19, FOR IT WAS THE
STUMBLING BLOCK OF THEIR INIQUITY, suggests that SILVER
and GOLD in the first part of the verse refer to silver- and gold-
plated idols, cf. Isa. 30.22. But the clause is a gloss, as are

also the words, added from Zeph. 1.18, THEIR SILVER AND
GOLD . . . THE WRATH OF THE LORD. The original reference
of the section was not to idolatry, but to money. We therefore
here revert to the idea of 12f., that money is useless. Indeed,
it is even worse than that: it is now actually loathsome—the
Hebrew word for AN UNCLEAN THING expresses the highest
degree of ceremonial impurity.

20. Their beautiful ornament they used for vainglory These
words are probably original, but the rest is from the same
commentator as added 19b.

21. The possessions of the people of Jerusalem are to be
made over to FOREIGNERS, that is, to the Babylonians, cf. 11.9,
where the reference is quite clear. Since the Babylonians are
the instruments of Yahweh, it may seem strange that they
should be called THE WICKED OF THE EARTH. However, the
description may be a stock one for the stereotyped 'enemies'
who are always associated with the Day of Yahweh, the
eschatological foes whose work is of cosmic range, and who
are depicted in terrible colours but not named. But Ezekiel
may also have had Isa. 10.5ff. in mind. There the Assyrians
are equally Yahweh's instruments, but their king is to be
punished for his lust for conquest, and his arrogant boasting
and haughty pride. The fact that God uses a man does not
whitewash him. 'In v. 21 $z\bar{a}r\bar{\imath}m$ (foreigners) is synonymous
with the expression $r\bar{\imath}\check{s}^{c}\bar{e}$ $h\bar{a}^{\,}\bar{a}re\d{s}$ "the unfaithful, the ungodly
of the earth". As a rule, the $r^{e}\check{s}\bar{a}^{\,}\bar{\imath}m$ are those who have be-
trayed the community of their own people (Ezek. 7.21). In a
wider sense of the meaning, viz., in connection with the world,
this qualification may be applied to the Babylonians. This
people outdo others in deeds of unlawfulness.'[7]

[7] L. A. Snijders, 'The Meaning of zar in the Old Testament' in
Oudtestamentische Studiën, 10, 1954, pp. 30f.

And they shall profane it   Probably a gloss by the commentator who expanded Ezekiel's original oracle about money to refer to idolatry. 'The desecration of a place consists of the breaking through of its privacy, by something else entering from the outside and asserting itself' (Snijders).

JUDGMENT ON THE TEMPLE

7.22-24

The oracle-series now reaches its climax, and announces the most terrible part of the judgment. I WILL TURN MY FACE FROM THEM means that Yahweh is to withdraw his favour and grace from them, cf. Num. 6.25f.; Ps. 104.29. This makes the profanation of the temple possible. It was in the Jerusalem temple, MY PRECIOUS PLACE, v. 22, that a worshipper 'sought Yahweh's face' (Ps. 27.4, 8-9). But now God's face is to be turned away. (In v. 22 THEM are the people of Jerusalem, THEY are the Babylonians, the ROBBERS.) No one but a Jew might enter the temple, and 'a sacred city, or temple, or other sanctuary was desecrated by the entrance of strangers, that is, persons who did not belong to the circle of worshippers of the deity of the place' (Toy). '. . . Even the degenerated cult is a secluded domain on its own, to which *zārīm* (i.e., strangers) do not belong, but into which they nevertheless force their way' (Snijders, *op. cit.*, p. 32). Profanation of the temple by the Babylonians would PUT AN END TO THEIR PROUD MIGHT— i.e. the last security of the people of Jerusalem (cf. Jer. 7) would prove as illusory as reliance on money or idols.

Since he was a priest, the profanation of the temple would evoke particular horror in Ezekiel. Yet in v. 23 the transgressions for which the desecration is punishment are social and therefore 'prophetic'. In v. 24 THEIR HOLY PLACES are the high places of ch. 6.

UNIVERSAL DESPAIR

7.25-27

A further description of the helpless panic. Yahweh not
only sets his face against the outward symbol of national
religion—or rather irreligion; he also (v. 26) withdraws the
recognized guides from whom, in the welter of calamities, the
people sought PEACE (v. 25). 'The basic meaning of the word
[peace] is "well-being", with a clear dominant emphasis on
the material side.'[8] 'Peace means the same as harmonious
community. . . . *Shālōm* [peace] under all circumstances
designates that which is free and intact. . . . To have *shālōm*
means to be unhurt and unchecked.'[9]

26. the law Here instruction in the Law. Part of THE
PRIESTS' duty was to interpret THE LAW, a function taken over
in post-exilic and NT times by the scribes.

the elders The office goes back to pre-Mosaic times. 'The
heads of the constituent larger families, or at least the most
respected of them, probably acted as elders of the clans.'[10]
After the settlement the tribes adapted the earlier clan office,
and we read of elders of the tribes (e.g. Deut. 31.28), and later
of 'elders of Israel' (e.g. I Sam. 4.3). They were the competent
authority for deciding certain military and political functions,
and also administered justice. They survived the break-up of
the tribal system, but in Deuteronomy their judicial functions
are local and there are other judicial officers alongside them.

---

[8] G. von Rad, *TWNT* II, p. 400.
[9] J. Pedersen, *Israel* I-II, pp. 264, 311, 314.
[10] M. Noth, *The History of Israel*, ET, 2nd ed. revised by P. R.
Ackroyd, London, 1960, p. 108.

Ezek. 8 shows that they also survived the fall of Jerusalem and were of importance in the exile, where they may have taken over the political functions exercised in the pre-exilic period by the 'wise men'.[11]

counsel De Boer gives 'some characteristics of the term. In the first place we notice a close connection with wisdom and understanding, a close relationship too between the counsellor and the wise. Secondly, it appears that the action of counselling points to the maintenance and restoration of life. Security, victory, recovery, salvation are the effects aimed at by counsel. Thirdly, counsel is a decision which determines the future. . . . True counsel, however, is never mere guess-work based on a calculation, nor an idea dependent on sentiments of one or more persons involved. It is a decision in a difficult situation given by an authorized person, and is meant to be followed ("done") on penalty of disaster or death. A fourth characteristic of our term is the identity of counsel and action. In the fifth place the passages surveyed lead to the conclusion that the counsellors form a special caste.'[12] ' '$\bar{e}\bar{s}\bar{a}$ (counsel) is a self-contained system of political wisdom,'[13] says McKane. He points out that there was bound to be a clash between those who wished to guide the state according to rational 'counsel' and the prophets who wished to guide it according to the word of Yahweh.

27. The king mourns These words should probably be omitted, as in some of the Versions. Since Ezekiel avoids the term 'king', and calls the ruler 'the prince', the phrase is the addition of a commentator who did not understand the pro-

---

[11] J. Fichtner, 'Jesaja unter den Weisen', *TLZ* 74, 1949, col. 77.
[12] P. A. H. de Boer, 'The Counsellor' in *Wisdom in Israel and the Ancient Near East*, ed. M. Noth and D. Winton Thomas (*VT*, Supplement III), 1955, p. 56.
[13] W. McKane, *Prophets and Wise Men* (SBT 44), 1965, p. 58.

phet's usage. If, however, MT is kept, as referring to Zedekiah, THE PRINCE, which follows, is to be taken collectively, as meaning the ruling classes.

All the official leaders, then, as well as the common people, THE PEOPLE OF THE LAND, are at utter loss in the universal panic of the Day of Yahweh.

A VISION OF EVENTS
IN JERUSALEM
8.1–11.25

Having foretold the imminent destruction of Jerusalem, in
a vision Ezekiel now sees it actually taking place, and describes it to his fellow exiles. The vision culminates in the
departure of Yahweh from the temple and the holy city.

Chs. 8-11 give the impression of being a carefully constructed unity. The sequence of events is:

8.1-4: the prophet is transported from Babylon to
Jerusalem;

8.5-18: he sees various forms of idolatry being practised in
the temple;

9: he sees executioners who destroy the inhabitants of the
city, though some are spared;

10.2-7: one of the destroyers scatters burning coals over
the city itself;

10.8-23: the prophet describes the heavenly throne, and the
departure of the glory of Yahweh from the temple;

11.1-13: he reports an incident at the east gate of the
temple, in which, during the course of his prophecy, a
man fell down dead;

11.14-21: he prophesies restoration to the homeland for the
exiles;

11.22-25: the glory of Yahweh leaves the city to stand
over the Mount of Olives, and Ezekiel is brought back
to Babylonia.

On closer analysis, however, the apparent unity is shown to
be composed of different, and even divergent, elements, some
of which are later additions to the original matter. The chief

problems which the chapters present are three. First, in ch. 10 many of the verses repeat, in most cases word for word, verses from ch. 1—cf. v. 1 and 1.26; v. 5 and 1.24; v. 8 and 1.8; vv. 9-12 and 1.15-18; v. 14 and 1.6, 10; vv. 16f. and 1.19-21; v. 21 and 1.6, 8; v. 22b and 1.9b: furthermore, there is considerable disorder and repetition in what is said about the heavenly throne. Secondly, 11.1-13 are obviously out of place. Pelatiah and his companions DEVISE INIQUITY (v. 2). But such sinners have already been destroyed (9.7f.) and the city burnt (10.2, 6-7). Also, the sins here are (most probably) social sins, while in ch. 8, they are cultic. Thirdly, 11.14-21 are also out of place, since down to the fall of Jerusalem (ch. 24), Ezekiel is a prophet, not of hope and restoration, but of doom and destruction (see above on 3.16-21).

The original form of chs. 8-11 was probably as follows: 8-9; 10.2, 7 (in part); 10.18-19; 11.23-25. This describes idolatries in the temple, the consequent destruction of the inhabitants of Jerusalem (with certain exceptions) and of the city itself, and finally, the departure of Yahweh from Jerusalem. In the commentary here, 10.2, 7, 18-19 and 11.23-25 will be treated immediately after the notes on 8-9.

ILLICIT CULTIC PRACTICES

8.1-18

The Book of Ezekiel is carefully planned—this may go back to the prophet himself. Chs. 6-7 have spoken of idolatry practised throughout the countryside of Israel (Judah) and in the capital. Ch. 8 advances to describe unlawful cults in the very environs of the temple itself. And so serious is the profanation that it results not only in the destruction of Jerusalem, but in the departure of Yahweh from the temple.

The death of Josiah, with its political consequences of domination first by Egypt and then by Babylon, could have suggested, amongst others, two lines of thought: either that Yahweh was less powerful than the gods of these two countries, who had given his land and people into the hands of their devotees; or that Josiah's reform had been displeasing to Yahweh, and that he was signifying this by bringing calamities upon his people (see here Jer. 44, especially vv. 17-18). With the idolatries mentioned in ch. 8 both lines of thought come into play. 'The effect of misfortune [i.e. the deportation of 597] on the southern kingdom was not atheism, but an outburst of violent superstition and fanaticism' (Lofthouse). People felt that they had to look for help in any direction that seemed to hold out promise of it, and so had recourse either to cults which, though foreign in origin, had made their entry into Yahwism, or to new foreign cults which were apparently of value to their new masters. Hopelessness was the seed-bed which forced the illicit practices now to be considered.

THE PROPHET IS TRANSPORTED FROM
BABYLON TO JERUSALEM

8.1-4

[On the general question of a ministry of Ezekiel in Jerusalem, see pp. 20ff.].

About a year after Ezekiel received his call and inaugural vision (cf. 8.1 with 1.2), THE ELDERS (see on 7.26), who are the leaders and representatives of the exiles, and to whom Jeremiah sent a letter (Jer. 29.1), came to Ezekiel's house seeking an oracle—they perhaps wanted further explanation of why it was necessary for Jerusalem to be destroyed. Ecstasy then overcame the prophet—THE HAND OF THE LORD GOD FELL THERE UPON ME (v. 1). The agents of his transportation to the temple area, A FORM THAT HAD THE APPEARANCE OF A MAN (v. 2) and THE SPIRIT (v. 3), are probably to be thought of as Yahweh himself—with 8.2 cf. 1.26f.—though the MAN may only be a heavenly being. Notice how once again, by using the terms FORM (vv. 2 and 3) and APPEARANCE (v. 2), Ezekiel seeks to avoid anthropomorphism in speaking of God. In the apocryphal book Bel and the Dragon the prophet Habakkuk is brought from Palestine to Daniel in the den of lions in Babylon (vv. 33-36) in exactly the same way as Ezekiel is here transported: cf. also II Cor. 12.2-4.

3. visions of God, i.e., as in 1.1 visions granted by God. The INNER COURT is the inner court of the temple. This, along with the temple itself, formed part of Solomon's great complex of palace buildings, and was separated from these by a wall.

The seat of the image of jealousy, which provokes to jealousy Albright takes the word rendered IMAGE as a figured slab, a '*stela* with hewn faces'.[1] 'Carving and painting cultic and

[1] *Archaeology and the Religion of Israel*, 3rd ed., Baltimore, 1953, p. 221.

D

mythological scenes on upright slabs (orthostates) set against the wall or built into it, were characteristic customs in northern Syria, southeastern Asia Minor and northern Mesopotamia between the twelfth and the seventh centuries BC' (*ib.* p. 166). He also thinks that the SEAT 'probably refers to the niche in the wall where the figured slab was placed' (*ib.* p. 165). WHICH PROVOKES TO JEALOUSY means that, as a heathen image, and one set up in the environs of the temple itself, it provokes Yahweh to indignation. This rendering depends, however, on altering one letter in the Hebrew. If the Hebrew is allowed to stand, it reads, 'the image of jealousy, the cane' (i.e. stalk, reed), and it has been suggested that this refers to 'the tree of life commonly used in the East as decoration for public buildings, but primarily symbolizing the goddess of fertility Ashera—Ashtoreth—Anath, or the heathen conception of Providence in general.'[2]

4. The verse breaks the connection between vv. 3 and 5, and has been inserted by an editor to prepare for ch. 10. THE VISION THAT I SAW IN THE PLAIN—cf. 3.23—refers to 1.1ff. THERE must mean somewhere near the north gateway.

Four kinds of idolatrous worship are then shown to the prophet (8.5-18).

GREAT ABOMINATIONS

8.5-6

The prophet's attention is drawn to the ABOMINATIONS by a divine question (v. 6, cf. vv. 12, 15, 17; 37.3; 47.6; Amos 7.8; 8.2). The ABOMINATIONS are not specified, but are apparently connected with THE IMAGE OF JEALOUSY. TO DRIVE ME FAR FROM MY SANCTUARY: if this rendering is kept, then it pre-

[2] H. Bar-Deroma, 'Kadesh-Barnea', in *PEQ* (July-December, 1964), p. 132.

pares the way for Yahweh's imminent departure from the temple (11.1, 22f.). But another translation is possible: 'who have withdrawn from my sanctuary', that is, who, despairing of help from Yahweh, have (presumably) erected this pagan altar just outside the temple.

IDOLATRY IN SECRET
8.7-13

The whole atmosphere suggests some hole-and-corner cult which the devotees would be ashamed to practise in public, but the details are not clear. Why should the prophet enlarge the hole in the wall—presumably in order to enter the chamber and take the idolaters by surprise—only to discover a door? Was it a door that 'otherwise could only be come to in a roundabout way and was not to be found by the uninitiated' (Ziegler)? And why was the hole there to begin with? LXX has a shorter text: 'and he brought me to the doors of the court, and said to me, Son of man, dig. And I dug, and behold a door.' 7-8 in the MT may have been expanded from 12.5, 7.

10. The animal cult is almost certainly a foreign one, though its derivation is not sure. It may have been Egyptian—the Egyptians held cats, crocodiles, the bull etc., as sacred—and introduced on political grounds: immediately after the death of Josiah, Judah was for a period under the domination of Egypt, and right up to the fall of Jerusalem there were those who looked to Egypt for deliverance from Babylon. The SEVENTY MEN (11) may then have been representatives of a pro-Egyptian party. The cult could however also be Babylonian. Seventy is a conventional number associated with the elders of Israel, Ex. 24.1, 9, Num. 11.16. The last part of 10, AND ALL THE IDOLS OF THE HOUSE OF ISRAEL, is probably a gloss.

11. Shaphan If this is Josiah's chancellor, who aided him in his reform (II Kings 22), what a falling away there has been in his son! The CENSERS were for offering INCENSE to the figures portrayed on the walls.

12. Every man in his room of pictures The meaning is uncertain. The words suggest that the room is divided up into cells, but this seems to be at variance with vv. 10f. They may however not be original. The word translated PICTURES means in Lev. 26.1 and Num. 33.52 'sculptured stones'. 'THE LORD DOES NOT SEE US, THE LORD HAS FORSAKEN THE LAND', cf. 9.9. 'The meaning of the worshippers is not that Yahweh would not approve of these rites, but that Yahweh has plainly ceased to care for the distracted state and people; they must look elsewhere for help' (Lofthouse). 'This [saying] is the key to the spiritual decline within the city and is the problem with which most of Ezekiel's early prophetic activity had to do. Men felt that God had forsaken them and that they were free to turn to other gods' (Howie). What the elders probably had in mind was the deportation in the time of Jehoiachin: this calamity, they imply, would not have taken place if Yahweh had still been regarding his people with favour. For other popular sayings of the time see 11.3, 15; 12.22; 18.2, 19, etc.

WEEPING FOR TAMMUZ

8.14-15

If the previous cult took place IN THE DARK (12), there is no secrecy connected with this third idolatrous cult; the women weep in the outer court of the temple. Jeremiah (44.17-19) mentions a similar women's cult, to 'the queen of heaven', Ishtar.

Tammuz was the widely venerated Babylonian god

Dumuzi ('true son'), one of the earliest figures in the Sumerian pantheon. He was parallel to, or identified with, Baal and Mot in Syria, and Adonis in Greece. Tammuz was a vegetation god, and it was supposed that, when plant life died down in summer, he too had died and gone down into the underworld, and cultic weeping was made for him at a festival in June/July. But after his sister Ishtar also went to the underworld and freed him, a sacred marriage took place between them, which resulted in the growth of the vegetation in spring, and this was celebrated by cultic joy. The weeping for Tammuz here mentioned may have been a recent introduction into Israel due to Babylonian influence. Even so, as Hvidberg points out, 'it was able to penetrate in Jerusalem just because it was not felt as something foreign.'[3] 'Cultic lamentation and cultic weeping, and all that went with them, were so deeply implanted in the life of Canaanite Israel that they left their stamp in various ways on Israelite belief and practice. No matter how great Yahweh became, and no matter how far Baal came to be in part absorbed in Him and in parts expelled by Him, nevertheless the songs of lamentation sounded over the withered pastures and there was weeping over the seed which had been "buried", as had happened in the old days over Baal and Mot. Weeping and lamentations were preserved through the years like other ancient customs which belonged to farming life.'[4] If this is so, the weeping represents a Canaanite infiltration into Yahwism.

SUN WORSHIP

8.16-18

The prophet is now brought into the inner court or nave of

[3] F. F. Hvidberg, *Weeping and Laughter in the Old Testament*, p. 115.
[4] Hvidberg, quoted in A. S. Kapelrud, *The Ras Shamra Discoveries and the Old Testament*, trs. G. W. Anderson, Oxford, 1965, p. 207.

the temple, between the porch at the east end of it (I Kings 6.3) and the altar of burnt offering (I Kings 8.64). 'This was the place where the priests offered prayer, Joel 2.17' (Cooke).

Worship of the heavenly bodies, of Mesopotamian origin, was much practised in the reign of Manasseh (II Kings 21.3, 5; cf. Jer. 8.2), and its abolition was among the reforms of his grandson Josiah (II Kings 23.5, 11). What is particularly offensive to the priest Ezekiel in the conduct of the TWENTY-FIVE MEN is that, in facing the rising sun, they turn their backs to the temple, and so dishonour Yahweh, cf. II Chron. 29.6, 'For our fathers have been unfaithful and have done what was evil in the sight of the Lord our God; they have forsaken him, and have turned away their faces from the habitation of the Lord, and turned their backs.' According to Dan. 6.10, the worshipper faces the temple. The sin of the twenty-five would be all the more heinous if the conjecture is correct that they were priests—according to I Chron. 24.7-19, there were twenty-four divisions of the priesthood: a representative from each of them with the addition of a high-priest would give the number twenty-five.

The insult to Yahweh is intensified by the fact that THEY PUT THE BRANCH TO THEIR NOSE (17). In spite of various suggestions, there is no certainty as to what the words mean. Probably some obscene rite is referred to. 'According to Jewish interpreters, THEIR NOSE is a silent correction (by the Jewish scribes) for "my nose" and BRANCH signifies *ventris crepitus*' (Cooke). Since this is the last idolatry to be mentioned, it is to be regarded as the most intolerable. 17b, THAT THEY SHOULD FILL . . . TO ANGER, is a later expansion. In this chapter the prophet is dealing wholly with cultic aberrations and not at all with judicial crimes.

THE EXECUTION OF JERUSALEM'S PUNISHMENT

9.1-11

Ezekiel now overhears Yahweh's command to seven angelic beings to execute the judgment upon Jerusalem already proclaimed (cf. 7.9 and 8.18 with 9.10). Eichrodt calls the chapter the 'metaphysical background' of the fall of Jerusalem as it came about in history. 'Usually he (Ezekiel) defines destruction as ordained of God to be carried out in the regular process of history, but not in this case. For the first time in biblical literature there is a well-developed apocalyptic (superhistorical) description of God's judgment. This sort of description becomes quite common in Zechariah and Daniel as well as in some inter-testamental books (for example, Enoch) and in the New Testament book of Revelation' (Howie, p. 30).

1. with a loud voice LOUD emphasizes the seriousness of this hour. DRAW NEAR, YOU EXECUTIONERS OF THE CITY carries the implication that the city's punishment is now imminent. EACH WITH HIS DESTROYING WEAPON IN HIS HAND has come in from the following verse.

2. Later Judaism knew of seven holy angels, with Gabriel at their head (Tobit 12.14; cf. Rev. 4.5; 8.1-11), and the Talmud identifies the seventh figure here with Gabriel. But a destroying angel was also known, and that in Israel's earliest history. In such a form ('the destroyer') Yahweh passed over the houses of the Israelites at the first Passover in Egypt (Ex. 12.23), and it was the 'angel of the Lord' who destroyed Sennacherib's army before Jerusalem (II Kings 19.35). But the story of the census taken by David shows that the angel could turn against Israel herself (II Sam. 24.16f.; I Chron. 21.15). Here the MAN CLOTHED IN LINEN (v. 2) occupies a middle place between the angel of Yahweh and the later Gabriel. LINEN is the material of priestly garments (cf. 44.17f.; Ex. 28.42; Lev. 16.4, 23), but here it probably signifies no more than the high rank of this heavenly being (cf. Dan. 10.5; 12.6). Ezekiel has, however, also been influenced by his Babylonian background: among the seven planetary gods there, Nebo was 'lord of the stylus or pen'. The WRITING CASE was probably a scribe's palette, such as we know from Egyptian monuments. The reason why the men came from the NORTH is primarily that this is the direction from which an army from Babylon would approach Jerusalem. There may, however, also be a reminiscence of the old mythological idea about the supposed dwelling-place of the gods on a mountain in the north, see on 1.4. THE BRONZE ALTAR: according to the general interpretation, 'this was Solomon's altar (I Kings 8.64; II Chron. 4.1), which had been moved to the north of the stone altar set up by Ahaz (II Kings 16.14); the space between the latter and the porch was occupied by the sun·worshippers 8.16; so the angels had to stand beside the old altar' (Cooke).

3. The first part of the verse, down to HOUSE, is obviously an insertion; in 3b, HE is Yahweh.

4. In spite of the widespread and indeed almost universal corruption in the city, there are still those WHO SIGH AND GROAN OVER ALL THE ABOMINATIONS THAT ARE COMMITTED IN IT. They are not more nearly defined—were they people like the prophet himself, or like Jeremiah? (On Ezekiel's individualism, see Introduction, pp. 34ff., and later on chs. 11, 18.) They recall the seven thousand who had not bowed the knee to Baal at the time when Elijah thought that he alone was faithful (I Kings 19.18). They are to be saved from the general slaughter by a mark put upon their foreheads (cf. the mark put upon Cain, Gen. 4.15, and the blood sprinkled on the doorposts and lintels at Passover, Ex. 12.7, 13). The mark here used was the last letter of the Hebrew alphabet, which then had the form of a X; it denoted that those so marked belonged to Yahweh (cf. Ex. 21.6, and Rev. 7.3f.; 13.16f., etc.).

5-6. 'The pitiless law of the holy war in its most extreme form (cf. Josh. 6.17ff.; Judg. 20.48; I Sam. 15.3; Deut. 13.16ff.; 20.16ff.) is here applied against Yahweh's own people' (Eichrodt). The punishment is to BEGIN AT MY SANCTUARY: 'There he was most present, there most fully known, there if possible most forgotten and provoked, and there his holiness and godhead will assert themselves with most terribleness against the sins of men' (Davidson). The sanctuary was also a place where, through the provision of asylum, one could be safe. But the presence of such sin as was described in the last chapter reverses all normal conditions, cf. Amos 3.14. And, if the holy temple is not to be spared, how much less the city itself! SO THEY BEGAN WITH THE ELDERS—that is, the elders who were sun-worshipping. But BEGAN probably implies that they were to go on to destroy the whole temple personnel.

7. The temple (THE HOUSE) is already defiled because of the idolatries described, but it is now to be further—we might perhaps say formally—defiled by the presence of dead bodies (cf. 6.4f.); GO FORTH must mean that, after defiling the temple, the angels were to go into the city itself and slay. But the verse is almost certainly the insertion of a later scribe who was appalled at such a profanation of the holy sanctuary, and wished to make clear that it was due to an explicit command given by Yahweh himself.

8. AND I WAS LEFT ALONE: the words are absent in LXX and are a gloss. The prophet's cry is generally taken as a

D*

prayer of intercession, but is better regarded as a cry of despair, to which Yahweh nevertheless gave an answer. ALL THAT REMAINS OF ISRAEL: in the OT, the 'remnant' is a technical term for the survivors of a calamity such as war (Josh. 13.12; II Sam. 21.2; Amos 9.12). Here however, it can hardly mean those who remained in the homeland after the deportation of 597. The sense is 'Wilt thou destroy Israel completely?' Verse 9b refers back to 8.12.

11. The angel reports back to Yahweh, as an official does to a king. The pronoun I may include the other six. If on the other hand it was meant to exclude the others, it emphasizes that a remnant does remain spared from the otherwise general slaughter, a remnant with whom Yahweh can later inaugurate his designs for his people's future.

THE BURNING OF JERUSALEM

10.2-7

The man clothed in linen is now given a fresh task. He is no longer to be a scribe, preserving, but the agent in the next stage of destruction, that of the city.

It is very probable that, before this incident was combined with the cherubim vision, what the angel entered was the temple itself, where he took coals from the altar (cf. Isa. 6.6) —this only a priestly figure could do, see on 9.2—and went out to scatter them on the city and so destroy it by fire. 'It is perfectly correct to suppose that fire taken from the holy place would have a particularly destructive power; what however is emphasized is that Yahweh himself turns the fire kindled in his honour into the fire of his wrath, in order to put an end to his own city' (Eichrodt).

YAHWEH'S DEPARTURE FROM THE TEMPLE

10.18-19

The original text was probably: 'Then the glory of the Lord went forth from the house and stood at the door of the east gate of the house of the Lord.' It did not however remain there.

YAHWEH'S DEPARTURE FROM THE CITY

11.23-25

the mountain which is on the east side of the city   The Mount of Olives, separated from Jerusalem by the valley of the Kedron. Yahweh's presence is thereafter to go with the exiles to Babylon (see p. 49).

GUILTY LEADERS

11.1-13

For the general question which this incident raises, see above, pp. 22 and 95.

The events described in 11.1-13 are not a continuation and further instalment of those of the previous chapter, for such sinners as the TWENTY-FIVE MEN (v. 1) have already been destroyed. This vision is also different in content: the iniquity here is no longer cultic, but social (see on v. 2). Originally independent, the section has been introduced at this point, perhaps by the prophet himself, because of its scene—like the rest of 8-11, it is connected with the temple.

1. Still in ecstasy, Ezekiel sees TWENTY-FIVE MEN (who are not the same as the twenty-five of 8.16-18, just as Jaazaniah is different from the man of the same name in 8.11), gathered at the east gate of the temple. A temple gate is also mentioned by Jeremiah as a meeting-place of the princes of Judah (Jer. 26.10). This suggests that these PRINCES OF THE PEOPLE were leading, influential citizens. 'The *sārīm* are the viceroys, the caste of officials who uphold the life of the city.'[5]

2. They DEVISE INIQUITY. Their iniquity is not defined. It is usually taken in the sense of plotting revolt against Babylon, but a similar expression in Micah 2.1 might suggest profiteering in land, and this fits in with a very probable interpretation of what follows.

3. The time is not near to build houses Various meanings have been suggested—the Hebrew is simply 'the building of houses is not near'. (i) Some take HOUSES metaphorically, in the sense of 'families'. After the deportation of the leading

[5] P. A. H. de Boer, 'The Counsellor' (see on 7.26), p. 49.

citizens in 597, some of those who were left behind, described
in II Kings 24.14 as 'the poorest people of the land', hoped
to capture the highest state offices, and their families would
thus attain to nobility (Ehrlich). (ii) Irwin thinks that the
words refer to a popular demand for the 'normal (building)
construction required by the common life of the city', which
the leading men oppose. 'The supreme need of the hour was
military; and the demands of the city's defense might not be
impaired by useless undertakings that could wait until the
crisis had passed' (p. 244). (iii) Following the Greek and Latin
versions, the words are read as a question: 'Have not the
houses (now) been rebuilt?' i.e. has not the damage done in
597 been made good?—in which case they reflect a feeling
of security over against Babylon on the part of the leaders
(in 28.26 the building of houses signifies peace and safety,
cf. Jer. 29.5), and, by implication, a sharp rejection of
Ezekiel's message of doom. (iv) The rich say that there is no
need to build houses: they have not only appropriated the
property of those already deported in 597, but are continually
enriching themselves at the expense of the socially weak, the
SLAIN of v. 6 (Fohrer). This interpretation would fit in with
a very probable interpretation of v. 15.

this city is the cauldron, and we are the flesh   Again the
meaning is quite obscure. The words may once more reflect
feelings of security: the people of Jerusalem (WE) will be
protected from the Babylonians by the city's strong fortifica-
tions (the CAULDRON). Or, on the principle that a pot is only
of use to cook meat, the saying is taken in the sense that
Jerusalem now exists for the advantage of those who were
still left in it, or, as Fohrer thinks, of the leading citizens.
Others believe that WE, the FLESH (the good part of the meat)
represents the contemptuous feelings of the people of Jerusalem towards the exiles of 597—the latter are no better than
offal (see on 11.15).

4-5. Ezekiel is commanded to prophesy against the men who utter these words, who are now called the HOUSE OF ISRAEL: the TWENTY-FIVE are regarded as representatives.

6-8. The meaning is not at once apparent. Who were the slain? Does the term simply mean 'the oppressed' (Fohrer, see above)? Some take it as referring to judicial murders, condemnation to death of political opponents—for example, not only Ezekiel, but Jeremiah too, threatened Jerusalem with destruction, and, while he himself was saved by the intervention of powerful friends, another prophet, Uriah, who used similar language, was put to death (Jer. 26). Others think of the slain as those who perished in the rebellion of 597, for whose deaths Ezekiel here holds the city's leaders responsible. But each of the two last suggestions goes far beyond the charge made in v. 2, and it is tempting to adopt Bertholet's emendation, 'I (i.e. Yahweh) will multiply your slain . . . and will fill' etc. This would allow of the omission of 8, which can hardly be genuine, for, however the saying in v. 3 is to be interpreted, there is no suggestion of fear in the attitude of the speakers.

7. How the SLAIN are the FLESH is obscure. The first part of the verse is generally taken as irony—when the city falls, as fall it will, the only people whom it will protect are those already dead—those who thought they were the flesh will be taken prisoner by the Babylonians and dealt with by them. Verses 9-12 are a later expansion, since they presuppose knowledge of what actually took place in 586, in particular, Nebuchadnezzar's putting to death of the leading citizens at Riblah AT THE BORDER OF ISRAEL (II Kings 25.20f.; Jer. 52.26f.). Verses 11-12 are also omitted by LXX—correctly, since v. 11 interprets the saying in v. 3 in a different way from v. 7.

13. The death of PELATIAH is often taken as meaning that Ezekiel possessed powers of clairvoyance. This may be so, but on the other hand, the incident is set in the context of a vision. Nor is it said that the death was the result of the prophet's words. It is much more naturally to be ascribed to the divine judgment. If Ezekiel had foreseen or foretold it, his reaction would not have been the dismay and horror that it was.

A PROPHECY FOR THE EXILES

11.14-21

This prophecy agrees with Ezekiel's general teaching on restoration, cf. 36.26, 28; 37.26ff. But it is largely a patchwork, and is certainly out of place here, for in chs. 1-24, that is, until Jerusalem has fallen, Ezekiel is a prophet of doom. It has been inserted to furnish an answer to the prophet's despairing cry in 11.13 following on Pelatiah's death, which seems to him to imply the complete annihilation of Israel. As R. Brunner says (p. 137), this cry is 'nothing less than dread (*Angst*) about the world's future'. Ezekiel refers to the belief that 'in you (Abraham) all the families of the earth will be blessed' (Gen. 12.3, RSV margin). But what if Abraham's seed perish utterly? He is shown, however, that, as well as being the avenger of sin, Yahweh is also a saving God who keeps his promises and who will make a new covenant with the remnant of his people.

What gave rise to the passage was a quite practical question. As Horst has shown,[6] THE INHABITANTS OF JERUSALEM (v. 15)—those who had not been deported in 597—were laying claim to enter into possession of the lands and property

[6] F. Horst, 'Exilsgemeinde und Jerusalem in Ez. VIII-IX', *VT* 3, 1953, quoted by von Reventlow, p. 51.

of those who had, and were justifying their act by appeal to
Yahweh's judgment upon the latter—for the words THEY HAVE
GONE FAR FROM THE LORD imply that it was Yahweh who had
driven them out as punishment for their sins (see next para-
graph). Yahweh however, through his prophet, takes the side
of the exiles who, as it were, cannot otherwise be represented
in court. Here, therefore, through Ezekiel's pronouncement
he acts as judge, and the 'form' in which the passage is cast is
that of a process in a court of law. (We have to remember that,
soon after the deportation there were, both in the homeland
and among the exiles, those who promised a speedy return
from Babylon and the restoration of the *status quo* previously
existing, see Jer. 24.27. But how were the returned exiles to
live if their property in Jerusalem and Judea had been
alienated?)

There are, however, wider questions to be considered.
(*a*) In the ancient East, it was believed that deity and land
belonged together. When Ruth said to Naomi, 'Your God
(shall be) my God' (Ruth 1.16), she meant it quite literally:
the writ of Chemosh, God of Moab, did not run in Judah,
which was Yahweh's land (cf. also I Sam. 26.19: David, and
II Kings 5.17-19a: Naaman). The exiles of 597 therefore
believed that, if they were to worship at all, it would necessarily be the gods of Babylon. The serious part of this was
that, FAR FROM THE LORD, they could have no forgiveness of
sins, since this depended upon participation in the cult of the
Jerusalem temple. (*b*) Was it, as suggested above, because
they were greater sinners than the men still in the homeland
that they had been driven away from Yahweh's portion?
Some twenty-five years before 597 Deuteronomy had been
published, and it contained the explicit threat of 'scattering
among the peoples' as the penalty for disobedience to
Yahweh's commands (Deut. 4.25ff.). (The religious viewpoint
of those who remained behind in Jerusalem 'was that the
exiles had gone into captivity because their sins had incurred

Jehovah's anger, and that now His wrath was exhausted and
the blessing of His favour would rest on those who had been
left behind in the land' [Skinner].) (c) The passage can also
be regarded as a discussion of the question, who is the true
'Israel'? The inhabitants of Jerusalem obviously thought of
themselves as such, for the promise to Abraham was bound
up with the possession of 'the land', and now they alone were
in possession. But Ezekiel, like Jeremiah (chs. 24, 29), sees
the people of God in the exiles. (The question of the true
Israel also arose in the early Church, see especially Rom. 11.)

15. With the words of the inhabitants of Jerusalem, compare
33.24, a passage which, in spite of its position in the book,
dates from before the fall of Jerusalem. For a different
religious outlook on the part of people in Jerusalem, see the
sayings in 8.12 and 9.9. The verse has been expanded to
include, by implication, those to be deported in 586 and,
explicitly, the exiles of 722 as well—THE WHOLE HOUSE OF
ISRAEL, ALL OF THEM. It should also be read as a series of
exclamations with no verb, not connected with v. 16. For
THIS LAND read THE LAND, i.e. Israel's peculiar possession by
the promise to Abraham.

16. Yahweh as it were admits what is implied in the utterance
of the men of Jerusalem—it is indeed he himself who has
driven them out—but shows that their conclusion is wrong.
YET I HAVE BEEN A SANCTUARY TO THEM FOR A WHILE: we
should render—if the word sanctuary is genuine[7]—something

---

[7] G. Jahn thinks that the text originally read '. . . scattered them
among the countries, and I became a stumbling block to them in the
countries etc.'. 'Stumbling block' was changed to 'sanctuary' as being
unworthy of God, and 'for a while' was added to restrict the punishment to the period of the exile (*Das Buch Ezechiel,* Leipzig, 1905).
The conjecture was not without its attraction, for it must be admitted
that the connection between a claim to enter into the possession of
land and Yahweh's being a sanctuary is not very direct.

like, 'I have only been to a small extent a sanctuary to them'.
'The presupposition of the words is that in the normal relationship between God and people, Yahweh actually becomes
a sanctuary, i.e. he offers himself for personal encounter in
the services of the temple' (Eichrodt, pp. 75f.). (The English
word 'sanctuary' perhaps suggests the wrong idea: not refuge,
but place of meeting, the place where Yahweh is present in
person, is what comes in question—though of course to know
that one could still meet with Yahweh was a 'refuge' in the
spiritual sense.) There were various ways in which Yahweh
was even for the exiles 'to a small extent a sanctuary'. For
one thing, they had a prophet among them, Ezekiel himself,
to make known his will to them—the situation was different
from that of Ps. 74.9, where 'there is no longer any prophet'.
Again, though they could not offer proper sacrificial worship,
they could observe the sabbath and circumcise their sons;
and they were free to meet together for lamentation and
prayer for the turning of their fortunes (Ps. 137), and for hearing the law. They were therefore not, as their opponents
alleged, completely cut off from Yahweh.[8]

17. Yahweh promises the exiles restoration to the land, and
(v. 18) 'restoration is to be the signal for reformation' (Cooke).
All idolatry, which had been the main cause of the exile, will
be put away.

19. During the half century or so before the exile, the ques-

[8] The Targum sees in this verse the origin of the synagogue—'and I
gave them synagogues which are different from my temple'. In the
temple at Jerusalem, worship was by means of animal sacrifice, while
the synagogue was a place of instruction, of exposition of the law.
After the exile synagogues could be established wherever there were
ten male Jews, and after the destruction of the Temple in AD 70 they
became what they still are, the focal point of Jewish life. The Targum
is, of course, anachronistic, but the synagogue may have derived from
forms of worship designed to meet the emergency situation of the
exile.

tion had begun to arise whether Israel was in fact capable of obeying God's commandments. For Deuteronomy it is hardly yet a serious problem. Completely divorced from the standards of Sinai as the nation was in the last quarter of the sixth century, Deuteronomy offered it fresh acceptance of the old covenant (Deut. 5.2f.; 29.2ff.), and, while the book is not without the sombre undertone that Israel may fail,[9] it generally regards the commandments as possible—and even easy—to obey (Deut. 30.11-14). But in the interval between 621 and the time of Jeremiah and Ezekiel, Josiah's reformation had proved unsuccessful, so that for them the question had become an acute one, and their answer to it was negative. Israel can no more do good than the Ethiopian can change his skin or the leopard his spots (Jer. 13.23), while for Ezekiel Israel is 'a nation of rebels' (Ezek. 2.3, etc.), whose disobedience began right at the moment of her election in Egypt (Ezek. 20.5-8). Both prophets therefore believe that the only way by which the chosen people will be able to obey the commandments is that God himself should make them able so to do. With them, 'both modes of conduct, obedience and dis-obedience, cease to be things over which men themselves can freely dispose. Obedience is created by the act of Yahweh, and comes from his hand equally with the blessing attached to it' (von Reventlow, p. 56). So both Jeremiah and Ezekiel think not in terms of a fresh offer of the old Sinai covenant, as does Deuteronomy, but in terms of a *new* covenant, and of a transformation of human nature. Unlike Jeremiah (31.31), Ezekiel never uses the actual words '*new* covenant', but this is implied in v. 20, for THEY SHALL BE MY PEOPLE, AND I WILL BE THEIR GOD (cf. 14.11; 26.28; 37.23, 27; cf. 34.30) is the old covenant formula, cf. Ex. 6.7; Deut. 27.9. For the covenant, see further Ezek. 37.24ff. As regards the transformation of human nature, the phraseology of both prophets is very much

---

[9] G. von Rad, *Old Testament Theology* I, p. 231.

alike. Ezekiel says I WILL GIVE THEM A NEW[10] HEART (RSV margin), AND PUT A NEW SPIRIT WITHIN THEM (cf. 36.26). Jeremiah says: I WILL GIVE THEM ONE HEART AND ONE WAY (Jer. 32.39). For Hebrew thought the HEART is the seat of thinking and willing. SPIRIT: principle of action, cf. Isa. 32.15; Zech. 4.6. ' "Flesh", impressionable and sensitive, is simply the natural opposite of the type of hardness and resistingness, "stone" ' (Lofthouse). STONE suggests obstinate refusal—perhaps even incapacity—to bend to the will of God. The result of the transformation—Ezekiel does not say how it is to be brought about—will be ability to keep the commandments (20). Thereafter, 'instead of being "only to a small extent a sanctuary", Yahweh will then again become completely his people's God and the people completely Yahweh's' (Zimmerli).

21. The Hebrew is unintelligible, and the verse is a later gloss referring to the inhabitants of Jerusalem.

Zimmerli has an interesting suggestion which, if accepted, makes the content of the passage even more pointed. He believes that vv. 17-18 are a later insertion into it (though possibly by the prophet himself). In that case, the divine action which makes the new covenant and the new obedience possible takes place not in Jerusalem with its (presumably rebuilt) sanctuary, but in the very exile in which it was believed that men could have no contact with Yahweh and where they had been abandoned by him. Thus, it is the place of apparent death that is the scene of new life; cf. 37.1-14.

---

[10] For A NEW HEART MT reads ONE HEART. This suggests disunity among the exiles, which is not in question. It is better to follow LXX (cf. Jer. 32.39) and read A NEW or 'another'. If MT is kept, it could have the meaning that 'their heart will no longer be divided between worship of God and images, but will be wholly loyal to Him' (Fisch).

SECOND CYCLE OF THREATS

12.1–19.14

A SYMBOL OF THE EXILE

12.1-16

Ezekiel is commanded to perform the actions of someone who is about to be deported. What he represents in his own person is the fate soon to overtake those who still remained in Palestine, and the point of performing the symbol publicly (IN THEIR SIGHT, six times, and BY DAY, v. 4) to the exiles in Babylon is to convince them of what, in spite of the events of 598, they still refused to believe, namely that Jerusalem would inevitably be captured, and they themselves be joined by those who were still in the homeland. Unwilling as they were to learn (v. 2), the re-enactment of what they had themselves experienced was intended to reiterate the message of the doom of Jerusalem from a fresh angle. And if they cherished any hopes of their own speedy return home (cf. Jer. 27.16; 28.3f.), these were fruitless.

The original oracle is composed of vv. 1-4, parts of 6 and 7, 8-9, and 11. It represents the coming general exile of 586. Then later, after the actual fall, v. 5, parts of 6 and 7, 10, 12-15, were added to take account of the fate of Zedekiah (THE PRINCE, v. 12) and his entourage.

(a) 1-4, parts of 6 and 7, 8-9, 11. The exile

3. An exile's baggage For the 700-mile trek to Babylon only a minimum could be taken, a staff, some food, a few cooking utensils and a water-bottle, no more than could be

117

carried on a bundle slung over the shoulder. TO ANOTHER PLACE means simply to some distance away, far enough to show what the action meant.

4. On the day of departure the exiles would perhaps be ordered to lay their bundles at the house-door: the actual march would begin at evening, to avoid the hottest part of the day. AND CARRY IT OUT IN THE DARK (v. 6b) belongs to the expansion; the words contradict the publicity (IN THEIR SIGHT) of the whole action, for the word for THE DARK, only again in vv. 7 and 12 here and Gen. 15.17, means complete darkness. The reference is to Zedekiah's flight by night, II Kings 25.4; Jer. 39.4; 52.7, and v. 12 here. COVER YOUR FACE: a sign of grief and shame. But the words may not be original. They are not repeated in the report of the carrying out of the sign in the next verse, and where they occur again, in v. 12, the reference is not clear. Verses 8, 9 and 11 report how on the next day the prophet, having returned to the midst of the exiles from 'the other place', performed what he was commanded to do.

(b) **5, parts of 6 and 7, 10, 12-15.** *The fate of Zedekiah*

5, 7. dig through the wall   The action prefigures the breach in the city-wall through which Zedekiah made his escape (II Kings 25.4).

6, 12. cover your (his) face   This can hardly refer, as does YET HE SHALL NOT SEE IT (v. 13), to the blinding of Zedekiah, for this took place only after his capture, at Nebuchadnezzar's headquarters at Riblah. Did Zedekiah make his attempted escape in disguise?

10, 12. the prince   For this title for Zedekiah see on 1.2 and 7.27.

16. An addition, on the model of 6.8-10, as the concluding formula in v. 15, AND THEY SHALL KNOW, etc., makes clear.

THE TERRORS IN STORE

12.17-20

This symbolic action, which refers to the coming Babylonian invasion, resembles the one already described in 4.10f., 16f., but its point is different. What is here stressed is not the shortage of food, but the terror in which food will be taken once the calamity supervenes. In 19 THE PEOPLE OF THE LAND are the exiles in Babylon. Eichrodt sees irony in the use of the term: some of the exiles were of the nobility and had possessed estates in the homeland, but 'they are now the "people of the land" without land'. THE INHABITANTS OF JERUSALEM in v. 19 may be a gloss, since v. 20 appears to have the whole land in view, not just the capital city.

In this action Ezekiel is probably not to be thought of as simply going through the motions of quaking and trembling; these represent an actual physical condition into which the prophet was brought by the action of the hand of Yahweh. After one of his visions Daniel says that 'my thoughts greatly alarmed me, and my colour changed' (Dan. 7.28); after another 'I was overcome and lay sick for some days' (Dan. 8.27); again, 'a (divine) hand touched me and set me trembling on my hands and knees' (Dan. 10.10), cf. Ezek. 21.6.[1]

---

[1] Von Rad, *Old Testament Theology* II, pp. 232f.

PROPHECY

12.21–14.23

SCEPTICS

12.21-25

The prophet prefaces some utterances on prophecy by dis-
cussing a popular current saying (A PROVERB THAT YOU—i.e.
people—HAVE). The exact reference of the passage is not perfectly clear. As ch. 13 and Jer. 28 and 29 show, prophecy was
at the time speaking with a double voice, both in the exile and
in the homeland. While Ezekiel and Jeremiah were announcing
judgment soon to come, others were prophesying weal, as for
example the speedy return home of those deported in 598
(Jer. 27.16; 28.1-4). But neither sort of oracle was being fulfilled. And since the accepted presupposition (Deut. 18.20-22;
Jer. 28.9) was that if a prophetic word was not fulfilled, then
it was false (COMES TO NAUGHT, v. 22), the whole institution
of prophecy was being called in question (cf. Jer. 5.13; 17.15).
(Smend may be right in suggesting that it was the non-
fulfilment of oracles of weal that had discredited prophecy.
Messel, who quotes him, notes that 12.21-28 do not suit the
date given in 12, because prophecies of doom 'had been
terribly verified a short time before', i.e. in the events of 597.
Ezekiel's whole message, however, in chs. 1-24, and passages
such as Jer. 28.2-4, suggest that these events had not been
taken seriously, and were generally interpreted as no more
than a temporary reverse. Thus, both kinds of oracles were
probably suspect.) If vv. 24-25a are in place here—and EVERY
VISION (22), i.e. *all* that the prophets say as a result of their
inspiration, suggests that they may be—then the reference of

the passage is to this general question. But if they are to be omitted (and this seems more likely, since they introduce a new theme, false prophecy, not delay in fulfilment of prophecy, which is at once dropped until the following chapter, and also because EVERY [v. 22] is lacking in LXX), the proverb then represents a criticism of Ezekiel's own prophecies of doom.

Ezekiel does not argue. And, indeed, in the case there could be no argument. The current test of the truth of a prophecy was fulfilment. So, like Amos when he was similarly challenged about the validity of his interpretation of the covenant (Amos 3.8), Ezekiel falls back on the inner certainty given him by his reception of the word of Yahweh, and with THE DAYS ARE AT HAND (v. 23) reiterates the announcement of the Day of Yahweh of ch. 7.

Such questioning of the authority of the prophets was not a new thing. Giving numerous references, Jannsen says: 'There is no pre-exilic prophet (of doom) of whom it is not said that there was opposition to him on the part of the people or their leaders.'[1] This attitude changed in the post-exilic period, largely for the reason given by Zechariah, 520 BC (Zech. 1.2-6), though this was not maintained (Zech. 13.2-6).

NOT IN OUR DAY

12.26-28

Here the current saying has a different reference: it is to the prophets' hearers rather than the prophets themselves. Even if what the prophets of doom say is true, people were saying, it does not concern us: when it is fulfilled, we shall not be here—cf. Hezekiah's attitude in Isa. 39.5-8. Ezekiel's answer is the same as before.

[1] E. Jannsen, *Juda in der Exilszeit,* Göttingen, 1956, p. 85.

(Irwin regards these last two sections as oracles of comfort, dating from 'after 586, and evidently long after, for the people must have lived through the first stunning effects of the disaster, have revived their faith in the Lord, but by long waiting were now falling into despair' [pp. 107f.]. If however the phrase THE DAYS ARE AT HAND [v. 23] is correctly taken as referring to the Day of Yahweh, this is unlikely, and the oracles are best taken as dating before 586.)

FALSE PROPHETS

13.1-16

This section deals with the general question of true and false prophecy, already raised in 12.24. If Ezekiel's theme in chs. 1-24 is false security, the belief that Jerusalem will not be captured, the false prophets are one of the main causes of it.

The distinction between the canonical prophets like Isaiah, Jeremiah and Ezekiel on the one hand and the 'false' prophets on the other is not altogether clear, for little is said of the latter in the OT. They have been taken as spokesmen of the Baalized popular religion, or as the representatives of the popular idea of Israel's election, whereby Yahweh would support his people even when they disregarded his ethical demands. Others look on them as the successors of the older ecstatic prophets, and argue that the difference between them and the canonical prophets consists in the fact that the latter made strong ethical demands. Or they may have been attached to the court, endorsing the king's policy. Eva Oswald suggests, possibly correctly, that the criterion of a true prophet is that he recognizes what Yahweh is planning to do at a definite point in history.[2]

[2] E. Oswald, *Falsche Prophetie im Alten Testament*, Tübingen, 1962, p. 29.

2. While Ezekiel does not refuse these men the title of PROPHETS (ISRAEL here means both the people in Palestine and the exiles), he says that what they utter is not God's word but their own thoughts; they PROPHESY OUT OF THEIR OWN MINDS (cf. v. 17).

3. and have seen nothing They have not had a vision such as Ezekiel himself had at his call (cf. Jer. 14.14). (Omit FOLLOW THEIR OWN SPIRITS AND as a variant gloss.)

foolish The rendering is misleading. In the OT foolishness is moral or religious superficiality or—often—practical atheism. That is, the charge is that 'they were self-deceived' (Davidson), not consciously false. 'Whatever there might be in their prophetic experiences that resembled those of a true prophet, there was nothing in their oracles that did not belong to the sphere of worldly interests and human speculation. If we ask how Ezekiel knew this, the only possible answer is that he knew it because he was sure of the source of his own inspiration. He possessed an inward experience which certified to him the genuineness of the communications which came to him, and he necessarily inferred that those who held different beliefs about God must lack that experience' (Skinner).

While false prophets were no new thing in Israel—cf. I Kings 22.8ff., the four hundred prophets who opposed Micaiah ben Imlah, c. 900 BC—they seem to have become particularly numerous and active in the last days of the Judean kingdom, because of the confusion and apprehension then prevailing. The fact that both Jeremiah (Jer. 14.13-16; 23.9-22, 25-32) and Ezekiel devote considerable space to them suggests that they were also influential.

The section falls into two parts, (*a*) 1-9 and (*b*) 10-16.

(*a*) **1-9.** The specific meaning of PROPHESY OUT OF THEIR OWN MINDS (2) is given in v. 5, an important verse, since it

contains by implication Ezekiel's definition of the office of
the true prophet. YOU HAVE NOT GONE UP INTO THE
BREACHES, OR BUILT UP A WALL FOR THE HOUSE OF ISRAEL,
THAT IT MIGHT STAND UP IN BATTLE IN THE DAY OF THE LORD
(v.5): the false prophets had shown lack of leadership, or
leadership of the wrong kind. They ought to have been ham-
mering home that the situation, religious, moral and poltical,
perhaps especially political, was a serious one. They should
have been using every means at their disposal—analysis of the
nation's peril, calls to repentance, threats, and perhaps also
intercession (Jer. 27.18)—to repair the damaged life of the
state, and so to ward off the judgment. But they had failed
in their duty, and left their fellow-countrymen with impaired
defences to meet the Day of Yahweh.

For Ezekiel, then, the true prophetic office is to provide
leadership to the nation in times of crisis, to be in the forefront of things. With this we may compare the description of
Elijah, 'The chariots of Israel and its horsemen' (II Kings
2.12).

4. As the change of person shows, this charge has been later
expanded by the addition of this verse. BREACHES in the walls
suggested RUINS: the prophets HAVE BEEN LIKE FOXES AMONG
RUINS. The exact point of the comparison is much debated.
Eichrodt thinks it lies in the fox's way of choosing such places
as ruins for its lair. 'Just as the fox makes its lair in ruins
and is in its element there, so Israel's outward and inward
collapse is not for these prophets a cause of dismay which
appals them and which they seek by all possible means to
restore, but they are quite happy about the dilapidation,
and even make themselves at home in it and draw advantages
from it. For the nation was never more ready to give (them)
credence . . . than when its security broke down and its
hopes lay in ruins' (cf. Fisch, 'in an atmosphere of insecurity
there is eagerness to listen to an optimistic speech'). This well

accords with what is implied, though not stated, in v. 5; the duty of going up into breaches might entail personal danger for the prophet himself, cf. Jeremiah (Jer. 20.2; 26.11; 37.14-15; 38.28). Jeremiah and Ezekiel were much more personally involved in their message and its fate than their predecessors had been.

6-7. Here, too, there has been expansion. Since v. 7 is in the second person and so links on with v. 5, v. 6 is a later addition. With vv. 6-7 cf. Jer. 14.14.

8-9. The original oracle may have ended with the simple statement, I AM AGAINST YOU, SAYS THE LORD GOD. Verse 9, which envisages the return, may be a later addition (Smith, Herntrich, etc.). It gives the punishment of the lying prophets, in which there are three elements: first, THEY SHALL NOT BE IN THE COUNCIL OF MY PEOPLE: the assembly or council is 'the free meeting together in time of leisure of the adult men. . . . It is the place where the news of the day is exchanged. It is the place where the plans for the coming days and for projects which lie ahead are discussed.'[3] They are to have no position of respect or influence in restored Israel. Secondly, they will not BE ENROLLED IN THE REGISTER OF THE HOUSE OF ISRAEL: i.e. in the roll of Israelite citizens, mentioned also in Jer. 22.30 and exemplified in Ezra 2=Neh. 7; they are to lose not only position, but even citizenship. This brings with it automatically the third thing, exclusion from the land of Israel, cf. Rev. 21.27. For a similar punishment of a 'false' prophet, see Jer. 29.29-32.

(*b*) **10-16.** These verses are a separate oracle, and bring in (v. 10) a further point, which can however be regarded as the obverse of that made in v. 5. The picture is different but still

[3] L. Köhler, *Hebrew Man*, trs. Peter A. Ackroyd, London, 1956, pp. 102f.

allied; the WALL is now not the wall of the city, but that of a house, possibly built without mortar. The soothing words of the false prophets—on PEACE (v. 10 cf. the note on 7.25)—are like WHITEWASH, which 'add(s) nothing to the solidity of the work' (Cooke); if it makes the building, i.e. the nation's dangerous state, more prepossessing than in fact it is, at the same time it covers up the weaknesses. Skinner gives the meaning of v. 10 as follows: 'When any project or scheme of policy is being promoted they [the prophets] stand by glozing it over with fine words, flattering its promoters, and uttering profuse assurances of its success.' THE PEOPLE BUILD . . . THESE PROPHETS DAUB; both parties think in the same way.

13-14. These verses are the original kernel of vv. 11-16, which have been much expanded. (In v. 13 read AND GREAT HAIL-STONES SHALL FALL TO DESTROY IT, and in v. 14 omit WHEN IT FALLS, YOU SHALL PERISH IN THE MIDST OF IT, as contradicting v. 9; even if 9 is not original, they can scarcely KNOW, if they are to PERISH earlier!)

12. Where is the daubing . . . ? That is, where is the security you promised? For similar pictures of destruction and its instruments cf. Isa. 8.17; 29.6; Job 38.22f.; Matt. 7.24-27.

SORCERESSES

13.17-23

Prophetesses are mentioned more than once in the OT: Miriam (Ex. 15.20), Deborah (Judg. 4.4), the wife of Isaiah (Isa. 8.3), Huldah (II Kings 22.14; II Chron. 34.22), Noadiah (Neh. 6.14). But the women mentioned in this chapter are better styled as practicers of magic and witchcraft. (It may not be without significance that Ezekiel calls them not prophetesses, but women WHO PROPHESY.) The reason why he brings them under the general concept of 'prophecy' is that, like the genuine prophetic word, their arts had power over life and death (see especially Zimmerli on v. 19). Belief in magic and its efficacy was widespread throughout the ancient east, particularly in Babylonia. Here again, as with their male counterparts, we see a reversion to superstition in a time of crisis.

Two originally independent oracles, 17, 22f., and 18-21, have apparently been combined.

17, 22f. The charge in v. 17 is the same as that against the male prophets (v. 1).

22. THE RIGHTEOUS and THE WICKED clearly link up with Ezekiel's 'doctrine of individual retribution' in ch. 18, in terms of which a man 'lives' or 'dies'—i.e. enjoys long life, a sign of Yahweh's favour, or is cut off prematurely—not because of the righteousness or unrighteousness of his ancestors and his involvement in that, but according to the measure of his own personal righteousness or unrighteousness. This also connects with the office of 'watcher' assigned to the prophet himself in 33.1-9, in virtue of which he is to warn the wicked to turn from his evil way and 'live'.

23. NOR PRACTISE DIVINATIONS: I WILL DELIVER MY PEOPLE OUT OF YOUR HAND is an addition designed to harmonize the originally independent oracles.

18-21. The details are not clear, but the hunt for souls certainly refers to magical practices.

18, 20. Magic bands The women tied these on the wrists of their clients—in 20 read THEIR ARMS for YOUR ARMS—and they in some fashion signified the sorceresses' power over those who consulted them. But the reason for putting veils or shawls over the head is quite uncertain.

18. Of every stature This suggests that the veil covered the whole body. Verse 19a is obscure. It may refer to divination by means of BARLEY and crumbs, a practice common among the Greeks. But FOR—i.e. for such a paltry fee—is much more likely. YOU HAVE PROFANED ME—the profanation consists in the women's claiming as their own that power over life and death which belonged to Yahweh alone. In v. 19b BY YOUR LIES TO MY PEOPLE, WHO LISTEN TO LIES is again a harmonizing gloss.

THE PROPHET AND IDOLATERS

14.1–11

The passage is probably, though not at all certainly, a unity (Hölscher, Zimmerli).

Some OF THE ELDERS come to consult the prophet (cf. 8.1; 20.1). They seek from him an oracle (INQUIRED, v. 3), the subject of which is not stated. But, since they are idolaters, no answer is to be given them by the prophet; Yahweh himself WILL ANSWER them (v. 4). The passage then passes over into a general call to Israel to repent, and punishment is threatened both for idolaters who consult prophets and for prophets who answer them. The purpose of the punishment is that the house of Israel may abandon idolatry and worship Yahweh alone. Then they shall be his people and he their God (v. 11). The idolatry in question is not defined. Since however, the elders dare to consult the spokesman of Yahweh, it is probably the private addition to a publicly professed Yahwism of continuing Palestinian cults which the exiles had brought with them, or of the worship of certain Babylonian gods, or of the wearing of amulets of them, such as have been found in numerous excavations, to ensure their aid in the foreign land. This has become a STUMBLING BLOCK (vv. 4, 7) to them, i.e. it has led them astray from Yahweh (see on 7.19).

3. taken . . . into their hearts These words 'might be translated "cherished"' (Cooke). SET BEFORE THEIR FACES is a synonym for this.

5. lay hold of the hearts of the house of Israel That is, 'lay hands on Israel, be her (sole) Lord; he will save her from the idols which, according to v. 4, dwell in Israel's hearts, and on whose account Israel has become estranged from him' (Messel). Ehrlich, however, following rabbinic usage, gives the meaning as 'in order thus to make them responsible for what they think in their heart, though they have not translated their thought into action or even expressed it'. Others again think that the idea is rather that of terrifying.

7. strangers Aliens resident within Israel, some of whom might have adopted Israel's faith.

8. a sign and a byword 'The exemplary punishment of the sinful among the Israelites will become proverbial and act as a deterrent' (Fisch).

The action of the elders is made the occasion of a general statement on idolatry. The main part of the oracle consists of vv. 6-8, and explains what is meant by I THE LORD WILL ANSWER HIM MYSELF (vv. 4, 7). The terminology has close affinities with that of the Holiness Code (Lev. 17-26), and this makes clear that the phrase I WILL . . . CUT HIM OFF FROM THE MIDST OF MY PEOPLE (v. 8) means the application of the 'ban', whereby the offender was excluded from membership of the chosen people, and so deprived of the possibility of expiation and forgiveness. To be put under the ban was as

E

bad as death. And physical death itself is actually threatened
(v. 9) for the prophet who gives an answer to such idolaters.

9. I, the Lord, have deceived that prophet For a similar
idea see I Kings 13 and 22. In the latter, Yahweh put a lying
spirit into the prophets of King Ahab, with the result that
they prophesied what Ahab wanted. Quell points out that here
the possibility of real obedience was open to the prophet,
since there was a clear word of Yahweh forbidding idolatry,
such as Deut. 13.1-5, and this should have warned him against
holding any communication with idolaters.[4] Davidson says
that 'in both cases (*sc.* here and with Ahab's prophets) this
enticement or deception (by Yahweh) was in punishment for
previous sin', i.e. the sin of entering into the thoughts and
purposes of wicked men. The OT way of thinking carries
everything back to Yahweh, whereas we today reckon with
secondary causes. But 'the case of prophecy was peculiar. It
was looked on as a real supernatural endowment (Deut.
13.1-5), and as such could come only from JHVH (II Kings
22.23). Yet in the Prophet's mind it was no less certain that
JHVH must punish all sin. He does not trouble himself to
solve the apparent moral contradiction, but wisely holds fast
to his two facts. It is his practical way of dealing with the
eternal question of divine absoluteness and human freedom'
(Toy).

The teaching of 14.1-11 is that God is resolved to stay with
his sinful people in order to heal them (Zimmerli).

THE PUNISHMENT OF JERUSALEM IS
REMORSELESS BUT JUST

14.12-23

Here Ezekiel seems to be answering a specific question. He
has announced the total destruction of the nation. But might

[4] *Wahre und falsche Propheten*, Gütersloh, 1952, pp. 99-102.

not the land be spared for the sake of the righteous men in it, on the principle laid down in Gen. 18.32—'for the sake of ten [righteous] I [God] will not destroy it [Sodom]' (see below)?

The section falls into two parts, (a) 12-20, teaching for the prophet himself and given to him directly—this deals with the general case of *any* land, not specifically Israel, that acts faithlessly, which means sins religiously, and (b) 21-23, an oracle introduced by the messenger formula and applying to the particular case of faithless Jerusalem. There is also a difference in content as well as form between the two parts. In (a) the point is that, if Yahweh punished a faithless land, the righteous in it WOULD DELIVER BUT THEIR OWN LIVES: THEY WOULD DELIVER NEITHER SONS NOR DAUGHTERS. But in (b) it is envisaged that some of the unrighteous will not only themselves survive, but will also LEAD OUT (presumably unrighteous) SONS AND DAUGHTERS. And also, the motif of consolation (22b, 23a) ill accords with (a)—but see below. (b) represents what in fact took place at the fall of Jerusalem, the exile of those who survived, good and bad alike, and was composed in the light of that event. It would appear that the prophet's expectation had been disappointed. He had believed that the fall of the city would follow the lines of (a). When it did not, he composed the rather artificial explanation given in (b)—when the original exiles of 598 were joined by those of 586, they would see that the wickedness of the latter was so great that Yahweh's punishment was completely justified. This was the purpose for which the exception had been made to the general principle laid down in (a). The point is not that sinners did escape, but that this was the unexpected method adopted by Yahweh to convince the earlier exiles of his justice. It is of course possible that (b) was composed not by the prophet himself, but by a later editor, the purpose being the same.

(a) **12-20.** Though it enters in, the subject of the teaching here is not the question of individual or collective retribution, that is, whether each man fares according to his own merits or demerits, or whether his fate is affected by his involvement in a guilty society (see ch. 18). The subject here—and it is a very human one—is whether, in the absolutely just action of Yahweh, the righteousness of a parent will avail to save (presumably wicked grown-up) sons and daughters. Gen. 18.22-33, Abraham's intercession for the righteous in Sodom, a passage of teaching already in existence (J), might have suggested that it would. However, for Ezekiel, the principle of strict individual retribution which he already holds leads him to an opposite answer. The righteousness of even paragons of righteousness like Noah, Daniel and Job would only avail to save them themselves: there is no transference of merit, cf. Ezek. 18.10-13. Zimmerli thinks that Ezekiel's experience as a priest may have contributed to his answer: in cases of disease, access to the sanctuary and participation in the life of the community depended on the actual condition of the individual himself, Lev. 13.

Jer. 15.1-3 should be considered along with the present passage, though the differences between the two are considerable.

As to structure, four typical cases are given of Yahweh's means of punishing a faithless land; they are famine (13f.), wild beasts (15f.; cf. II Kings 17.25f.), war (17f.), and pestilence (19f.) (cf. Ezek. 5.16f. and Jer. 15.2f.). Each one leads to the same conclusion that the righteous deliver only themselves. The cases are styled in the form of casuistic laws, and the fourfold, almost verbally identical, reiterations in vv. 14, 16, 18 and 20 are obviously intended to inculcate the inviolability of the norm proclaimed (Eichrodt). Four as the number of agents of destruction occurs elsewhere—Job 1.13-19; Zech. 1.18-21; Rev. 9.13-15, and also in the Babylonian Gilgamesh epic. It may signify that the punishment is complete and entire.

In Gen. 6.9 (P) and 7.1 (J) Noah is called righteous by
Yahweh. Daniel is not the Daniel of the OT, who is represented as a younger contemporary of Ezekiel himself (Dan.
1.1-7), but an earlier figure. In Ezek. 28.3, a poem on Tyre,
one Daniel is mentioned as wise. And the texts from Ras
Shamra, in the same quarter of the land, speak of a Dn'el, a
righteous king, who 'decides the case of the widow; (who)
judges the suit of the orphan'.[5] Here, therefore, Daniel is a
well-known and ancient type of righteousness. Job's righteousness is attested explicitly by God himself (Job 1.8;
2.3) and by implication in 1.2-5 which follows the doctrine
then current that prosperity is the reward of piety.

(In point of fact, Noah's righteousness did deliver his sons
from the Flood, though a grandson, Canaan, was afterwards
cursed for an act of wickedness [Gen. 9.20-27]. Dn'el could
not save his son Aqht from being murdered on a false charge
laid by the goddess Anat. And while Job's righteousness did
not save his sons and daughters [Job. 1.18-19], he did effect
deliverance for his friends against whom God's anger was
kindled [Job 42.7-9]. But these considerations are irrelevant
here. What is in question is only the men themselves as para-
digms of righteousness. It is however perhaps not irrelevant
that, where the subject is a land in general, and not specifically
the land of Israel, the examples chosen are non-Israelites.
Noah was pre-Israelite, Dn'el Syro-Phoenician, and Job from
'the land of Uz' [1.1], of 'the people of the east' [1.3].)

(b) **21-23.** *Any* faithless land is punished (vv. 12-20): how
much more severe must be the punishment of Jerusalem, the
capital city of the people to whom Yahweh had uniquely
revealed his will, cf. Amos 3.2. This is suggested by the fact
that not just one of the judgments of 12-20, but all four together, are to come upon her.

---

[5] Translation by John Gray, *The Canaanites,* London, 1964, p. 108.

As has been said above, the reason why some might be spared was that the exiles to whom they came might see their evil way of life (THEIR WAYS AND THEIR DOINGS), and so recognize that Yahweh's sentence was well-deserved. Verses 22b and 23a are wanting in LXX, and are an addition. The consolation is that their minds are set at rest, since they now have no doubts that Yahweh's punishment of Jerusalem, though remorseless, was completely justified. Of that there was no question, cf. 18.25-29; 33.17-20.

THE PARABLE OF THE VINE

15.1-8

The vine was at once the characteristic and the most choice product of the soil of Palestine, cf. Num. 13.23. In Jotham's fable (Judg. 9.7ff.) it is, along with the olive and the fig tree, the symbol of royalty, and in the oracle on Judah in the Blessing of Jacob (Gen. 49.11) it is used to indicate the paradise-like conditions of the coming time, 'binding his foal to the vine, and his ass's colt to the choice vine, he washes his garments in wine and his vesture in the blood of grapes'. The vine had also for long been used as a symbol for Israel. 'Israel is a luxuriant vine that yields its fruit' (Hos. 10.1); 'Thou didst bring a vine out of Egypt; thou didst . . . plant it. Thou didst clear the ground for it' (Ps. 80.8ff.). With Isaiah, however, a change begins. While elaborating the idea of Yahweh's care for his vine, he at the same time gave the image a new, and darker, colour by describing Israel as the unfruitful vine (Isa. 5.1-7). This continues in Jeremiah: Israel is the choice vine, wholly of pure seed, planted by Yahweh, that has turned degenerate and become a wild vine (Jer. 2.21). But in this progressive denigration Ezekiel characteristically (see chs. 16 and 20) goes further, and in two directions. First, he turns completely away from that which gives the vine its value and pride of place among the trees, its fruit, and concentrates on the part of it which is worthless, its wood. Second, he speaks of this wood as already half-burnt and scorched, thus making it of even less, indeed of trivial use. 'Exactly as if someone looking at a splendid mediaeval altar-painting were to notice only that the wood on which it was painted was worm-eaten, and on that basis passed his judgment on the picture.'[6]

[6] W. Zimmerli, 'Das Gotteswort bei Ezechiel' in *ZTK* 48, 1951, p. 251.

The background of the parable is, of course, Israel's election. She is the vine, the most valued in Yahweh's sight of the nations, THE TREES OF THE FOREST (v. 2). And what called forth Ezekiel's utterance may have been an objection to his prophecies of doom based on the fact of the covenant. Other nations might perish, but Yahweh would never allow the destruction of his own chosen people. The prophet refutes the argument by looking at the well-known figure of the vine Israel from a new angle.

The chapter falls into two clearly distinct sections, 1-5, the parable itself, and 6-8, its interpretation, introduced by the messenger formula.

2. The original may have been expanded, but the sense is: 'what superiority has the wood of the vine, the vine branch, over any other wood of the trees of the forest?'—a rhetorical question to which the answer must be 'None'. 'Judah never had any pretensions to be a powerful state, or to enter into competition in wealth or military resources with the kingdoms round about. As a tree among the trees, a state among the states, what was it good for?' (Davidson). It is useless even for making a peg to hang things on. But there is still more to it. When a piece of such wood is already half-burnt, it can have no value at all. Even without the interpretation in v. 6 the reference is perfectly clear, the hopeless state of Jerusalem now that FIRE HAS CONSUMED BOTH ENDS of the wood, that is, after the deportation of the leading citizens in 598. In 598 there had been no full-scale deportation, but in the FIRE soon to come, the destruction will be total. (Verse 8 falls out of the picture; it is a glossator's prosaic addition.)

JERUSALEM THE UNFAITHFUL WIFE

16.1-63

Ezekiel now adopts a fresh angle of approach to the necessity of Jerusalem's destruction—her history has been one of persistent unfaithfulness to Yahweh. He develops an image of Isaiah's, 'How the faithful city has become a harlot' (Isa.1.21), into a kind of allegory. The city, which stands at the same time for the whole nation, is personified as a foundling child for whom, when her parents abandoned her with complete ruthlessness, Yahweh cared, and ultimately married. But in spite of all he does for her, because of her inbred nature, she deserts him for other lovers. This brings terrible punishment upon her. Jerusalem is then compared, to her disadvantage, with Sodom and Samaria. The chapter ends with a promise of restoration. This is the first of three historical surveys given in the book, the others being chs. 20 and 23.

Westermann calls chs. 16 and 20 baroque expansions of the originally short oracle of judgment directed against the nation.[7]

The original kernel of the parable has been considerably expanded, in some cases perhaps by the prophet himself, in others by his disciples. The chapter divides as follows:

1-14: the foundling child who becomes the renowned bride of Yahweh.

15-34 (original kernel, 15, 22-25): Jerusalem's shameful requital of Yahweh's goodness.

35-43a (original kernel, 35, 39-41a): her punishment.

43b-58: the three sisters.

59-63: restoration.

In the chapter Ezekiel may be countering an objection to

---

[7] *Basic Forms of Prophetic Speech*, p. 182.

his teaching that Jerusalem must fall which is similar to that found in the Fourth Gospel: 'we are descendants of Abraham' (John 8.33ff.).

Ezekiel's view of his people's history is darker than that of any other prophet. Amos (5.25), Hosea (9.10), and Jeremiah (2.2f.) all think of the wilderness period as a time when Israel was loyal to Yahweh—Jeremiah calls it the honeymoon days —and reckon her apostasy as only beginning with the settlement in Canaan and the transition there made to the life of agriculture. For Ezekiel however the nation's sinful course began as early as her election in Egypt (see ch. 20). In this respect he stands closer to P, in whose view also the apostasy started in the wilderness (epecially Ex. 32, the golden calf).

FOUNDLING AND BRIDE

16.1-14

1-2. *Introduction*

The prophet is commanded to address to Jerusalem the kind of formal charges made in a court of law.

3-7a. *The foundling child*

In the matter of Israel's origins, Ezekiel here remarkably enough passes over the general tradition of a national derivation from Mesopotamia and an election in Abraham (Gen. 12.1-5, cf. Josh. 24.2-3). While he knows of it (33.24; 37.25), he prefers to link on to the history of Jerusalem, which remained a Canaanite city until its capture by David (II Sam. 5.6-9; cf. Amos 2.10: 'the land of the Amorite'). The AMORITES, represented as descended from Noah's grandson Canaan (Gen. 10.16), are here, as elsewhere in the OT, synonymous with the Canaanites. HITTITE is also used in the same sense. In spite of the strong polemic of Deuteronomy against any contact with the Amorites/Canaanites, Israel had in fact close affinities with them, since both were of Semitic stock. The Amorites had asserted themselves as a ruling class in Mesopotamia, Syria and Palestine about 2000 BC, and there founded a series of states. Abraham was an Amorite to the extent that he formed part of the Amorite migration westwards. The Hittites, who were not Semites, entered Anatolia, probably from beyond the Bosphorus, about the end of the third millennium BC, and were a dominant power from 1900-1200. Their influence was felt in Palestine, and Hittite names connected with Jerusalem make it probable that Ezekiel knew of traditions which spoke of Hittite influence on its earlier population. When he speaks of Jerusalem as Canaanite in origin and says: YOUR FATHER WAS AN AMORITE, AND YOUR MOTHER A HITTITE, what he means to imply is that heathenism was inherent in the nation from the very beginning—she was 'of a stained and corrupted lineage (in spite of the contention of ch. 18)' (Lofthouse), 'depravity was so to speak in her bones' (Ziegler). Of her origins Israel had no reason to boast. Though she regarded the Canaanites as accursed (Gen. 9.25) and unclean (Lev. 18.24f.), she was of the same stock as they were, and was later to display the same religious and moral characteristics. Anything that she has to be proud of comes from Yahweh: indeed, her very existence as a people—I SAID TO YOU . . . LIVE (v. 6)—is due to him, and him alone. (Yahweh is the giver of all life, Gen. 2.7.) Because, 'heathen by parentage, the child received heathen treatment at its birth' (Cooke), if Yahweh had not had pity on her, she would have perished like an unwanted child exposed to die, as weak or cripple or superfluous female infants frequently were exposed throughout the ancient East. Further, Israel has no natural claim upon Yahweh in the way that other nations supposed they had claims on their gods, as descended from them. It was a stranger who passed by, and did the kindly offices that gave her life. Zimmerli notes that in the OT 'life' carries the added implication of happiness, fulfilment, nearness to God.

4. Omit TO CLEANSE YOU. The rubbing with salt, which is still practised by the Arabs, may originally have been done to avert demons. Salt is also regarded as a 'giver of life' (W. L. Wardle in *Abingdon Bible Commentary*, London, 1929, *in loc.*).

7b-14. *Maidenhood and marriage*

When Yahweh passed by a second time, he again acted towards her in kindness. She had now grown up and reached the age of marriage.

7b. full maidenhood This denotes menstruation, and HAIR is the pubic hair. But she was NAKED AND BARE—i.e. poorly clad, like a Bedouin girl. 'Apart from life she possesses nothing, and has therefore no prospects of attracting a man and being married' (Fohrer). Yahweh however marries her with the customary legal formalities—i.e. gives her a unique position among the nations of the world.

8. SPREAD MY SKIRT OVER YOU: a symbol of betrothal and marriage, cf. Ruth 3.9; for the COVENANT, the oath sworn at this time, see Prov. 2.17; Mal. 2.14. YOU BECAME MINE: Israel now belongs to Yahweh. This implies faithfulness, cf. Hos. 3.3: 'You must dwell as mine . . . you shall not play the harlot.'

What is referred to in v. 8 is the making of the covenant at Sinai. We may notice how, like Hosea and Jeremiah, Ezekiel here boldly takes over the Canaanite idea of the sacred marriage of the god and goddess of fertility. In the ancient East the god was often regarded as a tribe's or nation's husband. But the prophets radically transform the idea: Israel's relationship to her God is not a natural one, but completely dependent on an historical act of choice. No reason is here given for Yahweh's act of choice, any more than in Deut.

7.7-8. But certainly all notion of any deserving on Israel's part is ruthlessly ruled out.

9. blood of the first coitus. 'Observe that everything is done for her by her protector' (Lofthouse).

10-13. These gifts figuratively signify Yahweh's self-revelation as expressed in law, the granting of the land of Canaan, the sending of prophets (cf. Amos 2.9-11), etc.

10. For the bride's fine clothing, cf. the princess's apparel in Ps. 45.13f. LEATHER: some kind of fine leather, such as was used for covering the tent when Israel was on the march (Ex. 26.14). SWATHED YOU IN FINE LINEN refers to a headdress. Fine linen was also used for cultic purposes (Ex. 25.4), so the suggestion may be that some kind of sanctity attached to Yahweh's bride.

12. a beautiful crown: the Song of Solomon mentions 'the crown with which his mother crowned him (Solomon) on the day of his wedding' (3.11).

13. Flour and honey and oil The three typical gifts of the divine beneficence, see Deut. 32.13f.; Hos. 2.10 (Cooke). They are also regal food: 'Solomon's provision for one day was thirty measures of fine flour' (I Kings 4.22), and Jeroboam I sent honey as a part of a gift (I Kings 14.3). This, and the mention of the crown in v. 12, led to a commentator to think —wrongly—that Ezekiel was referring to the institution of the monarchy, and so he added AND CAME TO REGAL STATE.

14. A reference to the splendour of the empire of David and Solomon.

This first section ends with the reminder that everything which the girl—Jerusalem—possessed had been bestowed on her by Yahweh.

YAHWEH'S GIFTS ABUSED

16.15-34

Prosperity makes Jerusalem wish for freedom and independence from Yahweh. Gratitude is not a sufficient motive to keep her loyal, and, at the same time, blood tells. And so she becomes an adulteress.

Harlotry is used in two senses in the passage: first, apostasy to the nature gods of Canaan (vv. 15-25) and, secondly, alliances with foreign powers, and reliance upon them instead of on Yahweh (vv. 26-29). The latter also led to the introduction of foreign worships and practices. Political relationships with another state involved some recognition of the other power's gods. In branding these two forms of defection from Yahweh as harlotry. Ezekiel, like Jeremiah, takes up a metaphor first used by Hosea (Hos. 1.2; 8.9). With v. 15 cf. Jer. 2.20, 23f.

15, 22-25. *The original kernel of the section*

24. vaulted chamber We learn from the Babylonian monuments that this was a low altar-pedestal on which cult-prostitutes lay as they offered themselves in the service of the goddess Ishtar (Astarte). LOFTY PLACE: Canaanite shrines were originally built on heights (see on 6.6); here it means the cult-prostitute's resort.

16-21. *The first expansion of the original kernel*

Its purpose is to underline the outrageousness of Jerusalem's conduct by stressing that the things which she used in the service of her wantonness were those which had been bestowed upon her by the husband to whom she owed everything (cf. Hos. 2.8). GAILY DECKED SHRINES (v. 16): cf. II Kings

23.7. IMAGES OF MEN (v. 17): probably phallic symbols, cf. Isa. 57.8.

20-21. Here we find a new element which the prophets regard as the culmination of outrage, namely, child-sacrifice. The first certain mention of this is in the reign of Ahaz (736-715): see also II Kings 23.10; Jer. 7.31; 19.5-6; Micah 6.7; Deut. 12.31; Lev. 18.21; 20.2. Though forbidden—cf. Josiah's reform, II Kings 23.10—it was occasionally practised in times of crisis. The reference here may be to the reign of Manasseh, who sacrificed his own son (II Kings 21.6) and apparently allowed others to do the same. Ezekiel again refers to child-sacrifice in 20.25f. This is Israel's culminating sin, for the children are Yahweh's. Implicit is the contrast between her conduct to her children and Yahweh's to her when she was a child.

26-29. *The second expansion of the original kernel*
Here the sin of Jerusalem is not religious apostasy, but lack of trust in Yahweh in the realm of politics. 'Alliances [with foreign powers] showed disloyalty towards God, or rebellion against His rule. They relied on physical power. They are like idolatry; both exalt the physical. Both turn away from God. An alliance with a military power showed a lack of faith in Him.'[8] Cf. Jer. 2.13. Instead of being a nation wholly devoted to her God and relying upon him alone for protection, as she did earlier in the time of the holy wars and as Isaiah in particular demanded of her, Israel had had recourse to statecraft. (One of the dilemmas which she had to face was how to reconcile statecraft, which relies on human wisdom, with the concept of charismatic leadership or of a divine word by which history was directed.)

[8] Israel I. Mattuck, *The Thought of the Prophets*, London, 1953, p. 102.

26. 'The policy of seeking help from Egypt had a natural attraction for the small states of Palestine, especially when they were threatened by Assyria and Babylon' (Cooke); see II Kings 17.4 (Israel); 18.21 (Judah); also Ezek. 29.6f. For overtures to Assyria, see II Kings 16.7ff.; Hos. 5.13; Isa. 7.1-20; Jer. 2.18, etc.

29. For HARLOTRY with the Babylonians, see 23.14ff. The Chaldeans were a tribe living in the country north of the mouth of the Euphrates, a situation suitable for trade, who gave great trouble to the Assyrians in the second half of the eighth century and eventually, along with the Medes, overthrew them. The father of Nebuchadnezzar, Nabopolassar (Nabium-apil-uṣur) founded the Chaldean or Neo-Babylonian dynasty, which lasted from 625 BC till its overthrow by Cyrus the Persian in 538. Since v. 27 anticipates the punishment of the harlot in vv. 35ff., it is itself a later insertion into 26-29. It is generally regarded as referring to Sennacherib's invasion of Judah in 701, of which he recorded: 'His (Hezekiah's) cities which I had plundered I separated from his land, and gave them to Mitinti king of Ashdod, Padi king of Ekron, and Silbel, king of Gaza, and diminished his land' (the Taylor Cylinder, col. iii, lines 22ff., quoted by Cooke). These three cities are Philistine. But Fohrer is probably correct in referring the verse to the events of c. 586 when, after the deportation, the Philistines occupied Judean territory lying on their borders, Ezek. 25.15-17. DIMINISHED YOUR ALLOTTED POR-TION: diminishing her allowance is also part of adulterous Israel's punishment in Hos. 2.9.

30-34. *A third expansion of the original kernel*
(Verse 31a takes up v. 24.) Jerusalem is not merely a harlot, but is unique in her behaviour as one. An ordinary prostitute charges for her favours, but Jerusalem actually paid her lovers! The reference is to the tribute which Judah had to

pay to foreign powers (Hos. 7.9; 8.9f.; 12.1; Isa. 30.6f.) in consequence of the political role she essayed to play.

THE HARLOT'S PUNISHMENT

16.35, 39-41a

As the original kernel of vv. 15-34 is 15, 22-25, so here the corresponding original kernel here consists of vv. 35 and 39-41a, the punishment of Jerusalem by her lovers. The remainder links up with the previous expansions. Yahweh summons Jerusalem's lovers—the foreign powers, not the foreign gods—first to tear down her buildings and then to act against the harlot herself.

39. they shall strip you of your clothes This means divorce—Yahweh frees himself from the husband's obligation to clothe the wife (H. W. Wolff).[9] Cf. Hos. 2.3. She is therefore back in the situation in which Yahweh found her at the beginning. She then suffers the penalty prescribed by the law for an adulteress, death by stoning (Lev. 20.10; Deut. 22.21ff.; John 8.1ff.; cf. Ezek. 23.47). For the burning, see Lev. 20.14; 21.9.

40. host Not foreign armies, but a legal assembly of Israelites. Deut. 13.6ff., a case of enticement to idolatry, says that the accuser's hand shall be the first in putting the accused to death (by stoning) and 'afterwards the hand of all the people', that is, the legal assembly.

The original text ends at MANY WOMEN (41a). The rest of the verse is out of context, and is a scribal addition.

In the expansion, 36-38, 41b-43, THE BLOOD OF YOUR CHILDREN (v. 36) refers back to the child-sacrifice of vv. 20f.

[9] *Dodekapropheton* 1 (*Hosea*) (Biblische Kommentar, Altes Testament XIV/1) 2nd ed., Neukirchen-Vluyn, 1965.

42b. I will be calm . . . angry   Probably the later comment
of a scribe who already had vv. 53ff. before him.

In 16.1-43 Ezekiel opposes all natural pride based on election. Israel's sole boast can be in Yahweh's free favour towards her. But since this has been grossly abused by her, she
must forfeit it. The end is about to come upon her; saving
history will either be at a standstill or cease altogether. Ezekiel is thus actualizing the words of Amos, 'The end has come
upon my people Israel' (Amos 8.2), 'Behold, the eyes of the
Lord God are upon the sinful kingdom, and I will destroy
it from the surface of the ground' (Amos 9.8).

THE THREE SISTERS

16.43b-58

A fresh subject now follows. The passage presupposes the
fall of Jerusalem, and is probably not from Ezekiel himself,
but the composition of a disciple who, starting from a proverbial saying, LIKE MOTHER, LIKE DAUGHTER, took up certain
expressions and thoughts in vv. 1-43a, in order to give an
additional but different ground for the rejection of Jerusalem.

Jerusalem is compared with two sister cities, Samaria and
Sodom. In terms of the allegory in vv. 1-43a, WHO LOATHED
HER HUSBAND AND HER CHILDREN etc. (v. 45) should mean
'who apostasized and offered child-sacrifice'. But while apostasy was true of Samaria, it was not true of Sodom. It might
then be supposed that the 'loathing' refers to the low moral
conditions obtaining in Samaria and Sodom. Yet surprisingly,
although Sodom, along with Gomorrah, is the OT type for
utter sinfulness (Gen. 18f.; Deut. 29.23; Amos 4.11; Jer. 23.14,
etc.), Sodom's sin in v. 49 is not sexual perversion, but pride,
luxury, and contempt for the poor, obviously a different tradition from that of Gen. 18f (J), and one which could very well

be applied to Samaria, cf. Amos 6.1-7. The confusion shows that the passage is secondary.

In comparison with Jerusalem, Samaria and Sodom seem RIGHTEOUS (v. 51, cf. Jer. 3.11; Lam. 4.6). 'The Prophet doubtless had in mind what he considered the greater nearness of JHVH to Jerusalem which made its neglect of Him the more heinous' (Toy). Jerusalem must, therefore, like them, BE ASHAMED and BEAR her DISGRACE (v. 52). This is meant to be an implicit prediction both of the destruction of Jerusalem, and of the completeness of this, since Samaria (722 BC) and Sodom (Gen. 19) were both destroyed. 'In all the preexilic passages Sodom and its sister cities are the stock terms for divine judgment on sin. They serve as the norm for punishment, inasmuch as these cities suffered the most terrible punishment ever meted out.'[10]

In such a situation, justice demands the restoration of Sodom and Samaria and their territory (DAUGHTERS, v. 53). But Jerusalem is to continue to bear her punishment (omit 53b and 55b, see below) and to be a consolation to her sisters —that is, the greater guilt of Jerusalem will make Sodom and Samaria feel that their own guilt is now less reprehensible. Before Jerusalem's punishment (BEFORE YOUR WICKEDNESS WAS UNCOVERED, v. 57a), she spoke of Sodom as the byword of iniquity. But now Judah, 'become worse than the worst' (Howie), is herself to be despised. The Edomites gloated at the fall of Jerusalem (Obadiah) and, like the Philistines, moved into Judean territory left depopulated by the deportation.

The rigour of this judgment upon Jerusalem was subsequently toned down by the insertion of a promise of restoration for Jerusalem, vv. 53b and 55b. Its author may have had vv. 59-63 before him, and to that extent be justified. But the addition completely spoils the point of vv. 53-58.

[10] N. K. Gottwald, *Studies in the Book of Lamentations* (SBT 14), 1954, p. 66.

RESTORATION

16.59-63

This is probably the latest section of the chapter. It picks up the COVENANT of v. 8 and the phrase THE DAYS OF YOUR YOUTH in v. 43, while v. 61 links on to vv. 46-58. Lateness is also shown by the fact that the term EVERLASTING COVENANT and the verb ESTABLISH connected with it are characteristic of P. The section also has affinities with Ezek. 34 and 37.

The verses seem to envisage Jerusalem as the capital of a new state which is to include Sodom and Samaria, cf. the boundaries of the restored community in 47.13ff., and also 37.15-22. Jerusalem's domination is expressed by the idea that her sisters are to become her daughters.

61. be ashamed 'She will blush for shame when he (Jahweh) returns good for evil by bringing her sisters under her domination—not because she has merited this by keeping faith, but of his pure grace' (Wardle).[11]

but not on account of the covenant with you The meaning is uncertain. It could mean, 'even though you (Jerusalem) did not keep the (Sinai) covenant which I (Yahweh) made with you'. But the words could also purport 'though they (Samaria and Sodom) shall not be in covenant with me as you are', that is, Jerusalem will have the place of pre-eminence as the capital city and perhaps also as the site of the temple which would, of course, be the sole place of worship in the restored community.

The idea of Jerusalem-Judah as a religious leader of other nations recurs in a more fully developed form in Trito-Isaiah,

---

[11] *Abingdon Bible Commentary*, p. 274.

cf. Isa. 60.1-7; 61.5f., but it did not maintain itself in the particularism of the post-exilic age.

The chapter is a good example of the 'actualization' of prophetic words. After his death, a prophet's oracles were not stored away among the archives, but were adapted—and sometimes even transformed—by his disciples for use in similar or different situations.

AN ALLEGORY

17.1-24

The subject of the allegory is Zedekiah's breach of his oath of loyalty to Nebuchadnezzar. Put on the throne by the latter in 597 in place of the deported Jehoiachin, about ten years later he rebelled, asking help from Egypt. For this Ezekiel was commanded to denounce him: his disloyalty will be punished by the Babylonian king. This however is still in the future, and vv. 1-21 are therefore to be dated to about 588. The chapter falls into three parts: vv. 1-10, the allegory of the two eagles; vv. 11-21, its interpretation; and vv. 22-24, the prediction of a ruler to come. The first two are closely connected, the third is probably not from Ezekiel.

THE TWO EAGLES

17.1-10

'Ezekiel is commanded to convey his message in the form of a riddle which requires some intelligence to solve, but at the same time to develop the application so as to bring it nearer to the form of a *mashal*, an allegory whose meaning is less disguised and more readily grasped' (Fisch).

3. A great eagle Nebuchadnezzar. The eagle is the symbol of strength and swiftness, and its description—the three parts of the plumage mentioned can be distinguished in many Mesopotamian sculptures—is meant to suggest the power of the Babylonian empire. G. R. Driver says that MANY COLOURS should rather be 'which has no markings', 'for the plumage of

the eagle is a uniform brown'.[12] Jeremiah, too, speaks of
Nebuchadnezzar as an eagle (48.40; 49.22).

Lebanon Jerusalem-Judah. Jeremiah again uses Lebanon
in connection with Jerusalem in the sense of splendour,
majesty (Jer. 22.6f.; cf. Isa. 10.33f.; Zech. 11.1-3).

the top of the cedar Jehoiachin and the nobility. THE TOP-
MOST OF ITS YOUNG TWIGS (v. 4); Jehoiachin was only
eighteen when he was taken into exile.

4. carried it to a land of trade A reference to the deporta-
tion of 598 (see II Kings 24.10-16) to Babylonia (cf. 16.29).
TRADE is probably used rather contemptuously. A CITY OF
MERCHANTS : Babylon itself.

5-6. The second stage in the action. Driver (*op. cit.*, p. 153)
renders v. 5 as follows:

> He took a native seed and put it in a seed-bed;
> a shoot by many waters, he made it a fruit-tree.

The metaphor changes from the cedar to the vine. SEED OF
THE LAND indicates that Jehoiachin was not replaced by a
foreigner, but by a native prince, Mattaniah, a son of Josiah
and therefore Jehoiachin's uncle, to whom Nebuchadnezzar
gave the throne-name of Zedekiah, the change signifying his
status as vassal—see II Kings 24.17 and the interpretations
in v. 13, where COVENANT and OATH (cf. Deut. 29.12) mean
oath of fealty, see Jer. 34.18f., and II Chron. 36.13. The nature
of the oath is nowhere stated. FERTILE SOIL; ABUNDANT
WATERS : Nebuchadnezzar had no wish to destroy Judah. A
reorganized state thriving under a loyal vassal could be of use
against intrigues on the part of Egypt. The language also

[12] *Biblica* 35, 1954, p. 152.

implies Ezekiel's belief that Judah could have lived happily as a part of the Babylonian empire, if only she had repressed her desire for independence.

6. Read 'that it might sprout'. While the vine had not the majesty of the cedar, it was nevertheless the choicest product of Canaan, and in 19.10ff. it is again employed of the royal house. But this was to be a LOW SPREADING VINE—Zedekiah was a vassal and might not pursue an independent foreign policy. ITS BRANCHES TURNED TOWARD HIM: 'Its policy was pro-Babylonian' (Muilenburg). ITS ROOTS REMAINED WHERE IT STOOD: 'The roots were not to seek other soil; there was to be no wavering of allegiance' (Cooke).

7-8. The third phase of the allegory. The second great eagle is Hophra, king of Egypt, who had just come to the throne in 588. The description suggests less magnificence than in the case of the first eagle, since Ezekiel regarded Babylonia as having greater power than Egypt, cf. chs. 29f. THIS VINE BENT ITS ROOTS TOWARD HIM—Zedekiah appealed to Hophra for help against Babylonia, see Jer. 37.7, and the interpretation in vv. 15-19 of this chapter. No reason is given for Zedekiah's action. (The text of vv. 7b and 8 is uncertain. Perhaps we should read with Cornill 'that he might water it better than the bed in which it had been planted' and omit v. 8. But Hitzig may be right in taking 'THAT HE MIGHT WATER IT' as a gloss due to the 'ABUNDANT WATERS' of v. 5.)[13]

9-10. The fourth phase. 'With the question, "Will it thrive?" the allegory turns to the future' (H. Schmidt). The text is again uncertain. Verses 9b and 10 are secondary. WILL HE NOT PULL UP. . . ?: unless the sentence should read as a passive, 'will not his roots be pulled up', HE signifies Nebuchadnezzar, as does also the EAST WIND (sirocco) in v. 10, cf. 19.12. For

[13] *Der Prophet Ezechiel*, Berlin, 1847, *in loc.*

CUT OFF ITS BRANCHES Köhler would apparently read 'make scaly its grapes'.[14] Ezekiel is writing before Nebuchadnezzar marched westward, but he is certain that the king will not overlook the action of Zedekiah.

THE INTERPRETATION

17.11-21

Verses 16-18, which are in prose, are a secondary addition.

17. As Jer. 37.5-11 shows, the PHARAOH did in fact send an ARMY and force the Babylonians to raise the siege of Jerusalem, but later withdrew, cf. Lam. 4.17. According to Josephus, (*Antiquities* X 7.3, quoted by Toy) he was defeated. Characteristically, however, Ezekiel goes behind the political reasons for Nebuchadnezzar's punitive action against Zedekiah. Politically, a vassal could rebel—he might even have the duty to do so if he could thereby regain his country's independence. Perhaps, too, Zedekiah was not a free agent in his rebellion (Jer. 38.5). However, his submission to Nebuchadnezzar had been by oath (Jer. 34.18), at the taking of which he had invoked the name of Yahweh (II Chron. 36.13). Therefore, when he broke the oath, he not only broke faith with his overlord, but he also transgressed against Yahweh—MY OATH AND MY COVENANT (v. 19). Through any covenant 'the two parties create something outside and higher than themselves, and its holiness appears from the fact that the divine power takes part in it and watches over it. But it is the same with . . . the *oath* . . . Hence the uttering of an oath is a holy act'.[15] 'Thus, Ezekiel does not make the reason for Zedekiah's imminent fall the logic of history, the fact that ambitions and breach of faith are wont to have a bad outcome, but sees it exclu-

[14] *Lexikon.*
[15] Pedersen, *Israel* III-IV, pp. 449f.

sively as the consequence of his trespass against Yahweh
who, as the guardian of law, does not allow breach of law
and covenant to go unpunished, since this is an offence
against his holiness' (Fohrer). The determining factor is,
again, Yahweh's honour. (Jeremiah's attitude to rebellion
against Babylon was slightly different: he believed that
Judah's submission to the foreign power was divinely ordained, e.g. Jer. 21.1-10; chs. 27-29; 34.1-7; chs. 37-38.)

18. he gave his hand: in pledge of fealty. For the figure in
v. 20, cf. 19.8; 32.3.

THE PREDICTION OF A RULER TO COME

17.22-24

Added to the oracle of judgment on Zedekiah is a prophecy
of salvation modelled upon parts of the oracle. Its purpose
was to show that in spite of all appearances, Yahweh remains
faithful to his promise to David made through Nathan (II
Sam 7).

Now it is Yahweh himself, not the eagle, who takes the
SPRIG, a future ruler of the royal line—the new Israel of the
future is not to come into being as a result of any power of
recovery still lingering within it, but solely as a result of the
divine action. With the SPRIG cf. Isa. 11.1.

a high and lofty mountain Originally the mythological
mountain of the gods (cf. note on 1.4), this is now Mount
Zion (cf. 40.2; Isa. 2.2=Micah 4.1; Zech. 14.10; Ps. 48.2).
The tree, too, is a mythological motif (cf. 31.1ff.; Dan. 4.4ff.).
The BEASTS and BIRDS are the Gentile nations, especially
those in Israel's immediate environment. Some sort of peace-

ful protection of these nations by Israel, and therefore a position of world importance for Israel herself, are envisaged, but not more nearly defined. (Isa. 2.2-4 is much more specific.)

24. the trees of the field shall know The Gentile nations 'shall be convinced of Jahweh's divinity and power by the change in Israel's fortunes. There is no thought of conversion to the true religion . . . Israel's restoration will lead the world to recognize Jahweh as He truly is, the only Lord of human life and the Controller of Israel's destiny; cp. Isa. 45.3, 5, 6 and Jer. 16.21' (Cooke).

GOD AND THE INDIVIDUAL

18.1-32

THE INDIVIDUAL AND HIS NATION

18.1-20

The starting-point of this oracle, in which the prophet discusses a theme as with pupils, is, as in 12.22, a popular saying which, as Jer. 31.29 shows, was also current in the homeland. Its meaning is that the generation of exiles was being punished not for its own sins but for those of the generations that had gone before it, cf. Lam. 5.7: 'Our fathers sinned, and are no more; and we bear their iniquities,' and also the Deuteronomist's statement in II Kings 24.1-4, that the destruction of Jerusalem and the exile were punishment for the sins of Manasseh. 'No doubt this popular and pithy summary teaching was used as much as an excuse as a protest; it proclaimed the exiles' innocence.'[16] In earlier Israel such a view would have been accepted as normal: the unit with which God was thought to deal was the family or the nation—e.g. Achan's whole family was put to death because of his sin (Josh. 7.24ff.). Now, however, with the increasing emergence of the individual in his own right, this idea of solidarity was leading on the one hand to questioning of the divine justice (vv. 25, 29), and on the other to a mood of moral paralysis and feelings of fatalism. This second factor Ezekiel seeks to counter in vv. 1-20 by asserting that 'the ancient solidarity is dead' (Auvray), and that the unit with which God deals is the individual taken in complete isolation from his heredity: THE SOUL (that is, the person) THAT SINNETH, IT SHALL DIE (v. 4).

[16] E. W. Heaton, *The Old Testament Prophets*, 1958, p. 99.

Innocent and guilty are not lumped together in calamity. Yahweh has complete freedom to deal with each man and woman by himself or herself. Ezekiel also here lays down a second proposition, namely the principle on which this freedom is exercised: a man who is righteous 'lives', while a wicked man 'dies'. 'Live' most probably means escape from, come through, the calamities of the times, and 'die' perish in them. At the same time, 'for Israel death's domain reached far further into the realm of the living [than it does for us]. Weakness, illness, imprisonment, and oppression by enemies are a kind of death.'[17] Lofthouse may therefore be right when he says, 'Since, in a period like Ezekiel's, death is so often associated with violence and misery, it comes naturally to be used for the loss of all that is worth having.'

4. all souls are mine 'All souls alike belong to God, and this "alike" guarantees the treatment of each by itself, the soul of the son no less than the soul of the father. According to former modes of thought the son had not personal independence, he belonged to the father, and was involved in the destiny of the father' (Davidson).

Ezekiel illustrates his propositions of individual responsibility and the divine measure of conduct by means of three model cases. As Zimmerli points out, the first (vv. 5-9) is in three parts: first a series of legal requirements, then a declaratory formula, HE IS RIGHTEOUS, and finally a promise of life, HE SHALL SURELY LIVE; the other two (10-13 and 14-18) are in the same form modified. Zimmerli therefore thinks that the cases are modelled on a procedure in the Jerusalem temple, the so-called liturgy of the gate. At the gate, pilgrims were stopped by a priest or priests and asked about their uprightness, if they had fulfilled the conditions necessary for entrance, cf. Pss. 15 and 24 and Isa. 33.14-16. If they had, they were declared 'righteous', that is, they might have access

[17] G. Von Rad, *Old Testament Theology* I, p. 387.

to the Temple. If so, Ezekiel, himself a priest, is here adapting a priestly function. Reventlow, however, denies this. He thinks of a different *Sitz im Leben*, the Israelite festival of the renewal of the covenant, where the proclamation of such series of apodictic commandments was the task of a prophet. Thus, in proclaiming life and death here, Ezekiel is exercising an integral part of the prophetic office. In either case, when Ezekiel announces a new divine dealing with the individual, he is not completely innovating, but does this in the context of ancient cultic usage, though, as Eichrodt notes, the old statutes are freed from connection with the soil of the Holy Land and the Jerusalem temple: 'On the model of the Book of the Covenant, Deuteronomy, and the Holiness Code in Lev. 17ff., he has extracted from the ancient covenant law an ethical and social norm for living which, for those staying in a foreign land, might put relationships with one's neighbour on a firm basis.'

5-9. *The first generation: a righteous man*

Righteousness, WHAT IS LAWFUL AND RIGHT (5) is defined by means of long-established regulations of the priestly law and other codes, particularly Deuteronomy and the Holiness Code, as the references listed below make clear. 'They may be classed under the three heads of piety, chastity, and beneficence' (Skinner), the cultic demands preceding the ethical as in the Decalogue. 'As always, the standard of assessment is practical conduct, which, for Israel's concrete way of thinking, is the visible expression of the inner attitude and disposition from which it arises' (Fohrer); cf. Job 31 and Matt. 25.31ff.

The following prohibitions and commands define 'righteousness'.

(i) EAT UPON THE MOUNTAINS: participation in sacrificial
      meals at the high places (see on ch. 6), implying
      communion with the deity (to Ezekiel a false deity).

We should probably however read 'eat with the blood' (cf. 33.25 and Lev. 19.26). The blood was regarded as the seat of life, and had therefore to be completely drained off from meat before it was eaten (it was then 'kosher'). Abstinence from blood would mark Israel off from her heathen neighbours and so serve to give the exiles solidarity.

(ii) LIFT UP HIS EYES TO . . . IDOLS: acknowledge, venerate, cf. Job 31.26.

(iii) For prohibition of adultery cf. Ex. 20.14; Lev. 18.20; 20.10; Deut. 5.18.

(iv) On sexual intercourse during menstruation cf. Lev. 18.19; 20.18. Breach of the prohibition caused cultic uncleanness.

(v) OPPRESS: cf. Ex. 22.21 and Lev. 19.33 (strangers) and Deut. 23.15f. (slaves), also Lev. 25.14, 17.

(vi) RESTORES . . . HIS PLEDGE: pledges had to be restored when they were something indispensable, cf. Ex. 22.26f.; Deut. 24.6, 10-13, 17.

(vii) COMMITS NO ROBBERY: cf. Lev. 6.4; 19.13.

(viii) GIVES HIS BREAD TO THE HUNGRY . . .: cf. Lev. 19.9f.; 23.22; Deut. 14.29; 15.7-11; 24.19-22; also Job 31.16-20; Matt. 25.31-46.

(ix) INTEREST . . . INCREASE: 'the reference is to interest on charitable loans; [the Deuteronomist] allows this in dealing with a foreigner, Deut. 23.20; but Ezekiel condemns it altogether. Interest in the modern sense, i.e. on money lent for commercial purposes, is an entirely different thing' (Cooke); cf. also Ex. 22.25; Lev. 25.35-37. On the difference between usury and increase the Jewish commentator Kimchi (quoted by Fisch) says that the former means lending money on the express condition of receiving interest, the latter, accepting interest offered voluntarily by the debtor on paying the debt.

(x) WITHHOLDS HIS HAND FROM INIQUITY . . . JUSTICE
  BETWEEN MAN AND MAN: the reference is to processes
  at law, see Ex. 23.1-3, 6-8; Lev. 19.35; Deut. 16.18-20.

The first clause of v. 9 sums up the series of positive
and negative commandments under the two common terms
for the Law, STATUTES and JUDGMENTS. Then follow the
declaratory formula and the promise of life.

10-13. *The second generation: an unrighteous man*

A wicked son of a good father derives no advantage from
the latter's righteousness; he falls because of his own conduct. The list of sins follows the preceding one fairly closely.
The son is not formally called unrighteous, and there is no
declaratory formula.

10b-11a. who does none of these duties The original text
has been expanded; the meaning is: does none of the things
his father did. Such a son must DIE (v. 13). HIS BLOOD SHALL
BE UPON HIMSELF: he, and he alone, and solely because of
his own conduct, brings death upon himself.

14-18. *The third generation: a righteous man*

If there is no transfer of righteousness, equally there is
none of unrighteousness: no man need feel his condition
hopeless as being engulfed in the guilt of his father. This is
the point to which vv. 1-18 lead up: 'God holds no man
responsible for the circumstances into which he was born, but
only for the use to which he puts them subsequently.'[18]

18. his brother Omit with LXX.

19-20. *The conclusion of the whole matter*

19. The prophet gives no answer to the question WHY SHOULD
[18] E. L. Allen, *The Interpreter's Bible* VI, p. 160.

NOT THE SON SUFFER . . . ?, which states the doctrine of family solidarity, but reiterates the doctrine that God deals with each individual on his merits.

20. 'Once he had said one generation cannot suffer for the sin of another, it was only a step further to say that one individual cannot suffer for the sin of another.'[19]

A FURTHER STEP

18.21-29

The passage revolves round another despairing current saying, THE WAY OF THE LORD IS NOT JUST (vv. 25, 29), where WAY means 'principle of action'. In vv. 1-20 Ezekiel asserted that a man is not benefited or handicapped by his *ancestral* past, his heredity; he now applies the same idea to a man's *own* past. When God confronts him with 'life' or 'death', what is decisive is his state *at that moment*; if, though once righteous, he is then wicked, his previous righteousness is of no avail to him, and he 'dies'. And conversely. God's ways are therefore perfectly just; it is human judgment that is illogical. (Verses 26-29 simply reiterate vv. 21-25.)

A CALL TO REPENTANCE

18.30-32

Repent, and turn from all your transgressions. It is to this call that the whole chapter has been leading up. No feelings of guilt due to solidarity or to one's own sinful past need paralyse

[19] A. S. Peake, *The Problem of Suffering in the Old Testament,* London, 1904. p. 27.

F

moral decision and effort. Later (36.26) Ezekiel speaks of the NEW HEART and the NEW SPIRIT as the gift of Yahweh. Here, however, his concern is to declare that a man can, by an act of will, change his mode of life.

This actual situation to which the prophet was addressing himself should be borne in mind when his doctrine of individual responsibility is stigmatized as atomistic, untrue to the facts of heredity and habit, and so on. Ezekiel was not the first to criticize the accepted solidarity idea (see Deut. 24.16; II Kings 14.6). But the situation in which he found himself was such that it required not merely to be more radically criticized, but even for the time being repudiated. *In and for this crisis* its operation is suspended. 'Ezekiel, like Jeremiah (the new covenant) is referring to the coming Kingdom and the coming Day of Judgment. . . . When he affirms that a son will not bear the iniquity of his father, he is not denying the Second Commandment and the facts of heredity and of national and family solidarity. . . .

'Similarly, when Ezekiel says (18.4): "The soul that sins, it shall die", and (18.5ff.): "If a man be just . . . he shall surely live", he is not asserting that good men always, or even usually, have long life and that bad men die young. He is referring again to the coming Judgment. The word "die" virtually means "be excluded from the coming Kingdom" while "live" means "be admitted to the Kingdom". Those to be excluded would actually, in consequence of the Judgment, suffer physical death, while the others would in fact remain alive and enter Palestine; the language is therefore quite apposite; the soul that sins shall die but the just shall surely live.'[20] The seeming inconsistency—the whole nation is condemned in chs. 16, 20, 23; none will escape (5.12; 7.10-27; 11.7-12 etc.)—is, again, an indication of the time: the problem was being felt acutely, but no satisfactory solu-

[20] C. J. Mullo Weir, 'Aspects of the Book of Ezekiel', *VT* 2, 1952, pp. 109ff.

tion had as yet emerged. In ch. 18 Ezekiel offers one that will at least temporarily give men back moral energy.

'There is a sphere within which natural laws have their course. . . . The physical effects of vicious indulgence are not turned aside by repentance, and a man may carry the scars of sin upon him to the grave. But there is also a sphere into which natural law does not enter. In his immediate personal relation to God a believer is raised above the evil consequences which flow from his past life, so that they have no power to separate him from the love of God. And within that sphere his moral freedom and independence are as much matter of experience as is his subjection to law in another sphere' (Skinner). It is with the second sphere that Ezekiel is here dealing.

'When the Prophets threatened that the spiritual faults and moral vices of the people would bring destruction on the nation, the people answered them with the proverb: "The fathers have eaten sour grapes, and the children's teeth are set on edge", either to exonerate themselves from blame for the impending calamity or to plead impotence to avert it, since according to the proverb its causes lay in the unalterable past. The proverb gave them both an alibi and an excuse for moral inertia. The Prophets answered them by refuting the proverb. But in denying its moral implications for the immediate situation, they could not have intended to reject the idea, and deny the potency, of historical continuity; they could only have meant that each generation has, by its moral character, sufficient power within the historical process to influence its direction, so that it must accept responsibility for its fate. The general tenor of their teaching clearly implies the doctrine of corporate responsibility (cf. Ezekiel 16.20; 47.21). Individual responsibility did not negate the fact of solidarity.'[21] This point of view differs somewhat from the one taken above.

[21] Israel I. Mattuck, *The Thought of the Prophets*, p. 88.

The topic is resumed in 33.10-20; cf. also 3.16-21. Notice that ch. 18 not only asserts the justice of God, but contains (in v. 23) one of the most evangelical utterances of the OT: HAVE I ANY PLEASURE IN THE DEATH OF THE WICKED, SAYS THE LORD GOD, AND NOT RATHER THAT HE SHOULD TURN FROM HIS WAY AND LIVE?

LAMENTS

19.1-14

The chapter is in the familiar *qinah* (dirge) metre (3:2).

LAMENTS OVER PRINCES OF ISRAEL

19.1-9

1-4. *The first lion whelp*

3-4. For BROUGHT UP ONE OF HER WHELPS read with Driver 'exalted one over [the rest of] her whelps'. For SOUNDED AN ALARM read 'were roused' with Noth.[22]

The LIONESS mother is Judah or the Judean royal house; in the Blessing of Jacob (Gen. 49) Judah is a lion's whelp, cf. also Num. 23.24; Micah 5.8. In the Blessing saying there is also mention of the VINE, as in vv. 10ff. here. The WHELP king is Jehoahaz, who, after a three months' reign as successor to Josiah, was deposed by Pharaoh Necho (THE NATIONS, v. 4) and taken TO EGYPT (II Kings 23.33f.; Jer. 22.10-12).

5-9. *The second lion whelp*

In v. 5 omit THAT SHE WAS BAFFLED and for MADE read 'appointed as' (Driver). In v. 7 the first clause (down to CITIES) is impossible in MT; perhaps read the whole verse, as Noth:

> 'He made palaces quake
> and terrified cities,
> so that the land and all in it was struck with amazement
> at the noise of his roaring.'

[22] M. Noth, 'The Jerusalem Catastrophe of 587 BC and its Significance for Israel', in *The Laws in the Pentateuch and Other Studies*, ET, Edinburgh and London, 1966. p. 272.

This WHELP-king is most probably Jehoiakim, Jehoahaz's successor. Jeremiah speaks of his violence and oppression (Jer. 22.13-19). He rebelled against Nebuchadnezzar who sent troops against him (II Kings 24.1f.). Verses 8b and 9a, where there has been textual expansion, refer to the lion hunts of the Assyrians and Babylonians.

THE VINE AND ITS STEMS

19.10-14

In v. 11 read for the first clause 'it grew strong branches serving as rulers' sceptres' and omit the rest as secondary addition.

The figure changes from the lioness to the vine (cf. ch. 17). Since, like vv. 1-9, this third lament begins with YOUR MOTHER, editors generally look for a reference to a definite king, some thinking of Jehoiachin, others of Zedekiah. But there is in fact no mention of one *single* rod (in v. 11 the plural 'rods' [AV] or 'branches' is correct as against RSV STEM), and since the vine is Judah or its royal house, vv. 10-14 are most naturally to be taken as a lament on the fall of the state, or the monarchy, generally. These verses had probably no original connection with 1-9. They were placed together partly because both are laments, partly because of the similar opening, YOUR MOTHER, (cf. Isa. 5.8-23 for a series of oracles each beginning 'Woe unto'), and partly also perhaps because of the conjunction of lion and vine in Gen. 49. Verses 13-14 may have been added after the events of 586. The fire would then refer to Zedekiah's breach of fealty, which brought the downfall of the state and the end of the monarchy. Then the last line of the chapter means 'What was composed as a lament over Zedekiah'—for so the scribe understood the verses—'is a lament founded on fact' (Bertholet).

FINAL PROCLAMATIONS OF
JUDGMENT AND PUNISHMENT

20.1–24.27

ISRAEL'S CONTINUOUS SIN AND ITS
RESULT

20.1-31

Some eleven months after the temple vision of ch. 8, the elders again approach the prophet, as in 8.1 and 14.1 (cf. also 33.31). They wish him to obtain for them an oracle from Yahweh (INQUIRE, vv. 1, 3). This they are refused, since they are in the state of cultic uncleanness (vv. 30f.). Instead, and in order to demonstrate their uncleanness, Ezekiel is to JUDGE THEM (v. 4), that is, 'set out the case against them' (Cooke). Thereafter follows a schematic review of Israel's history from its beginning, divided into four phases (vv. 5-9, 10-14, 15-22, 23-31), in each of which the central theme is the nation's refusal to obey Yahweh. 'Hardly anything more could be said than is done here about Israel's unfaithfulness, her indifference to the love of God, and her inability to render the slightest obedience.'[1] Like Ezekiel's other two historical retrospects, ch. 20 has been called a 'travesty' of the saving history—'the prophet had made the venerable tradition into a monstrous thing.'[2] But Ezekiel approaches the tradition with a different end in view from that of the canonical history as set forth in Genesis-Joshua. The latter is confession, Israel's avowal of Yahweh's goodness to her, and the way he had led her. But this is denunciation, Yahweh accusing and condemn-

---

[1] G. von Rad, *Old Testament Theology* II, p. 229.
[2] G. von Rad, *op. cit.*, p. 226.

ing his people as in a court of law. 'In the former, human confession, in the latter, divine reckoning' (Reventlow, p. 78). The canonical history is, however, the background of ch. 20.

It is sometimes supposed, on the basis of v. 32, that the reason for the elders' consultation of Ezekiel was a desire on the part of the exiles to build a temple or else to establish some kind of sacrificial worship in Babylon—Fohrer thinks of an image of Yahweh made of wood and stone. But, apart from the psychological unlikelihood of this latter suggestion, 'people who were intending to "become as the heathen" would hardly have resorted to such a person as Ezekiel' (Cooke). Kaufmann is almost certainly correct when he says: 'This is not faith in new gods, it is no faith at all. This is the desperate counsel of men whose spirit is broken and who have lost faith in the future. Despairingly they seek to live a life without God, like the nations. To this the prophet answers, "It shall not be." '[3] Moreover, Zimmerli has shown that on form-critical grounds v. 32 should go with vv. 33ff. and not with vv. 1-31 (see on v. 32).

To return to the theme: 'The principle that has ruled this history is that all through it Jehovah has acted for his name's sake. It is this principle that has given Israel a history, otherwise their sins would have cut them off' (Davidson).

THE FIRST PHASE: ISRAEL IN EGYPT

20.5-9

The election of Israel took place in Egypt (except in 33.24 and 37.25 Ezekiel ignores the patriarchs and the election traditions connected with them).

5. chose The Hebrew word *bāḥar* occurs only here in Ezekiel. But it plays a considerable part in Deuteronomy, a fact

[3] Yehezkel Kaufmann, *The Religion of Israel*, p. 441.

which leads Fohrer to surmise that, by using it here and then
going on immediately to speak of Israel's disobedience, Ezekiel indicates his belief that the Deuteronomic reform had
been a failure. The election is accompanied by (*a*) an oath (I
SWORE TO THEM, v. 5; cf. Ex. 6.8; Num. 14.30); (*b*) the revelation of the name Yahweh, in the covenant formula of Ex.
10.2, thus making cultic communion possible (v. 15); and (*c*)
the giving of the first commandment (v. 7), which, in the
canonical history, takes place only at Sinai. All this occurs in
the context of Yahweh's will to deliver ISRAEL, THE HOUSE OF
JACOB, and to bring it into a good land (cf. Ex. 3.7f.). Thus
the promise of grace to Israel is accompanied by a demand, a
demand which Israel forthwith failed to obey (v. 8). (The
only other reference to idolatry in Egypt, apart from 23.3 and
much later Jewish tradition, is Josh. 24.14.) Because of this,
Yahweh intended to pour out his fury upon them, but desisted FOR THE SAKE OF MY NAME, THAT IT SHOULD NOT BE PRO-
FANED IN THE SIGHT OF THE NATIONS AMONG WHOM THEY
DWELT (v. 9). Yahweh's name is here equivalent to his honour,
his reputation. Had Israel been destroyed immediately after
being promised deliverance, the Egyptians would have concluded that Yahweh was without the power to make the
promise good (Num. 14.13ff.; Deut. 9.28), and so his name
would be profaned among them. So he led them out into the
wilderness. (The same idea is present also in II Isaiah: the
reason there given for the return from exile, which is conceived as a second exodus, is 'that men may know . . . that
there is none besides me; I am the Lord, and there is no
other' [Isa. 45.6].) 'The grace shown in the deliverance from
Egypt, the basic datum of Yahweh's freely bestowed love to
his people in the old Credo (*sc.* Deut. 26.5-9), is here an act of
God's faithfulness to himself and of the maintenance of his
honour in the face of a sinful people' (Zimmerli).

8. Then I thought 'These words recur like a refrain through
F*

the chapter: in each case Yahweh's purpose is altered, lest his name should be "profaned" among the nations' (Lofthouse). The style of the chapter 'is monotonous, and reflects the gloom of the outlook; yet the very repetitions produce a solemn impression' (Cooke).

9. profaned 'To "profane" is the opposite of to "sanctify". (It is) to cherish any thoughts of Jehovah or to attribute any deed to him inconsistent with his being the one true God, or derogatory to him who is so' (Davidson). Ezekiel's great concern is that Yahweh's name should not be profaned but sanctified, cf. vv. 14, 22, 44; 36.21, 22, 23; 39.7, 25.

THE SECOND PHASE: IN THE WILDERNESS

20.10-14

See also notes on ch. 16 for Ezekiel's view of the wilderness period.

In the wilderness Yahweh gave his people further STATUTES and ORDINANCES, that is, the laws given at Sinai. BY WHOSE OBSERVANCE MAN SHALL LIVE: the same words appear in Lev. 18.5; cf. Ex. 20.12; Deut. 4.40; 5.16. Translating the last part of v. 11 as 'made them to know my demands which men must obey in order to live', Köhler says, 'There is no other Old Testament word which portrays so clearly the imperative nature of the law, the divine claim.'[4]

12. In addition Yahweh appointed the sabbath, its purpose being that the weekly pause from work might remind his people of their God. The sabbath was a day of rest even in pre-exilic times (Amos 8.5), but it assumed a new significance in the exile. 'The temple and its cult perished, but the commandment to observe the sabbath survived and now became

---

[4] *Old Testament Theology*, London, 1957, p. 205.

a very important part of the worship of Yahweh.'⁵ Ezekiel
himself mentions it nine times outside of this chapter. For
the sabbath as a sign, see Ex 31.12-17 (P). Ezekiel frequently
censures breach of the sabbath, 20.13, 16, 20, 24; 22.8, 26;
23.38, and demands its observance, 20.20; 44, 24. Two profana-
tions of the sabbath in the wilderness are recorded, Ex.
16.27-9 (gathering of manna) and Num. 15.32-36 (gathering
of sticks). For the post-exilic period, see Neh. 13.15-22.

13-14. But Israel again rebelled. And Yahweh again intended
to destroy her. But he refrained for his name's sake.

THE THIRD PHASE: THE SECOND GENERATION

20.15-22

15. Moreover The meaning is 'however' (Fohrer). Verses
15-17 apply to the people just mentioned in 10-14, and the
reference is to Num. 13f. and Deut. 1.19-46, where this generation was condemned to wander forty years in the wilderness
and not to enter into the promised land.

8. their children The next (that is, the second) generation
behaved as their fathers had done in the matter of the commandments, and with the same consequences.

THE FOURTH PHASE: IN THE PROMISED LAND

20.23-31

23-24. The punishment of this rebellion was to be eventual
exile from the promised land. Ezekiel apparently connects

⁵ E. Jannsen, *Juda in der Exilszeit,* p. 111.

this resolve to exile with the incident of the golden calf, which
ends with the order to Moses: 'Go, lead the people to the
place of which I have spoken to you (that is, the promised
land); . . . nevertheless, in the day when I visit, I will visit
their sin upon them' (Ex. 32.34). Other threats of exile occur
in Lev. 26.33-39; Deut. 28.36, 64-68. These Ezekiel sees as in
part already fulfilled in the exile of the northern tribes in 722
and, for the rest, as now finally, and with terrible actuality
for his hearers, in process of fulfilment with the events which
began with the deportation of Jehoiachin.

As well as threatening them with exile, Yahweh GAVE THEM
STATUTES THAT WERE NOT GOOD AND ORDINANCES BY WHICH
THEY COULD NOT HAVE LIFE (v. 25, contrast v. 11)—that is, he
gave them commandments designed to ruin them. The commandment in view is the law of the first-born (v. 26). Ex. 13.2
(cf. 34.19) reads: 'Consecrate to me all the first-born; whatever is the first to open the womb among the people of Israel,
both of man and of beast is mine.' Verses 13 and 15 of the same
chapter (cf. Ex. 34.20) prescribe, however, that the first-born
of men were not to be put to death, as were the first-born of
animals, but were to be redeemed, and Deuteronomy (12.31;
18.9f.) and the Holiness Code (Lev. 18.21; 20.2f.) expressly
forbid child-sacrifice (cf. Gen. 22, told as an explanation of
the redemption). But child-sacrifice had been resorted to in
the time of Ahaz and Manasseh (see on 16.20), and Ezekiel
seems here to interpret Ex. 13.2 and 34.19 in their literal
sense, as meaning that at Sinai Yahweh had in fact commanded the sacrifice of the first-born of men. Since this involved Israel in what Deuteronomy (12.31) calls 'Canaanite
abomination', it was a statute which, though commanded by
Yahweh, was NOT GOOD. Its purpose was THAT I MIGHT HOR-
RIFY THEM (v. 26). 'The penalty of sin is further delusion and
worse sin, the end of which is death' (Davidson). Cf. 14.9.
(With LXX omit the last clause, from I DID IT to the end of
the verse, as a later addition.)

As has been pointed out,[6] this is the one passage in the OT where the saving character of the law is called in question. (Jeremiah regards child-sacrifice as something 'which I [Yahweh] did not commanded them not, nor did it come into my mind', Jer. 7.31; 19.5.) This leads eventually to the Pauline discussion of the place and function of the law in Galatians and Romans.

25. statutes that were not good 'This striking expression must not be explained away; it is after all only in accordance with the general Hebrew view that God is the author alike of good and evil (Amos 3.6; Job 2.10), and that He can therefore even deceive men . . . Hence, since Israel has obviously been carrying out statutes that are not good, they must have been really given by Yahweh, but as a punishment, a judicially inflicted blindness' (Lofthouse). Cf. also von Rad on the hardening of the heart in Isa. 6: 'on the one hand, as far as this concept was concerned, he (Isaiah) inherited an outlook which was unchallenged in Israel, and indeed in the whole of the ancient world. But on the other hand, he voiced something entirely new and unprecedented. This was his radical opinion that Yahweh himself was to bring about Israel's downfall.'[7] To this Ezekiel added—in embryo—the further idea that Yahweh's means of judgment was the Law, as well as the thought that his motive in all his action on his people was regard for his own honour.

26. I defiled them   Cf. Rom. 1.24.

27-29. *The high place*
The verses are a later addition by a disciple who wished to fill out the picture of Israel's sinfulness after the settlement in Palestine.

[6] For instance, by F. Hesse, *Das Verstockungsproblem im Alten Testament*, Berlin, 1956.
[7] *Old Testament Theology* II, p. 154.

28. soothing odours Sacrifices designed to propitiate Yahweh.

29. Bamah The word seeks to bring contempt on the high places by a kind of punning on their name. In Hebrew *ma* means 'what' and *ba* means 'go' or 'come'. For the true etymology, see on 6.3.

30-31. *The reason for the retrospect*

The elders, being such as they are, and of such a race, need expect no answer from Yahweh.

A THREAT AND A PROMISE

20.32-44

The passage is best taken as composed shortly after the fall of Jerusalem. The word of the exiles in v. 32 reflects a feeling of hopeless abandonment by Yahweh rather than defiance of him. Their best plan, they mean, is to assimilate to and adopt the worship of the land, WORSHIP WOOD AND STONE. Yahweh however strongly asserts his continued sovereign claim upon them (I WILL BE KING OVER YOU, 33), and announces deliverance from exile, the return to Jerusalem, and the restoration of worship in the temple there, though this latter is to be preceded by a judgment of purification in the wilderness. 'In vv. 40ff. we see a step on the way to the concrete expectation of a new Temple in 40-48' (Zimmerli).

33. I will be king over you Van den Born[8] thinks these words have associations with I Sam. 8 where the monarchy was conceded to Israel because of her desire 'that we also may be like all the nations; and that our king may govern us' (I Sam. 8.20)—cf. LET US BE AS THE NATIONS, v. 32.

The prophet announces a second Exodus and a second period in the wilderness. Already Hosea had thought of the northern kingdom as to be brought again into the wilderness, and there renewed and then brought back to its own land (Hos. 2.14; 3.4f.; 12.9). There are, however, differences between the first Exodus and the second. The first meant Israel's deliverance from her enemies: the MIGHTY HAND and the OUTSTRETCHED ARM (33f.), expressions frequent in Deuteronomy, were then exercised upon Pharaoh. But these now act upon Israel herself. For in THE WILDERNESS OF THE PEOPLES (v. 35), the desert between Mesopotamia and Palestine, Yahweh is to enter into judgment with his people, as he did in the wilder-

[8] *Ezechiel* (De Boeken van het Oude Testament XI 1), 1954, *in loc.*

ness of Sinai (the reference is to v. 15 of this chapter), to PASS
them UNDER THE ROD (v. 37), as a shepherd does his flock to
count them (cf. Lev. 27.32; Jer. 33.13; Matt. 25.31ff.), make
separation among them (the obverse of v. 37), and purge out
the rebels (cf. 34.17, 20).

39. Ezekiel here addresses the exiles with reference to the
present time. The command is ironic. The meaning is that
they may do as they please, continue with their idolatrous
worship if they will, but (this is the meaning of the last clause)
if they continue in idolatry, they will have no share in the
return described in the preceding verses, and may even be
destroyed.

40. Next follows a description of the restored community—
the HOLY MOUNTAIN is Zion—with its offerings which are now
not only acceptable (contrast v. 26) but required. CONTRIBU-
TIONS and GIFTS are technical terms: the first is 'something
lifted off a larger whole and dedicated to religious purposes,
such as land for the temple (45.1, 6f.; 48.8-20), or dues for
the priests (44.30), or material for the public sacrifices (45.13,
16). . . . In what way *contributions* differed from *gifts* is not
known; Eissfeldt suggests that the former may have been
binding, the latter voluntary' (Cooke).

**41. I will manifest my holiness among you in the sight of
the nations** At the fall of Jerusalem the Gentiles might have
supposed that Yahweh lacked power. But now that he delivers
his people from their midst, they will recognize that he does
have power.

43. And there you shall remember Cf. 6.9; 16.61, 63; 36.31.
'The restoration will impress not only the heathen (v. 41),
but Israel itself; it will awaken penitence (v. 43), and a fuller
belief in Jahveh's nature' (Cooke).

If vv. 43-44 were spoken shortly after 586, their juxta-position with vv. 1-31, perhaps effected by Ezekiel himself, shows how, even with the most devastating judgment on Israel's history in the whole of the OT, hope is still held out for the future. Judgment and grace go step by step together. Even in the hour of apparent death, the exiles must not let go the hand by which they have been smitten, for there is no other hope. If Israel assimilates, she ceases to be Israel. But this is not God's will. He remains her king, and also her shepherd.

THE SWORD

20.45–21.32

In MT 20.45-49 form the beginning of ch. 21. The section consists of literary units which have been placed together because most of them have a common catchword, THE SWORD.

AN ORACLE AGAINST THE SOUTH

20.45–21.7

There are two parts to the oracle, 20.45-48 and 21.1-7. The second interprets the first, and 20.49 gives the reason why interpretation is necessary: Ezekiel is reluctant to utter 45-48, since people complain that he speaks ALLEGORIES which they cannot understand (cf. 33.32 and 17.1-10, 11-21). But, as Cooke says, 'the people could hardly fail to understand Ezekiel's figurative language; what they refused to believe was its application to themselves. Their attitude was represented by the deluded Hananiah, Jer. 28.'

46. the south Jerusalem and Judah, according to the interpretation (21.2). Jerusalem could be regarded as south by exiles in Babylon, just as Jeremiah perhaps speaks of Babylon as 'the north' (Jer. 1.11-15).

47. fire An image of destruction by war as again in 30.8, 14, 16; 39.6, cf. Amos 1.4ff. The image of a forest fire had already been used by Isaiah (9.18; 10.16-19) and Jeremiah (21.14), cf. Zech. 11.1-3; Ps. 83.14f. The GREEN TREE and the DRY TREE are the RIGHTEOUS and the WICKED (21.3f.). 21.4f. is probably a later gloss.

21.6-7. To the oracle and its interpretation is appended a symbolic action. Jerusalem's fate is so certain that the prophet expresses the emotion with which the news will be received.

6. Sigh . . . with breaking heart HEART is literally 'loins'; 'the loins, which are girt with the sword for war, and with sackcloth for grief, are the place of strength (Job 40.16; Nahum 2.1). If they are "broken" . . . then this strength is at an end' (Zimmerli). The TIDINGS are the news coming to the exiles of the fall of Jerusalem.

'One of the most important factors affecting the prophets of this time [that is, the Babylonian and early Persian period] is the way in which their office increasingly invaded their personal and spiritual lives.'[9] 'And this [Ezek. 33.1-9] is not the only instance of the kind; there are other passages as well which show how for Ezekiel the prophetic office was a matter of life and death, and how the offence of the message he was charged to deliver reacted first upon his own person, and had sometimes to be most strangely and painfully expressed in symbolic actions. "And you, son of man, groan. With trembling loins and bitterness shall you groan before their eyes" (Ezek. 21.6, 21.11 in Hebrew).

'Things of this kind were not cheap playacting. Here the coming disaster, the destruction of Jerusalem, is casting its shadow before it and harnessing the prophet, body and soul alike, with a hard yoke of suffering. Yet Jahweh had so decreed, for Ezekiel was to be made "a sign for Israel" (Ezek. 12.6b). He was not to present a symbolic action which did not involve him personally; his own condition was to prefigure the suffering of the coming judgment (so also Ezek. 12.17ff.).'[10]

[9] G. von Rad, *Old Testament Theology* II, p. 274.
[10] *Ibid.*, pp. 232f.

THE SONG OF THE SWORD

21.8-17

The text is badly preserved, and there has been expansion, though this may be due to the prophet himself, if what he did was to take up an old popular sword-song such as Gen. 4.23f., or a prophetic word of judgment in which the sword figured, and apply it to the contemporary situation. In this case the original kernel, in verse, would be found in vv. 9-10, 14a, 16-17 (so Fohrer). Verses 9b and 10 should be translated:

> A sword, a sword is sharpened and also burnished.
> It was sharpened to cause slaughter, burnished to
> flash like lightning.

(10b is hopelessly corrupt.)

11. The original probably read: 'And it was given to a slayer to wield with the hand.' 'The rest of the verse consists of marginal notes' (Cooke).

12. Smite . . . upon your thigh This is a sign of grief in Jer. 31.19 also.

13-14. The sense of v. 13 is quite obscure.
Omit the second half of v. 14 (after YEA, THRICE) as uncertain.

15. Read: 'That all (so LXX) hearts may melt, and those that stumble be many. In all their gates they are given up to the slaughter of the sword (so LXX), that is made like lightning, burnished for slaughter.'

THE SWORD OF THE KING OF BABYLON

21.18-24

The sword of Yahweh is THE SWORD of Nebuchadnezzar, THE SAME LAND (v. 19) being Babylon. The prophet is instructed to perform another symbolic action. He is to MARK TWO WAYS: that is, he is to draw, or trace on the ground, two roads starting from the same point and going in different directions, the one leading to Ammon, east of Jordan, with its capital Rabbah (modern Amman), the other to Judah and its capital Jerusalem.

19b-20. Read: 'And thou shalt set up a signpost at the head of each way, that the sword may come to Rabbah of the Ammonites or to Judah and Jerusalem in her midst.'

Nebuchadnezzar is already on the march westwards to subdue the rebellious Palestinian states, Ammon and Judah among them (Jer. 27.1-3), and he stops where the roads divide, as was common before a battle, in order to use various oracular techniques to decide against which of the two powers to proceed (cf. I Sam. 23.1-4; 30.7f.).

21. he shakes the arrows Two arrows with names written on them were shaken in a quiver, and either the one which fell out first gave the requisite answer, or, by another method, the one here used, the arrow which the RIGHT HAND drew out indicated the place to be marched against.

he consults the teraphim The teraphim (lit. 'vile things') were household gods, tutelary gods of the hearth (cf. Gen. 31.34), later identified with representations of the mother goddess of fertility. 'Although [the Babylonians] made their prayers to the gods, it was the guardian figures to whom the householder looked for protection. Popular belief and practice show that no god in the pantheon was of much use in daily life.'[11]

he looks at the liver Throughout the ancient world, inspection of an animal's liver was a regular means of obtaining an indication of the divine will. 'After the performance of certain rites and the slaughter of the animal, the diviner exposed its liver and, by the examination of its parts or the markings on its surface, was able to predict the future.'[12]

23. to them it will seem like a false divination THEM means the people of Jerusalem, to whom the DIVINATION seems FALSE bceause 'they expect that this advance will bring no good to Nebuchadnezzar, since they have their defences and the looked-for help of Egypt' (Lofthouse). THEY HAVE SWORN SOLEMN OATHS: the meaning is obscure. Verse 24, which is addressed to the nation and not, like 18-23, to the prophet, is probably a gloss.

ZEDEKIAH TO BE DEPOSED

21.25-27

27. A ruin . . . I will make it IT is Jerusalem, Zedekiah's capital and place of residence. For the obscure sentence THERE SHALL NOT BE EVEN A TRACE OF IT read: 'Woe unto her, so will she remain' (LXX, Bertholet, Fohrer, etc.). The words UNTIL HE COMES WHOSE RIGHT IT IS are reminiscent of Gen. 49.10 (reading *shilot*—i.e. the place Shiloh—as *shello*, 'to whom it belongs'. The meaning is uncertain. Some, e.g. Hölscher and Herrmann, interpret it messianically. Mowinckel takes it as a prophecy about the coming scion of David in the age of restoration.[13] Fohrer thinks it refers to the resto-

---

[11] A. Guillaume, *Prophecy and Divination*, London, 1938, p. 27.
[12] A. J. Heschel, *The Prophets*, London, 1962, p. 454.
[13] *He that Cometh*, trs G. W. Anderson, Oxford, 1956, p. 175.

ration of Jehoiachin to his former rights. Zimmerli, on the basis of Ezekiel's usage of the word translated RIGHT, renders 'since he comes who is due to punish it and I make it over (to him)'; that is, HE refers to Nebuchadnezzar and this is then an oracle of doom, not of hope.

AGAINST THE AMMONITES

21.28-32

Though the Babylonian king has decided to go against Jerusalem rather than Ammon, the latter, too, will eventually be blotted out. The verses are the work of a redactor, who felt that something should be said at this point as well as in 25.1-7 about Ammon. REPROACH refers to the *Schadenfreude* with which the Ammonites greeted the fall of Jerusalem, 25.3, 6; cf. Zeph. 2.8. The SWORD is best—though not usually —taken as Nebuchadnezzar's, and not as belonging to the Ammonites (with reference to some otherwise unknown attack by them on Judah).

28. concerning Better 'against'. Then read: 'Sword, sword, drawn for slaughter, burnished to destroy, to flash lightning, in order to be laid—while they [the Ammonite soothsayers] see false visions concerning you and divine lies concerning you—upon the neck of the unhallowed wicked,' etc.

31-32. The rest of the oracle speaks of the punishment of Nebuchadnezzar in his own land, reminding us of what Isaiah said of an earlier foreign king used by Yahweh as his instrument of chastisement: 'Ah, Assyria, the rod of my anger, . . . When the Lord has finished all his work on Mount Zion and on Jerusalem, he will punish the arrogant boasting of the king of Assyria' (Isa. 10.5, 12).

JERUSALEM ARRAIGNED

22.1-16

This chapter, 'the most stately of Ezekiel's orations' (Skinner),
is composed of three oracles: 1-16, the sins of Jerusalem,
especially idolatry and bloodshed; 17-22, punishment under
the figure of smelting; and 23-31, the guilt of the various leading classes in the city. The purpose is, once more, to show
that 'the destruction of Jerusalem is not only just, but also
necessary'.[14]

THE BLOODY CITY

22.1-16

2. As in 20.3, the prophet, again addressed as SON OF MAN,
is once more commanded to JUDGE (cf. 20.4). Here, however,
what is given is not, as in ch. 20, a review of history, but a
catalogue of contemporary sins stated in apodictic form. The
verses have close affinities with the Holiness Code.

Nahum had called Nineveh 'the bloody city', thinking of
the Assyrians' power politics and cruelty (Nah. 3.1). 'Ezekiel
thus equates Jerusalem with this depraved and now destroyed
heathen city (cf. 16.1-43)' (Fohrer). And Isaiah had said of
the people of Jerusalem, 'Your hands are full of blood' (Isa.
1.15), having in mind, as the verses following make clear,
social sins. Again, P has much to say about blood in connection with cultic matters. Ezekiel here combines moral and
cultic offences under the term 'bloodshed'—'the keyword of
the entire passage is blood (vv. 2, 3, 4, 6, 9, 12)' (Muilenburg).
The catalogue of sins recalls 18.5-18.

[14] Heinisch, *Das Buch Ezekiel* (Bonner-Bibel 8.1), Rome, 1923, *in
loc.*

4. your day Your time of judgment, the Day of Yahweh for Jerusalem. THE APPOINTED TIME means 'the end'. The two chief sins are idolatry (cf. chs. 16 and 23) and bloodshed.

5. will mock you 'What Ezekiel says here is remarkable, for only in the chapter before [i.e. 21.28ff.] we have been told that this same God intends to punish a heathen country because it mocked at the calamity which overtook Jerusalem' (Brunner). FULL OF TUMULT: cf. Amos 3.9.

6. the princes of Israel Zedekiah and his court. Cf. 23.37; 24.7. 'The meaning is not that they shed blood to the utmost of their power, but that they were arbitrary; their power, lit. *arm*, was the only law' (Davidson). For their conduct to the prophet Uriah, see Jer. 26.20ff., and to Jeremiah himself, Jer. 38.4-6.

7-12. *Particular sins*

7. Conduct towards parents: see Ex. 20.12=Deut. 5.16; Ex. 21.17; Deut. 27.16; Lev. 19.3; 20.9 (the Holiness Code=H). Oppression (EXTORTION): cf. 18.7, 18; of THE SOJOURNER: cf. Ex. 22.21; Deut. 27.19; of THE FATHERLESS AND THE WIDOW: cf. Ex. 22.22; Deut. 24.17.

8. Despising HOLY THINGS: cf. v. 26. Profanation of the sabbath: see on 20.12.

9. SLANDER and perjury: cf. Jer. 6.28; 9.3. Slander is forbidden in Lev. 19.16. EAT ON THE MOUNTAINS: see on 18.6. LEWDNESS introduces what follows in vv. 10f.

10. UNCOVER THEIR FATHERS' NAKEDNESS: marriages with a step-mother were forbidden in Lev. 18.7f.; Deut. 22.30; 27.20; cf. also II Sam. 16.20ff. HUMBLE WOMEN WHO ARE UNCLEAN IN THEIR IMPURITY: see on 18.6; cf. Lev. 18.19; 20.18.

11. Adultery: see on 18.6 and Lev. 18.20; 20.10. DEFILES
HIS DAUGHTER-IN-LAW . . . : cf. Lev. 18.15; 20.12; II Sam.
13.12.

12. BRIBES leading to bloodshed: cf. Ex. 23.8; Deut. 16.19.
INTEREST AND INCREASE: see on 18.8. GAINED . . . BY EXTOR-
TION: cf. Jer. 6.13; 8.10.

13-16. *The threat*
STRIKE MY HANDS: see on 6.11.

15. The exile is to have a purifying effect; cf. 11.14-21.

16. Read: 'And I shall let myself be profaned because of you
in the sight of the nations.' See note on 20.9.
   As in ch. 20, Jerusalem's judge is the law, the enactments of
which she has contravened in the list of sins given in vv. 7-12.

CONSUMED IN THE MELTING POT

22.17-22

The house of Israel had become like a mixture of dross—
'that has been proved by the enumeration of her [Jerusalem's]
crimes and the estimate of her social condition' (Skinner)—
fit only to be put in the furnace and destroyed. Isaiah had
already said, 'your [Jerusalem's] silver has become dross' (Isa.
1.22), while Jeremiah (Jer. 6.27-30; 9.7) and Deutero-Isaiah
(Isa. 48.10) use the figure of smelting to represent Yahweh's
purifying of the nation. But here 'the idea of any purification
whatsoever—separation of the silver from the other crude
metals—is to be completely ruled out' (Spadafora). 'The
whole house of Israel has become dross, from which no
precious metal can be extracted; and the object of the smelting is only the demonstration of the utter worthlessness of

the people for the ends of God's kingdom' (Skinner)—and, one should add, of the justice and inevitability of their destruction.

'In ancient times silver was obtained by a two-fold process. . . . First came the smelting of the argentiferous lead-ore, which was placed in a furnace provided with a forced draught by means of bellows. The ore was mixed with fluxes to ensure fusion, and melted with sufficient heat; then the furnace was tapped; the metallic lead was run out with the slag, which would float on the top, and, when cool, could easily be removed. The slag or dross contained the sulphides of *copper, tin, iron, lead*, and the other impurities of the ore. This is as far as Ezekiel goes, and he points to the result of the operation. A further process, however, was required to obtain pure silver. The metallic lead produced by the smelting was cut up and placed in a cupel, or crucible, made of bone-ash, and heated; the cupel absorbed the baser elements, as a sponge absorbs water, until silver alone remained' (Cooke).

18. In MT SILVER comes at the end of the verse. RSV is probably correct in putting it at the head of the list of metals. G. R. Driver, however, would keep it at the end and, with a slight emendation, translate 'dross without silver'.[15]

19-22. *The threat*

19. I will gather you into the midst of Jerusalem It is not just Jerusalem that has become dross, but THE HOUSE OF ISRAEL, the whole nation. So with these words Ezekiel is probably thinking of the country folk who would take refuge in the city as Nebuchadnezzar's army advanced. Verses 21-2 largely repeat 20: Jahn thinks that v. 20 was inserted for the purpose of setting aside the idea that the one who melts is God himself.

[15] *Biblica* 19, 1938, p. 69.

With vv. 17-22 cf. v. 15. Zimmerli notes that there is a slight logical inconsistency in the passage. In Isaiah, the dross is to be purged away (1.25) and the city restored to its pristine purity. But in Ezekiel the city is already dross. So that the kindling of the fire in v. 21 is not for refining, as in Isaiah, but for destruction.

CORRUPTION IN ALL CLASSES

22.23-31

Princes, priests, officials, landed gentry—all are corrupt. As v. 31 shows, the passage dates from after the fall of Jerusalem. Its writer knew Zeph. 3.1-4, 8.

24. Read with LXX, 'you are a land that is not rained upon nor wetted in the day of indignation.' Palestine depends upon its rainfall (Lev. 26.4; Deut. 11.14), drought is God's warning (Amos 4.7f.; Isa. 5.6; Jer. 14.1ff.; I Kings 17.1).

25. Begin as LXX 'whose princes in her midst are like . . .' The PRINCES are the members of the royal house. With the verse cf. Zeph. 1.8; also Ezek. 19.2-9.

26. The PRIESTS, who 'handled' the law (Jer. 2.8), were arbitrary in their exposition of it. Profaning holy things is mentioned in Lev. 19.8; 22.15 in connection with unlawful eating of sacrifice. One of the priest's main duties was that of teaching the laity what was clean and what unclean—for example, what food could be used, what animals could be offered in sacrifice, matters of cleanliness and health etc., cf. 44.23; Lev. 10.10; 11.47; Hag. 2.11-13. On profanation of the sabbath, see on 20.22. With 26 cf. Zeph. 3.4b.

27. princes The Heb. word is different from the PRINCES of v. 25, and here means state officials, perhaps in particular the judges, cf. Zeph. 3.3b. For dishonest gain, cf. Jer. 6.13; 8.10.

28. Cf. Zeph. 3.4a and Ezek. 13.9ff. The PROPHETS have falsely backed up the 'princes'.

29. The people of the land They were the landed gentry of Judah.

30. a man among them THEM must refer to all classes, not just to the prophets, as in ch. 13. The verse is reminiscent of Jer. 5.1-5. 'In this passage Ezekiel is thinking of a "Saviour of Society", who cannot be found' (Lofthouse).

A THIRD HISTORICAL REVIEW

23.1-49

This retrospect deals principally with the period of the monarchy. Samaria and Judah-Jerusalem are pictured as two sisters, Oholah and Oholibah, who became the wives of Yahweh, yet lavished their favours on others, that is, made alliances with foreign powers, the former with Assyria, the latter with Babylonia. In form and content ch. 23 has close affinities with ch. 16, and is even more realistic, but the main ideas are developments of Jer. 3.6-10. Both Jeremiah and Ezekiel may be taking up a folk-tale. In the literature of Ugarit the god El has two wives.

Verses 1-21 are a divine communication to the prophet himself, and the address to Jerusalem only begins at v. 22.

THE TWO SISTERS

23.1-4

2. The two kingdoms are already sisters in Jer. 3.7. Cf. also Ezek. 16.46.

3. they played the harlot in Egypt In the chapter harlotry is used in the sense of seeking foreign alliances and not of idolatry, but in this verse it has the general meaning of apostasy—Israel entered on her sinful course right at the very beginning of her history.

4. Oholah Often taken as meaning who has 'her tent in her', referring to the northern kingdom with its own shrines, and Oholibah as 'my tent is in her', referring to the legitimate

temple in Judah-Jerusalem. (The Hebrew word for 'tent' is
'*ōhel*.) More probably however they are simply two names
rather similar in sound—Ewald (quoted by Cooke) cities
Hasan and Husein, the two sons of Ali. 'The point is that the
sisters were alike, as in name so in guilt' (Cooke). THEY BE-
CAME MINE, they became Yahweh's spouses, cf. 16.8, 20. THEY
BORE SONS AND DAUGHTERS: they grew and became strong
(Fohrer). The last clause of v. 4 is a later gloss.

OHOLAH-SAMARIA

23.5-10

Verses 7-8 are a later addition, as is also 10b, AND SHE
BECAME, etc.: the words have been taken from 16.14 and
inserted here.

Menahem paid tribute to Assyria (II Kings 15.19; cf. Hos.
5.13; 7.11; 8.9; 12.1). With v. 9 cf. 16.37.

OHOLIBAH-JUDAH

23.11-21

Verses 12-14a are a later addition—v. 12 largely repeats
vv. 5f. They were inserted by an editor who remembered that
Judah had made overtures to Assyria in the time of Ahaz
(II Kings 16.7ff.). But Ezekiel's interest is in his own day,
and in Judah's relationships with the Babylonians (Chaldeans) since their rise in 621.

Judah did not take a lesson from the fate of Samaria, but
made overtures to Babylon. She did this when she saw men
PORTRAYED UPON THE WALL, etc. (v. 14), though what this
means is no longer clear.

16. Zimmerli thinks that SENT MESSENGERS TO THEM may refer to feelers put out to Nabopolassar when the Assyrian empire was beginning to fall.

19-21. A reference to Judah's appeals to Egypt for aid against the Babylonians, Jer. 2.18; 37.7. 'For the comparisons, which had become proverbial, see Hos. 8.9; Jer. 2.24 (the wild ass), and Jer. 5.8; 13.27 (horses). The prophet describes the Egyptians with greater repugnance than he feels for the Babylonians, vv. 14f.; the lasciviousness of the Egyptians was abhorrent to the Hebrews, cp. 16.26; Gen. 39.7ff. J' (Cooke).

THE THREAT AGAINST OHOLIBAH

23.22-35

There are four threats: vv. 22-27, 28-31, 32-34 and 35; each is introduced by THUS SAYS THE LORD GOD.

22-27. Yahweh now directly addresses Oholibah, threatening to ROUSE her LOVERS AGAINST her. Omit v. 23b (from AND ALL THE ASSYRIANS to ON HORSES); the words have been inserted to take account of v. 12. The identifications of PEKOD etc. are uncertain.

24. from the north Cf. Jer. 4.6f. I WILL COMMIT THE JUDGMENT TO THEM: I will entrust them with the judgment. 'The heathen are to be the judges; Jahveh commits to them the right to punish His people' (Cooke); cf. Isa. 10.5f.
25. cut off your nose 'The punishment awarded by Egyptians to adulteresses (Diodorus Siculus, 1.78); Assyrian wall-sculptures bear out all these atrocities, and more' (Lofthouse).

28-31. The allegory of the two sisters probably ended originally with v. 27. Verses 28-30 are a doublet or later expansion of vv. 22-27. 'In sharp contrast to the concrete detail, 28-31 are general, though the motif of harlotry is pronounced' (Muilenburg). Verse 31 makes the transition to the next section.

32-34. These verses are a later addition, in which the judgment of the two sisters is represented as a cup of destruction. Unlike the rest of the chapter, this passage is in verse. The original poem may have run somewhat as follows, though the text is very uncertain.

> Thy sister's cup shalt thou drink, the deep and wide one,
>   that holdeth much.
> Thou shalt be filled with breaking and sorrow: a cup of
>   terror (is) the cup of thy sister Samaria.
> Thou shalt drink it and drain it, and swallow its dregs;
> For I have spoken it, saith the Lord Yahweh.

34. For AND PLUCK OUT YOUR HAIR, AND TEAR YOUR BREASTS G. R. Driver has suggested 'Its sherds thou wilt gnaw and thy breasts thou wilt tear out'; 'in other words, in remorse and revulsion she will smash the cup as the cause of her downfall and gnaw its very fragments, and she will tear out her own breasts as the peccant members through which she has sinned.'[16] In the second line of the poem 'the cup of thy sister Samaria' may be a gloss. If original, it means the cup which Samaria drank at her destruction in 722.

The figure of the cup of Yahweh's wrath is employed in Jer. 25.15ff.; 49.12, and also in Isa. 51.17, 22; Hab. 2.16; Obad. 16; Pss. 11.6; 75.8; Lam. 4.21. Cf. also Matt. 20.22; 26.39; Rev. 14.10.

35. An independent oracle of judgment.

[16] *Biblica* 34 (1954), p. 155.

G

A RECAPITULATION
23.36-49

'The oracle in verses 37-49 must be understood as a different piece from the Oholah-Oholibah story. It deals concurrently with both sisters as if punishment were impending for both. They are considered together, probably as a result of Ezekiel's unwillingness to accept the division between Israel and Judah as either valid or final' (Howie).

The passage, however, is later than Ezekiel, and largely composed in dependence on chs. 16 and 20. It therefore needs little commentary here.

(*a*) **36-44.** The first sin, ADULTERY (v. 37) refers to idolatry, the second, BLOOD(shed), to child-sacrifice. The text of vv. 40-44 is very corrupt. THEY EVEN SENT (v. 40) refers to 23.16, the embassy to Babylon.

42b. Cf. 16.11, also Prov. 7.14ff. DRUNKARDS: MT is uncertain ' "From the wilderness" may refer to embassies of Bedouin tribes asking for alliance in revolting from Nebuchadnezzar' (Lofthouse). 43 has had no satisfactory meaning given it.

(*b*) **45-49.** Again composed from chs. 16 and 20. In 16.37f. it is the lovers who execute judgment, here it is RIGHTEOUS MEN.

46. host See on 16.40. With 47, 48a, cf. 16.40f.; 23.25-27.

48. We now pass from the allegory of the two sisters, the actual history of the two kingdoms, into a warning against adultery in general, with the sisters as examples or types. The passage is a good specimen of the way in which prophetic texts were 'actualized' for later generations, even though the historical situation in the texts no longer applied.

THE FALL OF JERUSALEM
24.1-27

The chapter concludes the first section of the book. It has three parts: 1-2, the noting of the date; 3-14, a parable and its explanation; and 15-27, Ezekiel's sorrow at the death of his wife, which is a sign.

A DAY TO BE NOTED

24.1-2

The prophet becomes aware that ON THIS VERY DAY Nebuchadnezzar has begun the siege of Jerusalem, and he is commanded to note down the momentous event, which in post-exilic times was observed as a fast (Zech. 8.19). In what way did Ezekiel—in Babylon—become aware of this? Some (e.g. Kraetzschmar, Kittel, Cooke) have supposed the prophet to be endowed with second sight; others (e.g. Toy) regard it as a *vaticinium ex eventu*, or as redactorial (Hölscher, Messel), and, on form-critical grounds, as dependent on II Kings 25.1. Muilenburg suggests that 'knowing that the Babylonian army was on the march, he may well have had a premonition that it was on that day that they would strike' (so substantially Fohrer). It is best taken as redactorial. See also Introduction, p.22).

THE BOILING POT

24.3-14

The text is hard to interpret in detail. Bertholet thinks there are two separate poems (3-5 and 6-14) with the common theme of Jerusalem as the pot. Zimmerli connects 9-10a with 3-5, and regards 6-8, 10b-14 as an insertion. A possible reconstruction, which largely follows Cooke, and for which there is here no space to set out justification, gives the following as the first poem:

(3b) SET ON THE POT, SET IT ON,
and POUR WATER into it ALSO;

(4) PUT PIECES OF FLESH IN IT,
ALL kinds of GOOD PIECES, THIGH AND SHOULDER;

(5) TAKE THE CHOICEST sheep,
also PILE up LOGS beneath it,
bring its PIECES to the boil,
and cook ITS BONES IN IT.

(6b) Take it out piece by piece.

'The flesh is cooked, and the pot can now be emptied: in other words, the siege is followed by the expulsion of the inhabitants' (Cooke). In MT 6 ends 'a lot has not fallen upon it'. This 'can only be understood by supposing that, when the deportation of 597 took place, lots were cast in some instances to decide who should go and who should remain: this time, says the prophet, there will be no alternative; everybody will have to go' (Cooke). But the words are an explanatory gloss.

Second poem: the now empty pot (Jerusalem) is itself to be melted

(6) WOE TO THE BLOODY CITY,
THE POT WHOSE RUST IS IN IT,
whose RUST departs not from it.

(9b) I ALSO WILL MAKE THE PILE GREAT,

(11) and I will set it EMPTY on its COALS,
THAT IT MAY BECOME HOT AND ITS COPPER BURN,
and ITS FILTHINESS melt in it, ITS RUST CONSUME.

(14) I Yahweh, have SPOKEN; it comes,
I WILL DO IT; I WILL NOT refrain nor SPARE.
ACCORDING TO YOUR WAYS AND YOUR deeds I judge
YOU
SAYS THE LORD Yahweh.

7f. Explanatory glosses on BLOODY and RUST. Verse 10, where
the text at the end is not clear, is a secondary addition
suggested by v. 5. In vv. 12f. the text is again very uncertain,
and the verses are a secondary explanation.[17]

EZEKIEL'S BEARING AT THE DEATH
OF HIS WIFE
24.15-24

The section contains a command (vv. 15-17), the account
of how it was carried out (vv. 18-19), and the interpretation
(vv. 20-21, 24).

The prophet is told that his WIFE (18), THE DELIGHT OF
YOUR EYES (16), is to die suddenly, and that he is to perform
a kind of negative symbolic act, by refraining from all the
external signs of mourning. As with Hosea's marriage (Hos.
1, 3), and Isaiah's (Isa. 8.1-4, 18), so Ezekiel's is introduced
not for any biographic interest, but solely in the context of
his prophetic activity. Because of it, Ezekiel becomes a SIGN
(v. 24).

---

[17] On 24.1-14 see also J. L. Kelso, 'Ezekiel's Parable of the Corroded
Copper Cauldron', in *JBL* 64, 1945, pp. 391-3.

17. Sigh, but not aloud The sense of AV, 'forbear to cry', is also sound. For mourning customs, see II Sam. 15.30; Micah 3.7; Jer. 16.7. 'Grief was shown by the reversal of ordinary habits of dress: head and feet were left bare, and the beard, the ornament of manhood (cf. II Sam. 10.4) was covered out of sight. The friends of the family were invited to a funeral feast' (Toy).

19-24. 'When the astonished neighbours enquire the meaning of his strange demeanour, he assures them that his conduct *now* is a sign of what theirs will be when his words (*sc.* the prophecies of chs. 4-24) have come true' (Skinner). Ezekiel himself interprets his experience: the DELIGHT OF his EYES becomes the Jerusalem temple (MY SANCTUARY, v. 21; THE DESIRE OF YOUR SOUL is the exiles' longing to see it again), and his mourning their mourning for their SONS AND DAUGHTERS still in Jerusalem. Zimmerli comments that a present-day interpreter may ask whether it was not subsequent reflection in view of the people's question that made what he had done at God's behest into a message and a symbolic act. Brunner, perhaps correctly, sees more in the verses: 'What is he (Ezekiel) to answer to them all who do not now recognize that, with Jerusalem destroyed, God is in the same case as is the prophet with his dead wife? He suffers deep distress, and he may not show his suffering.'

Verses 22-23 interrupt the words of Yahweh; they are an editorial addition based on v. 17. YOU SHALL PINE AWAY IN YOUR INIQUITIES: 'For while their sorrow will be too deep for words, it will not yet be the godly sorrow that worketh repentance. It will be the sullen despair and apathy of men disenchanted of the illusions on which their national life was based, of men left without hope and without God in the world' (Skinner).

THE PROPHET'S DUMBNESS

24.25-27

For the questions raised by these verses see the Introduction and the Commentary on 33.21f.

With 24 we come to the end of Ezekiel's message of judgment on his own people. Auvray well sums up chs. 1-24: 'Jeremiah had had occasion to express himself equally clearly on the same near future. Jeremiah's line was to consider the calamity as avoidable, and to preach the conversion of men's hearts and the return to a sane political policy as the means of re-establishing the situation again. For Ezekiel, the perspectives are without hope. All he can do is to explain the inevitable disasters. But in explaining them the prophet draws new conclusions from them. In emphasizing that, amid the ruin of the nation, individuals might still save themselves, he allows for the safety of the "little remnant" already foreseen by Isaiah, and prepares for a better future.'[18]

[18] *Ezechiel*, 1947, pp. 74ff.

II

ORACLES AGAINST FOREIGN
NATIONS

25.1–32.32

Between the announcement in 24 that Jerusalem was soon to
be captured and the note in 33.21 of the receipt of the news of
its actual fall is inserted a series of oracles against foreign
nations. Such oracles are found even in the earliest of the
'writing' prophets (Amos. 1.3–2.5). They probably derive from
a cultic cursing of Israel's enemies, which in turn very likely
had as background the Egyptian practice of execration which
'seems to have involved the writing on bowls the names of
enemies to be cursed. With the smashing of the pottery the
curse was believed to become effective by sympathetic magic
on the enemies themselves.'[1] As here in Ezekiel, so too in
Isaiah (13-22), Jeremiah (MT and EVV 46-51, but in LXX,
which preserves the original order, after 25), and Zephaniah
(2), the oracles against foreign nations are placed between
the prophecies of doom and the prophecies of salvation.
Various reasons for the divine punishment are given in the
various oracles here, but the general purpose of the chastisement is stated, on the one hand as it affects Israel, that the restored nation may dwell in security (28.24, 26) and, on the
other, as regards the foreign nations themselves: first, 'Then
they will know that I am the Lord' (25.17; 28.24), secondly,
closely allied to this, that they may recognize that Yahweh has

[1] J. B. Pritchard, *Archaeology and The Old Testament*, Princeton
and London, 1958, p. 66.

power (36.36); and thirdly that, since they put Israel to shame, they must themselves suffer shame (36.5-7). In connection with 28.26 Bertholet points out that for the Deuteronomist 'rest from all your enemies round about' is the precondition for the erection of the legitimate place of worship (Deut. 12.9f.; I Kings 5.4f.), and this may have been in Ezekiel's mind also, since 40-48 deal with the restored temple. Like Jeremiah, Ezekiel gives seven oracles against foreign nations: this number too may go back to Deuteronomy (7.1), where seven nations are to be driven out to allow the people of Israel to settle in the promised land. The first four oracles, against neighbours of Judah (cf. Amos 1-2), Ammon (25.1-7), Moab (8.11), Edom (12-14), and Philistia (15-17) are all short, conventionally phrased, and in form threats, BECAUSE . . . THEREFORE, but the sustained denunciations of Tyre (26.1–28.19) and Egypt (29-32) show Ezekiel at his most powerful.

It may seem surprising that there is no oracle against Babylon. The reason for this may have been prudence. Much more probably however is it due to Ezekiel's regarding Nebuchadnezzar as the instrument of Yahweh.

THE AMMONITES

25.1-7

Two oracles are conjoined (1-5 and 6-7), each introduced by the formula, THUS SAITH THE LORD GOD.[2]

Ammon is north of Moab, east of the Dead Sea and Jordan, lying between the Jabbok and the Arnon. There was a long history of hostility between the Israelites and the Ammonites, going back to the time of the conquest (Judg. 3.13; 11.4ff.; II Sam. 10.1ff.; 11.1; 12.26ff.; II Chron. 20.1ff.). II Kings 24.2 shows them in alliance with the Babylonians against Judah, after Jehoiakim's revolt, but at the beginning of Zedekiah's reign they were one of a coalition of neighbouring peoples trying to persuade the Judean king to rebel against Babylon (Jer. 27.1ff.), and the fact that the Ammonite king instigated the murder of Gedaliah, whom the Babylonians had appointed governor of Judah, suggests that they remained anti-Babylonian.

3-5. The charge brought against them in the first oracle is gloating over the profanation (i.e. the destruction) of the sanctuary, the desolation of the land of Judah, and the exile of its people, cf. Zeph. 2.8; also Lam. 2.15. For this they are to be handed over to THE PEOPLE OF THE EAST, i.e. the Bedouin of the desert south-east of Damascus (Judg. 6.3, 33; 7.12, 8, 10; I Kings 4.30; Isa. 11.14). On Rabbah, the capital city (modern Amman) see on 21.20.

6-7. The second oracle is more general, and may not be original. For the gestures, see note on 6.11. Here Ammon is to be given over to the nations—perhaps the Babylonians are meant—and perish (omit I WILL DESTROY YOU as a gloss).

---

[2] The arrangement of ch. 25 follows the structure of the Egyptian execration texts, see Fohrer, 'Modern Interpretation of the Prophets', *JBL* 80, 1961, p. 311.

MOAB

25.8-11

Moab's territory lay south of Edom, between the Arnon
and the Zered. As with the Ammonites, it is for their conduct after the fall of Jerusalem that the Moabites are to be
punished, though again there was a record of enmity between
the two peoples. (See Num. 22-4; Judg. 3.2ff.; II Kings 3. For
other oracles against Moab, see Amos 2.1-3; Isa. 15f.; Jer.
48.) Moab's offence was in effect a denial of Israel's election
and special status: BEHOLD, THE HOUSE OF JUDAH IS LIKE ALL
THE OTHER NATIONS (v. 8). It had suffered the same fate as
they had, so that it could not have been protected by its God.
'God's judgment becomes a way of proving that there was no
history of God dealing with his people' (Zimmerli). Because
of this the mountain slopes which formed Moab's western
boundary towards the Jordan are to be laid open. The text of
v. 9 is uncertain, but the meaning is that Moab will be laid
open by the destruction of the frontier-cities, and so exposed,
like the Ammonites, to the incursions of the Bedouin. Beth-
jeshimoth is the modern Tell el-'Azemah, about two and a
half miles north-east of the Dead Sea; Baal-Meon is the
modern Ma'in, about nine miles east of the Dead Sea; and
Kiriathaim is el-Qereijât, about ten miles below Baal-Meon.
'The road described by the places thus leads from the depths
of the Jordan valley through Kiriathaim on the way up to the
plateau to Baal-Meon on the plateau itself' (Zimmerli).

EDOM

25.12-14

Edom lay to the south of Moab. The later oracle against

Edom (ch. 35) speaks of a 'perpetual enmity' of Israel on
Edom's part (v. 5; cf. Num. 20.14ff.; Judg. 11.17; II Sam.
8.13f.; I Kings 11.14ff.; II Kings 8.20; 14.7; 16.6; 24.2; Jer.
27.1ff.; 49.7-22).

Edom's offence is worse than mere gloating. It had taken
bitter vengeance on Judah for all the reverses it had suffered
at the latter's hand—Obad. 10ff. speaks not only of gloating,
but of preventing fugitives from escaping: see also Ps. 137.7.
The penalty is complete devastation, from Teman in the north
to Dedan in the south, and the execution of it is committed
not, as before, to the Bedouins, but to Israel herself. Many
editors however regard 14a as a later addition.

Glueck identifies Teman with Ṭawilan, near Petra.[3] Dedan
is el-'Ula in northern Arabia, far south of the Edomite border.

PHILISTIA

25.15-17

From Judah's eastern neighbours Ezekiel now turns to one
on her west.

The Philistines, a part of the 'sea-peoples', who eventually
gave the land the name Palestine, arrived there in the Amarna
age, c. 1200 BC, settling in five main cities on the coastal plain.
Until their incorporation into David's empire—and even
afterwards (I Kings 15.27; 16.15)—they were Israel's most
dangerous enemies (Judg. 13-16; I and II Sam.). Their actions
at the time of the fall of Jerusalem are not known, but v. 15
suggests conduct such as the Edomites'. Verse 16 contains a
paronomasia, since I WILL CUT OFF is *hikhrathi*. The
Cherethites (and the Pelethites) are mentioned in II Sam.
8.18; 15.18; 20.7, 23; and I Kings 1.38, 44, as foreign mer-

[3] *PEFQS*, 1934, p. 186.

cenaries recruited into David's troops, and part of the Negeb was called the Negeb of the Cherethites (I Sam. 30.14). Here and in Zeph. 2.5 CHERETHITES is apparently synonymous with PHILISTINES. For other oracles against the Philistines see also Amos 1.6-8; Isa. 14.28-31; Jer. 47.

15. never-ending Lit. 'from of old'; ' "perpetual" and therefore "implacable" ' (Spadafora).

TYRE

26.1–28.26

In the time of David and Solomon there were trade relations between Tyre and Israel (I Kings 6; 9.10-14, 26-28), and Ahab had married a Tyrian princess (I Kings 16.31). Tyre too had joined the embassy to Zedekiah in 594 (Jer. 27.3). In the end she must have risen against Babylon, which led to a siege which lasted thirteen years, from 585 to 572 (Josephus, *Antiquities* X.11.1; *Contra Apionem* 1.21). It appears to have been inconclusive, although Babylonian texts suggest that the city finally capitulated. The long resistance was due to Tyre's strong position on a rocky island, with a half mile of water between it and the mainland. The name Tyre means 'rock'.

To no other foreign nation, Egypt excepted (chs. 29-32), does Ezekiel devote so much space. Zimmerli thinks the reason is that, after 587, only Tyre and Egypt, apart from Jerusalem, continued to oppose Nebuchadnezzar, and that therefore, since Ezekiel, like Jeremiah, regarded Babylon as Yahweh's chosen instrument, it was inevitable that he should give quite special treatment to Yahweh's judgment upon these two powers. But Bertholet is surely also correct when he says that the prophet saw both in Tyre's opulent commerce and in her resistance to Nebuchadnezzar 'a supreme example of offensiveness to God, whose punishment in the eyes of all the world could not fail to come to pass'.

Ezekiel's knowledge of Tyre and Egypt is so detailed that it has been supposed that he visited these places.[1] Zimmerli however, gives a conjecture by Mazar (communicated verbally) that possibly the deportees from Judah were settled

---

[1] L. Finkelstein, *The Pharisees*, Philadelphia, 1946, I, p. 321, II, p. 688, n. 29, mentioned by Fohrer.

near groups of exiles from Tyre, and that this may have contributed to the particularly vigorous formulation of the oracles
and possibly also to the use of Tyrian traditions.

Other oracles against Tyre are Amos 1.9f.; Isa. 23; Jer.
25.22; 47.4; Joel 3.4ff.; Zech. 9.2-4.

THE OVERTHROW OF TYRE

26.1-21

The chapter divides into four parts: (*a*) Yahweh resolves on
the overthrow of Tyre (vv. 1-6); (*b*) Nebuchadnezzar's army
is to raze the city (vv. 7-14); (*c*) the dismay of the princes of
the sea (vv. 15-18); (*d*) Tyre's descent into the underworld
(vv. 19-21).

YAHWEH RESOLVES ON THE OVERTHROW
OF TYRE

26.1-6

1. In the eleventh year That is, of Jehoiachin's captivity.
Jerusalem has already fallen (v. 2), but according to 33.21
news of this only reached Ezekiel in Babylon in the twelfth
year. Therefore many follow LXX A and read 'twelfth' here.
But at 32.1, where MT reads 'twelfth', LXX and Syriac
change to 'eleventh'. Probably 'eleventh' should be read
throughout. 'This emendation would solve the lapse of
eighteen months between the Fall of Jerusalem and the news
of that event reaching Babylonia by reducing the time required
for the trip from eighteen to less than six months. It might
well have taken a fugitive six months to find his way to the
Jewish colony at Tel-Abib, but not eighteen months.'[2] No
month is given. Jeremiah however says that Jerusalem was
destroyed in the fifth month (Jer. 52.12). So we should think
of the eleventh or twelfth month.

2. Aha, the gate of the peoples is broken, it has swung open

[2] C. G. Howie, *The Date and Composition of Ezekiel*, p. 39.

to me Tyre was a great trading city; the reason why she exulted is probably not because she would now be able to collect the tolls which Jerusalem, on account of her position on the trade route from the south to Tyre, had imposed on passing commerce, but rather because since the time of Solomon the carrying trade from Asia Minor and Mesopotamia had been largely an Israelite monopoly (Fohrer).

5. in the midst of the sea A reference to Tyre's location on an island. DAUGHTERS ON THE MAINLAND (v. 6): Tyrian settlements on the mainland.

NEBUCHADNEZZAR'S ATTACK ON TYRE

26.7-14

'The judgment becomes concrete' (Muilenburg).

7. from the north See on 1.4.

king of kings A regular title of the later Persian kings (Ezra 7.12); since it had been adopted by the earlier Assyrian kings, it may also have been used by Nebuchadnezzar.

8. siege wall A rampart. 'Siege-works were, of course, as useless as horses and chariots (vv. 7, 10) against the island-city; but Ezekiel pictures an attack from the mainland; and his description, so far from being "fantastic", as Hölscher calls it, agrees exactly with what Esarhaddon did in 673, and Asshurbanipal in 668 BC, when they besieged Tyre. . . . The city itself could only be taken by a blockade from the sea, or by building a mole from the mainland. Sennacherib tried the first method in 701 without success . . . ; Alexander the Great adopted the second in 332, and thus brought up his

troops and engines to the walls, but even then not without
help from a fleet' (Cooke). ROOF OF SHIELDS: 'something of
the same sort as the Lat. *testudo*, a covering of interlocked
shields beneath which the attacker can approach the walls of
a fortified city in comparative safety.'[3] 'To attack the island
of Tyre with mounds and siege wall, or to enter it with
chariotry as depicted here, would seem a physical impossibility. This does not necessitate the assumption that the
oracle is spurious, for the prophet may be deliberately using
the conventionalized symbols of siege, or referring in part
to the daughters on the mainland' (May).

10. His horses . . . render as Cooke, 'From the surge of
his horses their dust shall cover thee.' HORSES 'would be as
strange in Tyre as in Venice' (Lofthouse).

11. pillars 'The word is almost always used of a pillar having
religous meaning' (Davidson). Herodotus (II 44) says that
there were two pillars in the temple of Melkarth of Tyre.

THE LAMENT OF THE PRINCES OF THE SEA

26.15-18

This poem is largely parallel to 27.28-36. When Tyre's
prosperity was at its zenith, the COASTLANDS of the Mediterranean (15) with whom she traded and their rulers (THE
PRINCES OF THE SEA, v. 16), were afraid of her power: now
they are appalled at her ruin. Verse 16 describes the usual
signs of mourning. For sitting on the ground, cf. Isa. 47.1;
Job. 2.12, and for putting off everyday clothing, cf. Jonah 3.5f.
EVERY MOMENT: the meaning is doubtful.

[3] Driver, *Biblica* 35, 1954, p. 156.

17-18. A dirge in the *qinah* measure. It has been expanded, and the original may have run something as follows:

HOW HAVE YOU VANISHED FROM THE SEAS, O CITY RENOWNED
WHO IMPOSED YOUR TERROR ON ALL THE MAINLAND!
(But) NOW THE coastlands TREMBLE ON THE DAY OF YOUR
FALL.

TYRE'S DESCENT TO THE UNDERWORLD

26.19-21

The verses have close parallels in 31.14-18 and 32.17-32, and may not be original.

The waters of the sea (vv. 3, 12) now become the waters of the deep (Hebrew Tehom), cf. 31.15; Amos 7.4, which Yahweh put under restraint at Creation. 'Ezekiel expands [the picture in v. 3] from a simple storm to a cosmic catastrophe' (Fohrer). 'Rather than conquer the chaotic waters like Yahweh or the Canaanite Baal, Tyre would be conquered by them and descend to the lower world' (May). Verse 20 brings a fresh image. THE PIT is Sheol, the Underworld, the abode of the dead, Job. 17.16; 33.18ff.; Pss. 28.1; 88.3-6; Isa. 14.15, etc.

A LAMENT OVER TYRE

27.1-36

Tyre is pictured as a magnificent ship which suffers shipwreck in the midst of the sea. The poem is one of Ezekiel's
finest. Into it has been inserted a catalogue of the merchandise
that was brought to Tyre (vv. 3a, 9b-25a), which is not
original.

THE POEM

27.1-2, 3b-9a, 25b-36

'The island-city, bounded only by the sea, suggests the picture of a ship under sail' (Cooke). YOUR BORDERS . . . etc.
(v. 4): Some read: 'In the midst of the sea you were built
great.'

5-7. *The construction of the ship*

Senir Mount Hermon (Deut. 3.9), a projection of the Anti-
Lebanon range.

6. Bashan East and north-east of Galilee; for its oaks cf.
Isa. 2.13; Zech. 11.2. PINES: perhaps rather 'cypresses'.

7. blue and purple Blue-purple and red-purple. Purple was
extracted from the murex. The land of Canaan means 'the
land of the red-purple wool', and Phoenicia comes from the
Greek word for purple, *phoenix*—so important was the purple-
industry. 'The purple suggests luxury and regal splendour'
213

(May). ELISHAH has not yet been certainly identified, but may be Cyprus.

8-9a. *The ship's crew*

Other Phoenician cities manned the ship. SIDON, twenty-five miles north of Tyre, had earlier been more important than Tyre itself.

9a. Read: 'The elders of Byblos were in you to repair your seams', and omit the rest of the verse. Byblos is the Greek name of Gebal; it lies northwards of Tyre.

25b-28. *The shipwreck*

25b. in the heart of the seas 'On the high seas' (Cooke).

27. Read simply: 'YOUR RICHES, YOUR WARES, YOUR MERCH-ANDISE SINK INTO THE HEART OF THE SEAS'. The rest has come in from vv. 10f. On the phrase INTO THE HEART OF THE SEAS Muilenburg comments: 'Where Tyre had deemed itself supreme . . . The sea destroys the mistress of the sea; this is the irony of the whole lament.'

28. countryside The pasture-land round a town.

29-31. 'The whole shipping world laments the loss of the splendid vessel' (Cooke).

32-36. The lament CAME FROM THE SEAS (v. 33): rather, 'went out by sea' (Cooke). AND SHALL BE NO MORE FOR EVER (v. 36): 'This figure of the mighty and over-laden ship, proudly venturing out into the waters which are to be her ruin, is the most striking example in the Bible of the thought familiar to Hebrews and Greeks alike—that pride prepares the way for its own fall' (Lofthouse). 'It (Tyre) stands in history as a noteworthy example of how weak and transitory is all human greatness' (Schumpp).

THE CATALOGUE OF MERCHANDISE

27.3a, 9b-25a

10. Lud (Gen 10.22): Lydia in Asia Minor. PUT: uncertain, perhaps Cyrene or Somaliland. 'The names thus have no geographical connection; they are chosen to show that Tyre was powerful and rich enough to supply her army from the most distant lands' (Cooke).

11. Helech Possibly Cilicia. MEN OF GAMAD: perhaps the Kumadi of the Tel-el-Armarna letters, in northern Syria.

12. Tarshish Generally taken as Tartessos, a Phoenician colony in Spain, but it may be in Sardinia.

13. Javan, Tubal, Meshech Cf. Gen. 10.2. The first is Ionia, the second and third lay, the one on the east, the other on the west, of the Anti-Taurus mountains in Asia Minor. BETH-TOGARMAH (v. 14, cf. Gen. 10.3): probably in Armenia.

18. Helbon Thirteen miles north of Damascus, and famous for its WINE.

19. Uzal Sana in the Yemen. The spices CASSIA and CALAMUS (sweet cane) came from Arabia. DEDAN (v. 20): near the north-east coast of the Red Sea. KEDAR (v. 21): northern Arabia. SHEBA and RAAMAH (v. 22): both in southern Arabia.

23. Haran a city in north-west Mesopotamia: from it Abraham set out, Gen. 11.31, 12.4f. CANNEH: also in Mesopotamia, but not as yet located. EDEN: probably a district near Haran. Omit ASSHUR, which is probably not Assyria, but a town on the west side of the Tigris. CHILMAD is unknown.

THE RULER OF TYRE

28.1-19

AN ORACLE OF JUDGMENT

28.1-10

2. the prince of Tyre Not so much the ruling king, Ithbaal II, but rather a personification of Tyre itself. 'It is of the character and achievements of a people rather than of a single definite monarch that Ezekiel thinks, even when he uses the term "king of Tyre", "king of Egypt", in prophecies that have several contacts with this poem [that is, with Isa. 14.4b-21].'[4] The monarch's sin—and therefore, since king and people were most closely linked together, Tyre's sin—is *hybris*, thinking himself to be a god, or even God (2, 9), priding himself on his wisdom and the riches he has gained by trade. For this he is to be shown that he is only a man, and to be slain shamefully by the Babylonians; his pride is to be punished in the same way as in the fall of the tyrant in Isa. 14.13-15. In Phoenicia, as widely throughout the ancient East, the king was also regarded as in some sense divine, though here 'I am a god' is 'hardly a boast of divine descent,[5] but a blasphemous word of self-exaltation' (Cooke). Again, 'for the Phoenicians, as the Ras Shamra poems prove, Yaman, the sea, was divine. The king of Tyre, representative of the city, could believe that he had the right to claim that his empire which had conquered the sea had a divine power inherent in it' (Steinmann).

[4] G. B. Gray, *Isaiah I-XXVII* (ICC), 1912, p. 251.
[5] So Frazer, *Adonis, Attis, Osiris*, 2nd ed., London, 1907, p. 13.

the seat of the gods The dwelling-place of the gods, called EDEN in v. 13 and THE HOLY MOUNTAIN OF GOD in v. 14, cf. Isa. 14.13, where the Babylonian king says he 'will sit on the mount of assembly in the far north' (cf. 1-4). 'The prince identified Tyre with it. The beauty and splendour of the place, its richness and renown, possibly also its isolation, make it something not of the earth' (Davidson). But the comparison is not particularly apt, and there is much to be said for Bruno's emendation (p. 125): 'Behold, wise one, you wanted to be in the image of God, from whom no secret is hidden. To what end did you get wealth for yourself by your wisdom and understanding, and gather gold and silver into your treasuries!'

3. Daniel See on 14.14. The verse is intended ironically. The king's WISDOM is explained in vv. 4f. as his skill in commercial enterprises. The meaning of v. 3b is uncertain: Zimmerli suggests: 'No secret thing can dumbfounder you.' UNDERSTANDING (v. 4): prudence, cf. Prov. 2.11; 14.29.

7. therefore, behold, I will bring strangers upon you The Babylonians, as in 7.21 (see note there); cf. 30.11; 31.12; 32.12. THE BEAUTY OF YOUR WISDOM: the splendours which he had got by his commercial acumen. DEFILE: rather 'profane', (cf. 7.24) with reference to the king's claiming equality with God.

8. THE PIT (so also 31.15-17; 32.18-32): see on 26.20.

10. uncircumcised Cf. also 32.17ff. According to Herodotus (II 104), the Phoenicians were circumcised, and this Ezekiel must have known. Zimmerli explains that 'in each instance in Ezekiel, in the "death of the uncircumcised" and "lying with the uncircumcised" is to be found a division (*Kategorie*) of the underworld that does not in every case agree with the state in the upper world of the people thither consigned. . . . Not merely death is threatened, but a dishonourable death, rejection into the sphere of uncleanness and absence of rest even in the underworld below, shame amid the "people of old" (26.20)'.

'The fate of the king of Tyre as depicted by the prophet has in it much of the fate of the First Man. In both, pride, the will to be like God, is the chief cause of the profound fall. The connections are unmistakable' (Schumpp).

A DIRGE

28.11-19

The poem is particularly difficult, partly because of textual corruption and partly because we do not understand some of the allusions. The mythology has clear connections with Gen. 2, but there are also striking differences. The Tyrian king is equated with a being in Paradise, almost certainly the primaeval man, who, because of his sin, was driven out to meet a terrible end. At the same time he is a seal or signet ring, cf. Jer. 22.24; Hag. 2.23, an image intended to represent the splendour of Tyre embodied in its ruler.

12b. read, following Driver, 'thou wast a seal of perfection', i.e., an exquisitely carved seal, 'a crown of beauty'. 'Thus the prophet, using two Babylonian words characteristic of Nebuchadnezzar's period describes the king of Tyre, somewhat ironically, as a perfect work of art, a carved seal or a diadem set with precious stones, in his royal splendour.'[6]

13. Eden, the garden of God Called in v. 14 THE HOLY MOUNTAIN OF GOD. An elevated position is also required for

[6] Driver, *Biblica* 35, 1954, p. 159.

the paradise of Gen. 3, since the four world-rivers flow from it. EVERY PRECIOUS STONE: the list is an insertion on the basis of the stones on the breast-plate of the high-priest, Ex. 28.17-21=39.10-14—LXX in fact gives the twelve stones of Exodus. We are to think of a robe ornamented with precious stones: in Babylonia the statues of certain gods were so draped. The last part of v. 13 is hopelessly corrupt, and the first part of v. 14 should probably be rendered, 'to thee I joined the guardian cherub', cf. Gen. 3.24. Steinmann however, reading 'I made you a cherub', says, 'It may even be asked whether Ezekiel does not here have in view what the later apocalypses are to call "the angel of Tyre", that is to say, the heavenly guardian of the city or rather what we today would call "its soul". This soul personified, and at the beginning angelic, would have become demonic by a fall very closely recalling that of the first man in Paradise.' STONES OF FIRE: uncertain; they may be stars, or angelic beings among whom the first man lived. Ziegler also suggests that they may refer to glistening precious stones enclosing the mountain, cf. Zech. 2.5.

15-17. Just as the first man sinned and was driven forth from the garden, so the king of Tyre is brought to ruin. As vv. 16-18 show, the sin consisted in injustice and pride.

18-19. The city is now addressed. If YOUR SANCTUARIES (or, with many MSS and Versions, 'sanctuary') is kept, 'the reference is to the whole island (SEAT OF THE GODS, v. 2) rather than to the temples raised to the gods. The profanation was due to gifts acquired by fraud, the fruit of injustice and acts of oppression' (Spadafora). If 'my sanctuary' (Bertholet) is read, then the reference may be to the paradise of Eden (Steinmann).

ORACLE AGAINST SIDON

28.20-23

Sidon (modern Saida) lies twenty miles south of Tyre. In earlier times it had been more important than Tyre, and after Nebuchadnezzar's siege of the latter it may have resumed something of its earlier glory. Since the oracle is composed of stock-phrases and mentions no specific changes against Sidon, it may have been added later by an editor who wished to bring the number of oracles against foreign nations up to seven.

23. the slain shall fall The rare form of the Hebrew verb suggests the translation 'fall in heaps'.

TWO LATER ADDITIONS

28.24-26

24. A general summary of the oracles against foreign nations and the effect of their punishment upon Israel. For the figure, cf. Num. 33.55; Josh. 23.13.

25f. Restoration to the homeland and peace for Israel, cf. 34.28; 38.11, 14; Jer. 23.6; 32.15, 37.

ORACLES AGAINST EGYPT
AND PHARAOH

29.1–32.32

The oracles against Tyre are followed by a series of seven oracles against Egypt, all of them dated except 30.1-9, and in chronological sequence (Jan. 587-585 BC) except for 29.17-21 (571 BC). Egypt differed from Tyre in that it was a world power, and Babylon's only possible rival. Ever since the time of Josiah it had been a dominant factor in Israelite politics. Wishing to re-assert its old hegemony over Palestine and Syria, it had to prevent the small states there from being incorporated in the Babylonian empire, or, when they did come under Babylonian influence, it had to incite them to rebellion. There were also those in Jerusalem and Judah who pinned their hopes against Babylon on alliance with the Nile power, which indeed was the only state able to offer any effective opposition to the Mesopotamian empire. But since in Ezekiel's view Babylon was Yahweh's instrument and Judah ought to submit to it, he goes to great lengths to make clear that reliance on Egypt is reliance on a 'broken reed' (29.6b-9a).

THE GREAT DRAGON

29.1-6a

A poem in the *qinah* measure.

The date is January 587, about half a year before the fall of the city (though LXX reads 'the twelfth year'). Albright[7] conjectures that it would be about January 587 that news

[7] 'The Seal of Eliakim and the Latest Pre-exilic History of Judah, with some Observations on Ezekiel', *JBL* 51, 1932, p. 94.

would come to the exiles of Hophra's campaign against the
Babylonians who were then besieging Jerusalem (Jer. 37.5).
Hophra, otherwise Apries, 588-570, is the Pharaoh of v. 3.
He is compared with THE GREAT DRAGON (i.e. the crocodile)
THAT LIES IN THE MIDST OF HIS STREAMS. There is no need to
see mythological associations here, either with the chaos-
dragon of Mesopotamia or the Leviathan of Ras Shamra. The
crocodile typifies Egypt. Just as the Tyrian king claimed to be
a god because of the site of his city, so Pharaoh exalts himself because of the Nile (which alone gives Egypt prosperity),
claiming that he had made it, and so, as the creator, asserting
a divine status. For this megalomania Yahweh is to punish
him. With the threat in v. 4 cf. 38.4, also Herodotus II 70.
In v. 4, where there is possibly expansion of the text, the FISH
OF YOUR STREAMS are possibly the inhabitants of Egypt, who
are to share the fate of their ruler, though some think of
mercenary troops or of subjects.

5. wilderness 'The "wilderness" is at once the battlefield on
which Egypt will be defeated and the environment in which
a crocodile must necessarily perish' (Lofthouse). NOT . . .
GATHERED AND BURIED (cf. Jer. 8.2; 25.33): 'Pharaoh's body
will undergo the last indignity, and forfeit the rites of burial,
cp. Isa. 14.20' (Cooke); to the ancient world this was something terrible. Or the meaning may be: 'Driven away from
the Nile, the Egyptian people will be destroyed' (Fisch). The
flesh of the crocodile is useless for food. The oracle ends at
6a: I AM THE LORD.

THE BROKEN REED

29.6b-9a

6b. REED: The papyrus reed, which grows by the Nile (cf.

Isa. 19.6f.), is the symbol of untrustworthiness, cf. Isa. 36.6=
II Kings 18.21.

7. THEY: the house of Israel. The reference in v. 7 is to
Hophra's expedition, see above. The oracle ends at I AM THE
LORD (v. 9a).

THE DESOLATION OF EGYPT

29.9b-12

Like the preceding, the oracle begins BECAUSE.

10. from Migdol to Syene MIGDOL, which means 'tower',
was on the northern border of Egypt, either Tell el-Heir,
twelve miles south of Pelusium, or Tell es-Samat, near Kan-
tara, while SYENE is on the southern border. The phrase is
thus equivalent to 'from Land's End to John o' Groats'.

12. a desolation in the midst of desolated countries 'Egypt
will become like the Arabian and Libyan deserts on either
side of it' (Cooke). FORTY YEARS: cf. Judah's punishment in
4.4-6. Jeremiah thinks of the Babylonian supremacy over the
Jews as lasting seventy years (Jer. 29.10). The Egyptians are
also to be exiled.

THE RESTORATION OF EGYPT

29.13-16

The FORTUNES OF EGYPT are to be restored, but the Egyptians are to be confined to THE LAND OF THEIR ORIGIN, Pathros,
which is Upper Egypt, and there the kingdom is to lose all its

former might, so that Israel will never again be tempted to any policy of alliances with it (v. 16). Thus, Egypt's sin is not only *hybris*, but tempting God's people to look away from him as their confidence. RECALLING THEIR INIQUITY: cf. 21.23f. Jeremiah also prophesied the restoration of Egypt, Jer. 46.26.

AN APPENDIX

29.17-20

The oracle (in prose) is directed to the prophet himself. Its date is the spring New Year of 570, and this is the latest date in Ezekiel. Nebuchadnezzar besieged Tyre for thirteen years. In chs. 26-28 Ezekiel had prophesied the capture and destruction of the city. The latter at any rate did not take place, in spite of all the efforts made by the Babylonians.

18. made his army labour hard against Tyre   This may refer to an attempt to build a causeway from the mainland to the city. Thus, though Nebuchadnezzar was Yahweh's agent, he got no WAGES (19), no great spoil. But now, 'on the principle: the workman is worthy of hire' (Ziegler), he is to be compensated, and to be able to pay his troops, with booty taken from Egypt, which he in fact invaded in 568, though with what success is unknown. In v. 20 omit the last clause (from BE-CAUSE to GOD) as a gloss.

'This oracle allows us to see a process which is of importance for the understanding of prophecy, of significance far beyond the immediate context in Ezekiel. On the one hand it shows how one element in the prophet's message, the announcement of judgment upon Tyre, which had a very direct urgency in earlier years, can in the march of history fade into the background. We cannot ascertain how far Eze-kiel was able to see in the ending of the siege of Tyre a ful-

filment of his threats against the city and its princes, or how
far there were still unfulfilled expectations. But it is clear in
any case that in the combined Tyre-Egypt oracles, the expectation of judgment for Tyre falls into the background. The
true prophet knows (this is particularly clearly seen in Isaiah)
that Yahweh remains Lord over the history he creates, and
has also power, in the case of announcements that were apparently capable of only one meaning, to take them back into
his own freedom or even let them fall into the background.
At the same time, however, we can see how in this oracle the
announcement of judgment upon Egypt gains a new actuality
due to the influence of the ending of the siege of Tyre. What
dominates 29.17-20 is not the taking back of an earlier word,
but the declaration which the prophet is enabled to make of
a new validity for an earlier prophecy in a new present, the
virtual seal set upon the saying against Egypt' (Zimmerli).

A WORD CONCERNING ISRAEL

29.21

ON THAT DAY: that is, after Nebuchadnezzar's capture of
Egypt. The HORN is the symbol of strength (I Sam. 2.1; Ps.
75.10; Jer. 48.25; Luke 1.69). The reference is either to the
revival of Israel or the restoration of the Davidic line (cf. Ps.
132.17). The meaning of the second clause, I WILL OPEN YOUR
LIPS AMONG THEM (cf. 16.63) is obscure. It probably does not
refer to the prophet's 'dumbness' (3.26; 24.27; 33.22). 'In the
judgment upon Egypt, now soon to be accomplished, and the
turning of the fortunes of the house of Israel which will
follow in connection with this, fresh credence will be given
to the prophet, and he will again be free to claim a hearing'
(Zimmerli).

H

THE DAY OF YAHWEH UPON EGYPT

30.1-19

No date is given, and this, together with the reminiscences of other parts of the prophecy (with 6, cf. 29.10, with 7, 29.12), suggests that the verses are, if not wholly, at least to a very great part, the work of later disciples.

For the Day of Yahweh, see on ch. 7.

3. a time of doom for the nations The day of judgment of the nations (cf. 7.7, 12), probably not all the nations of the world, but Egypt's allies.

5. An expansion. On the three lands ETHIOPIA, PUT (Libya) and LUD (Lydia), see on 27.10. THE PEOPLE OF THE LAND THAT IS IN LEAGUE: uncertain, probably meaning peoples in league with Egypt, though some think of Israelite mercenaries, understanding the LEAGUE (Heb. covenant) as the Sinai covenant.

6. THOSE WHO SUPPORT EGYPT: her allies. MIGDOL TO SYENE: see on 29.10. With v. 7 cf. 29.10, 12. With v. 9 cf. Isa. 18.2.

12. TO DRY UP THE NILE means famine for Egypt, cf. 29.10; Isa. 19.5ff.

13-19. *The destruction of the principal cities of Egypt*

13. MEMPHIS, the ancient capital of Lower Egypt, ten miles south of Cairo.

14. PATHROS, see on 29.14. ZOAN (Greek Tanis), in Lower Egypt in the eastern Delta, now San-el-Hagar. THEBES, the modern Luxor and Karnak.

15. PELUSIUM, on the north-east frontier.

17. ON: Heliopolis, seven miles north-east of Cairo. It was renowned for the worship of the sun practised in it, Jer. 43.13. PIBESETH, Bubastes in the eastern Delta, modern Basta, forty miles north-east of Cairo. According to Herodotus (II 66f.) it possessed the finest temple in the whole of Egypt to which (he says) seven hundred thousand pilgrims resorted every year.

18. TEHAPHNEHES: Greek Daphne, in the east of the Nile Delta, cf. Jer. 2.16. It had a royal palace (Jer. 43.8ff.).

PHARAOH'S ARM BROKEN

30.20-26

The date is three months later than 29.1, and so three months before the fall of Jerusalem. The breaking of Pharaoh's arm refers to Hophra's defeat when he attacked the Babylonians when they were besieging Jerusalem (Jer. 37.5-10). The original oracle was probably v. 21 only (so Hölscher), but it has been rather confusedly expanded (23=26a, 24a= 25a, 25b=26b, so Spadafora) to indicate that Egypt is to suffer further defeats. Not just one of Pharaoh's arms (v. 21), but both of them (v. 22), are to be broken, since Yahweh is to STRENGTHEN THE ARMS (cf. Hos. 7.15) of Nebuchadnezzar, and the Egyptians are to be beaten and driven from their land.

AN ALLEGORY

31.1-18

The greatness and splendour of Pharaoh is compared with

a lofty pine-tree whose top reaches to heaven and whose foliage shelters the birds and beasts of the earth. But it is to be cut down, its branches spreading over the land, and to be brought to the lower world, to the astonishment of all nature.

Many mythological elements are gathered together in the chapter, the world-tree whose roots are watered by Tehom the primaeval deep, the garden of God, Eden, etc.

1-9. *The beauty of the tree* (verse)

2-3. Read:

> 'Whom art thou like in thy greatness?
> Behold, (I will liken thee to) a pine-tree with fair branches,
> and of great height,
> and its top is among the clouds.'

Omit A CEDAR IN LEBANON, which has come in to explain the unusual Hebrew word for 'pine-tree'. FOREST SHADE: very uncertain, and best omitted with LXX B.

4. The waters nourished it The waters of the Nile. THE DEEP is Tehom, cf. 26.19, the waters under the earth which made the world-tree grow tall. MAKING ITS RIVERS FLOW: the DEEP made its streams encircle the place where the pine-tree was planted. TO ALL THE TREES OF THE FOREST can hardly be right, as other trees do not come into question. The words have probably come in from the following verse; or we may read 'unto it', that is, the pine-tree. Omit v. 5 with Jahn as a secondary addition.

6. 'This is a picture of the prosperity of Egypt' (May). Its empire gave shelter to many small peoples. BIRDS and BEASTS: cf. the tree in Dan. 4.10ff.

8. For THE GARDEN OF GOD see on 28.13. Verse 9 is probably

a later addition intended to point out that the tree's beauty
was the work of Yahweh.

10-14. *Its fall* (prose)

10. For the last clause read: 'and its heart rose in its loftiness'
(Cooke).

11. a mighty one of the nations   Nebuchadnezzar.

12. For FOREIGNERS see on 28.7. THE MOST TERRIBLE OF THE
NATIONS: cf. 28.7; 30.11. Cf. also the fate of the dragon, 29.5.
The VALLEYS and BOUGHS are the peoples to whom Egypt
gave protection.

13. dwell   Settle; 'as on a carrion, the nations gather in
Egypt to despoil it' (Ziegler).

14. The verse is a later gloss, and should be omitted. The
figure changes somewhat to 'trees of water' (Heb.), and 'those
that drink water' (Heb.), which are not to exalt themselves,
as they are doomed to the underworld. The second half of
the verse clearly anticipates vv. 15ff. It is a general observa-
tion, the TREES now possibly signifying potentates of all
nations.

15-18. *The descent to the underworld* (prose)
    Cf. 26.19-21; Isa. 14.5-21.
    The text is uncertain. The following is a possible recon-
struction. (Verse 17 disturbs the image of the tree and its fall,
and is best omitted as a gloss.)

15. 'In the day when it (the pine tree) went down into Sheol,
I made Tehom mourn over it, and held back its streams, and
the many waters were held back. And I darkened Lebanon
in sorrow for it, and all the trees of the field pined away for

it. 16. At the sound of its fall I made nations quake when I made it go down to Sheol with those who go down to the Pit. But in the underworld all the trees of Eden were comforted, the choice one of Lebanon, all that drink water. 18. Whom were you like in glory and greatness? So you shall be brought down with the trees of Eden into the nether world; you shall lie among the uncircumcised, with the slain of the sword.'

15. 'And I darkened Lebanon . . .' (RSV: I WILL CLOTHE LEBANON IN GLOOM . . .): this was because there was no longer water to keep them alive.

16. 'I made NATIONS QUAKE': the nations allied to Pharaoh, who were to share his fate. 'Were COMFORTED': because the mighty Pharaoh is as mortal as they, cf. Isa. 14.8. It is not, however, apparent why THE TREES OF EDEN have been brought down into the underworld (again in v. 18). The words may refer to some myth now unknown.

18. On UNCIRCUMCISED see on 28.10. The Egyptians were circumcised, cf. 32.19, 32.
'All nature shudders in sympathy with the fallen cedar; the deep mourns and withholds her streams from the earth; Lebanon is clothed with blackness, and all the trees languish. Egypt was so much a part of the established order that the world does not know itself when she has vanished' (Skinner).

A 'LAMENTATION' OVER PHARAOH

32.1-16

1-8. *The capture of the dragon*

The poem is a new, but more vivid and terrible, version of

the lamentation over the crocodile in 29.3-5, of which it may
be only a doublet. It is dated IN THE TWELFTH YEAR, though
LXX A and Syriac read 'eleventh'. In either case it is after
the fall of Jerusalem.

'Brief as it is, this lamentation is one of the most con-
summate in Ezekiel, by virtue of the concentrated force, the
colour and violence of its imagery. The prophet here attains
to the grandeur and power of the most famous poets of his
race.'[8]

2. The opening figure, YOU CONSIDER YOURSELF A LION AMONG
THE NATIONS, does not suit the one which immediately follows. The most likely emendation is Bertholet's, 'Woe to thee,
Pharaoh, how art thou perished!' The DRAGON is taken by
many to be the crocodile (cf. 29.3), in which case THE SEAS
and RIVERS are the Nile and its canals, cf. 31.4. But it could
also be the mythological dragon of the waters of chaos. YOU
BURST FORTH IN YOUR RIVERS: Ewald's emendation is
generally accepted, 'and didst snort with thy nostrils'. 'The
vitality of the monster and his violent activity are suggested
by his troubling the waters and fouling the streams' (Davidson). But more specifically the reference is to Egypt's efforts
to induce the Palestinian states to revolt against Nebuchadnezzar.

3. Such pride, which is indeed rebellion against Yahweh, if
the Babylonians are his appointed instrument, must be
punished. Delete, following a hint in LXX B, WITH A HOST OF
MANY PEOPLES; it is a glossator's explanation of Yahweh's NET
(cf. 12.13; 17.20; 19.8), the Babylonians. With v. 4 cf. 29.3-5.

5. The reference is now to Egypt rather than to Pharaoh
himself. Verse 6 is probably an expansion. The word rendered

[8] Steinmann, p. 130. (I owe this translation to the kindness of my
colleague, Professor A. J. Steele.)

BLOOD occurs only here, and means 'outflow'. Bertholet renders: 'I drench the Nile with your issue, and the watercourses
with your blood.'

7-8. 'The destruction of Egypt is on such a scale that it
darkens the sky and the stars as with garments of mourning,
cp. 30.18; the hyperbole goes further than 31.15' (Cooke).
Such apocalyptic traits as the darkening of the sun, etc., are
common in connection with the Day of Yahweh, cf. 30.3; Isa.
13.10; Amos 5.18; 8.9; Joel 2.10, 31; 3.15. 'The destruction of
the dragon of chaos was associated with the Day of Yahweh'
(May). 'The judgment of Egypt is a prefiguration of the world-
judgment, 30.2f.' (Ziegler). (Smend thought that in these two
verses Ezekiel had suddenly gone over to a new figure: the
dragon, as well as being a mythological monster, was also a
star which Yahweh now put out. But this cannot be proved.)

9-10. *The effect of the capture*
The section is in prose and contains nothing original; cf.
26.16; 27.35.

11-16. *The sword of the king of Babylon*
Again in prose, although rhythmic, and certainly, like vv.
9f., no part of the original lamentation. Not only is Pharaoh
to be destroyed, (vv. 11-12a), but the land of Egypt is to be
devastated (vv. 12b-15).

11. With the words THE SWORD OF THE KING OF BABYLON cf.
21.19; 29.8. The words interpret the NET of v. 3. With the
SWORDS of v. 12 cf. 30.11. Verse 13b seeks to interpret the
last part of v. 2, but the DRAGON there has now become
BEASTS.

14. Since the WATERS are no longer trampled, the mud will
settle and they will run CLEAR and smooth (LIKE OIL). Verse

15 (probably later than the rest) prophesies further desolation for Egypt. With v. 16 cf. 19.14; 31.18. The LAMENTATION refers only to the poem in vv. 2-8.

EGYPT'S DESCENT TO THE UNDERWORLD

32.17-32

'This last elegy rises to a more general concept: the descent of Egypt into Sheol is symbolic of her future ruin, and at the same time of the end to which all the arrogant have come in the past and will in the future (cf. v. 18). Hence the list of rulers and empires who have already fallen or who will finish ingloriously through their own cruelty (vv. 22-30). The more cruel they have been in life, the deeper they will plunge into hell, when the divine justice pursues them even after death. Egypt is in the same case: she has no preferential treatment: she will share the same fate' (Spadafora).

The prophet is to sing a dirge over Egypt as she descends to the underworld, Sheol, THE PIT, and is received by the nations already there. Sheol here is 'the aggregate of all the burying-grounds scattered over the earth's surface' (Skinner), and is without moral distinctions—good and bad alike go down to it as their final destiny. Ezekiel pictures each nation as having its own place of habitation in the nether world, 'just as on earth the members of the same family would usually be interred in one burying-place' (Skinner). The graves of the individuals of each nation are gathered round that of the king who is their representative.

'The prophet desires to express by his representation a moral truth. The nations which he mentions are those that have come into conflict with Israel, although their sin is regarded as more general than this. . . . Their fate is the judgment of Jehovah upon them, his verdict in regard to their

H*

life as nations. Their common sin is violence: they put their
terror in the land of the living. And their fate is but the
nemesis of their conduct: taking the sword they perish by it.
The history of nations is the judgment of nations. But the
nations like individuals continue to subsist, they bear their
shame in Sheol for ever' (Davidson).

The text of the section is in considerable disorder.

18. For HER AND THE DAUGHTERS OF THE MAJESTIC NATIONS
probably read, with Zimmerli, 'her among mighty nations'.
On UNCIRCUMCISED (v. 19) see on 31.18. The text of vv. 20-21
is very corrupt, and no satisfactory reconstruction has been
proposed. The verses are best omitted.

22-28. Various nations receive Egypt as it comes down to
Sheol.

22. ASSYRIA: The Assyrian empire fell in 612. Omit the
second part of the verse, THEIR GRAVES etc., as a gloss which
has come in from the next verse.

24. Elam An ancient and sometimes important kingdom
lying east of Babylonia to the north of the Persian Gulf. It
was conquered by Asshurbanipal c. 650. By the time of Jeremiah it had regained independence (Jer. 49.34ff.). It later became a province of the Persian Empire, its capital city, Susa,
becoming the capital of the empire (Neh. 1.1; Dan. 8.2). Verse
25 should be omitted. All that stands in LXX is AMONG THE
SLAIN.

26. Meshech and Tubal See on 27.13, and cf. 38.2ff.; 39.1.

27. And they do not lie If the reading of the Hebrew text
is kept, then the meaning is that MESHECH AND TUBAL are
given a position inferior to THE FALLEN MIGHTY MEN OF OLD

(reading with LXX and Old Latin OF OLD for MT 'uncircumcised'). But LXX and Syriac omit the negative, correctly: the reason for the fate of Meshech and Tubal is no different from that of the other peoples, namely that they have spread terror on the earth (Bertholet). FOR THE TERROR OF THE MIGHTY MEN: if the clause is kept, THE MIGHTY MEN must mean 'their mighty men'. In v. 28 the change to the second person makes the verse suspect.

29-32. These verses were probably added later (Jahn, Hölscher). EDOM, THE PRINCES OF THE NORTH, THE SIDONIANS, 'minor nations on the Jewish borders, could hardly be ranked among the mighty dead, such as Assyria, Elam and Meshech, states which had fallen and belonged to the past; but here was an opportunity to plunge into Sheol the detested enemies of the present!' (Cooke).

III

ISRAEL'S RESTORATION

33.1–39.29

With ch. 33 begins the second period of Ezekiel's activity,
which is concerned with restoration. The fall of the city
(33.21) produced feelings of hopelessness and abandonment
by God among the exiles—for even if Lamentations was
composed in the homeland, the mood it reflects (e.g. 1.12; 2.13)
must have been that of the exiles as well. Their condition was
spiritual death (37.1-14), when God's saving action was at a
standstill. But, bereft as they now were of all on which they
had formerly relied, the promised land, the temple and its
sacrifices, as well as the monarchy and state, the possibility
was opened up that some might at last look to Yahweh and be
ready to listen to the promises of a prophet whose threats had
been so terribly fulfilled. Thus, like the Servant, Ezekiel's task
now was to foster faith wherever he might find it. His promises include a new heart and a new spirit for the nation, the
return of Israel and Judah to the promised land, a new
covenant and royal leadership, and the destruction of all
enemies. Then (40-48) follow the vision of the new temple
and its restored worship.

THE PROPHET AS WATCHMAN

33.1-9

The verses have affinities with 3.16-21.

'The figure of the watchman is drawn from the daily experience of the people. On his watchtower he guards the vineyards (Isa. 5.2); as shepherd he protects his flock (I Sam. 17.34-6); in time of war he sounds the alarm of the approaching enemy (II Kings 9.17ff.; Jer. 4.5f.; 6.17; Hos. 5.8; Amos 3.6)' (Muilenburg).

2. The sword Cf. 21.9ff.; 30.4, 21f.; 38.21.

3-6. The duty of a watchman is to give warning, the responsibility of alerting the city to danger is his. He is not, however, responsible for the way in which his warning is received. Two cases are then given. First (vv. 4-5), if a warning is given but has no heed paid to it, the watchman has no responsibility for any deaths. Secondly (v. 6), if the watchman fails to give warning, Yahweh holds him responsible for those who perish.

7-9. The figure is then applied to the prophet and his office, cf. 3.17ff.; he is to warn both Israel as a whole, and wicked individuals within her, to keep the commandments, and if he fails to do so, Yahweh will hold him responsible for the death of the wicked. On Ezekiel's prophetic office, see also notes on 13.1-16.

FREEDOM TO REPENT

33.10-20

The subject has already come up in 18.21-32 (see notes

there), and, like the discussion in ch. 18, it starts from a popular saying (v. 10), OUR TRANSGRESSIONS AND OUR SINS ARE UPON US, AND WE WASTE AWAY BECAUSE OF THEM; HOW THEN CAN WE LIVE? The exiles realize that they are paying the penalty for their rebellion against Yahweh, and are in hopeless despondency: they have not yet come to repent. The prophet is to counter this mood with the saying already given in 18.23 and 32, that Yahweh has NO PLEASURE IN THE DEATH OF THE WICKED, but the wicked should TURN FROM HIS WAY AND LIVE. 'But if the words were in the form of a question in 18.23, and of a simple statement in 18.32, they are here an impassioned oath of asseveration' (Zimmerli). Verse 12 departs from the theme of comfort and takes up the principle of God's justice, already treated more fully in 18.21-29, q.v. With v. 13 cf. 3.20; 18.24. With v. 14 cf. 3.18; 18.27. With v. 15 cf. 18.7; 20.11. With v. 16 cf. 18.22. With vv. 18f. cf. 18.26f.; with v. 20 cf. 18.25, 29.

'For the first time a general conviction of sin, a sense of being in the wrong, was produced in Israel. That this conviction should at first lead to the verge of despair was perhaps inevitable. The people were not familiar with the idea of the divine righteousness, and could not at once perceive that anger against sin was consistent in God with pity for the sinners and mercy towards the contrite. The chief task that now lay before the prophet was to transform their attitude of sullen impenitence into one of submission and hope by teaching them the efficacy of repentance. They had learned the meaning of judgment; they have now to learn the possibility and the conditions of forgiveness. And this can only be taught to them through a revelation of the free and infinite grace of God, who has "no pleasure in the death of the wicked, but that the wicked should turn from his way and live" (v. 11). Only thus can the hard and stony heart be taken away from their flesh and a heart of flesh given to them' (Skinner).

NEWS OF JERUSALEM'S FALL

33.21-22

21. For TWELFTH read with Hebrew and LXX Mss. and Syriac 'eleventh' (see on 26.1). An ecstatic experience on the evening before the fugitive's arrival removed the prophet's 'dumbness'.

THOSE STILL IN THE HOMELAND

33.23-29

The date of the passage is probably some months after the fugitive's arrival, when the new conditions in Judah were beginning to take shape.

Those who had not been deported possessed themselves of land that was now ownerless (cf. 11.15; Jer. 52.16; II Kings 25.12), and tried to justify their conduct by saying that ABRAHAM, to whom the land was given, was ONLY ONE individual, while they were MANY. Since part of the promise to Abraham was a land in which his posterity should dwell for ever, they regarded their present possession of it as indicating that they were Abraham's true heirs, the elect, the section of the nation whom Yahweh favoured. While Ezekiel does not say explicitly that Abraham's title to the land was his righteousness, he implies this in the list of sins (vv. 25f.) and the threat (27f.) which follow; like Jeremiah (Jer. 24), he rejects the claims made by those who had not been deported. With vv. 25f. cf. 18.5f. With v. 27 cf. 5.12, 16f.; 14.13ff.

26. You resort to the sword A slight emendation would give 'You stand upon (i.e. possess) your waste places.'

Jannsen remarks that vv. 24-29 set the tone for the judg-

ment which future generations were to pass on the time of
the exile: the future was with the exiles alone.[1]

EZEKIEL AS MINSTREL

33.30-33

The fall of Jerusalem accredited Ezekiel in the eyes of the
exiles, and now they talked about him, and came to listen
to him, the more eagerly since he now spoke of hope and of
God's care for individuals.

31. But the success was a hearing without understanding
(Isa. 6.9): they did not yet realize that the promised salvation had moral preconditions attached to it, while they themselves were still self-seeking (THEIR HEART IS SET ON THEIR
GAIN), and did not do what Ezekiel demanded of them. They
were merely hearers of the word and not doers (cf. Isa. 29.13;
Jer. 12.2; also Mark 3.35). (Omit AS MY PEOPLE with LXX
and Syriac, and for WITH THEIR LIPS THEY SHOW MUCH LOVE,
BUT . . . read 'for lies are in their mouth, and . . .'.)

32. The prophet is no better than one who SINGS LOVE SONGS
to them. But they will yet realize that a prophet has been
among them.

33. When this comes THIS is not defined, but in the context
it can only mean the prophecies of salvation and of the destruction of the wicked which are now Ezekiel's theme. 'The
prophet's function is to interpret history in the light of God's
purpose for His people. However insensible and shallow the
present generation, a new Israel will carry out God's purpose
in the age which is about to dawn. Cp. Isaiah's declaration,
Isa. 29.13, 14' (Cooke).

[1] *Juda in der Exilzeit*, p. 69.

SHEPHERDS AND SHEEP

34.1-31

The chapter is not a unity, but rather a collection of utterances having the common theme of shepherd, that is, ruler, as occasionally in the OT (I Kings 22.17; Isa. 44.28 [Cyrus], and especially in Jeremiah and the writers after him), and commonly throughout the ancient East. Jer. 23.1-6 is the basis of Ezekiel's thought here.

THE FALSE SHEPHERDS AND YAHWEH THE TRUE SHEPHERD

34.1-10

1-6. Like Jeremiah (Jer. 22.13-30), Ezekiel is critical of the Judean kings of the period immediately before the fall of Jerusalem, especially of Zedekiah (cf. 17.1-21; 19.10-14; 21.25-27; and also 19.2-9). Three charges are brought against them:

2b-3. First, they exploited their subjects for their own advantage.

fat Read 'milk' with LXX and the Vulgate.

4. Secondly, they neglected their proper duties. WEAK: 'sickened' (Cooke). For the last clause of the verse read 'and the strong you treated too harshly' (cf. LXX).

5-6. Thirdly, because of bad leadership the state fell a prey to ALL THE WILD BEASTS, that is, the surrounding nations, especially the Babylonians, with the result that the people were taken into exile (SCATTERED OVER ALL THE FACE OF THE EARTH).

7-10. Yahweh, the owner of the flock, punishes the shepherds by removing them from their office. This prepares the way for a different form of state government in the restoration, cf. vv. 23-24; 45.8f.

YAHWEH HIS PEOPLE'S SHEPHERD

34.11-16

'However, a flock cannot be left to itself; so a promise is added' (Fohrer). Yahweh is himself to rule his people, directly and with no delegation of authority, and to lead them back from exile, tend them in their own land, and give them peace.

12. On a day of clouds and thick darkness Cf. 30.3; the day of the Lord as represented by the fall of Jerusalem and the exile.

15. The pronoun I is emphatic; Yahweh himself acts directly (cf. Isa. 40.11; Jer. 31.9). With v. 16 cf. v. 4.

THE JUDGMENT OF THE FLOCK

34.17-22

In the preceding section, the shepherds oppressed the flock. Now, judgment (linking on with the same word in 16) is to be made within the flock itself (20.33-38 also speak of a judgment among the exiles). Yahweh is to judge between the individual sheep (SHEEP AND SHEEP, vv. 17, 22), who in v. 20 are classified as FAT and LEAN. The strong overreach the weak —as in 22.29, oppression by the rich and powerful. The end of v. 17 is not clear. The phrase RAMS AND HE-GOATS is most probably a gloss explaining FAT (strong).

19. 'Jahveh's sheep are the helpless and weak, as distinguished from the fat and the strong. The common rights of humanity are invaded by these selfish oppressors' (Cooke).

DAVID AS THE ONE SHEPHERD

34.23-24

Originally the verses were probably independent of what precedes them. Under Yahweh as shepherd, there is to be a human shepherd, David, who is to be their prince. This does not mean the historical David resurrected or *redivivus*, for the verb SET UP has no connections with raising from the dead (cf. Amos 9.11, the fallen booth of David; II Sam. 7.12, the seed of David). It means a king (less probably a line of kings) such as David was. Taken in conjunction with 37.21ff., ONE refers to the reunion of the divided nation in the restoration; there is to be one ruler over one people. His subordination to Yahweh, and the fact that he is to be no more than Yahweh's vice-regent, is secured by the use of the words SERVANT—a servant is at the complete disposal of his lord— and PRINCE, the latter avoiding the title king. (David is styled servant in II Kings 8.19; Ps. 89.3, 20.) The words AMONG THEM, not 'over them' or 'their prince', are also probably deliberate—he is to be one with his people.

24. AND I, THE LORD, WILL BE THEIR GOD (cf. 11.20; 37.27) is the covenant promise, cf. Ex. 29.45f.

With the passage cf. 17.22-24; 37.24-25.

THE COVENANT OF PEACE

34.25-31

'The word "peace" (came) to be practically a synonym of the word "covenant". "Peace" refers to the state of those who are united in harmonious society; "covenant" refers to the community and all the privileges and obligations which it implies. We are not surprised, therefore, to find the two words used together. "A covenant of peace" is merely a stronger expression for the covenant itself (Ezek. 34.25; 37.26; Isa. 54.10).'[2]

In the new age the covenant is to be restored, accompanied by ideal conditions in the land (Palestine). With the driving out of the WILD BEASTS, which would have multiplied during the depopulation of the exile, cf. Lev. 26.6; Isa. 11.6-8; 65.25; and, with a slight difference, Hos. 2.18. THE WILDERNESS is the uncultivated pasture-land. SLEEP IN THE WOODS: 'in ordinary times this would be dangerous, Jer. 5.6; Ps. 104.20f.' (Cooke).

26a. The text is uncertain, but THE PLACES ROUND ABOUT MY HILL (i.e. Zion) can scarcely be original, for the context is the security and fruitfulness of the land. With v. 27a (down to SECURE IN THEIR LAND) cf. Lev. 26.4; Amos 9.13f.; Zech. 8.12; also Ezek. 36.34f.; 47.1-12.

29. prosperous plantations   Perhaps 'a planting of salvation'.

[2] G. Ernest Wright, *The Challenge of Israel's Faith*, London, 1946, p. 94.

30. Omit WITH THEM (as LXX) and read 'that I, Yahweh, am their God'.

The conventional language of the passage and its connections with Lev. 26 suggest that it may be the composition of a disciple.

ORACLES AGAINST EDOM

35.1-15

An oracle against Edom has already been given in 25.12-14. The main reasons for a re-occurrence here are two. First, ch. 35 presupposes a later historical situation. The general terms of Edom's offence in 25.12-14 are now specifically defined as occupation of Judean territory after the fall of Jerusalem (vv. 10, 12; cf. 36.5). Secondly, ch. 35 is addressed to MOUNT SEIR (Edom) and ch. 36 to the 'mountains of Israel'. If the returned exiles are to dwell in their land in safety, then it must be cleared of foes (cf. also chs. 38, 39): the Edomites, who were in possession of large parts of it, and who also, of Israel's neighbours, had done most to harm her, must be driven out; and for Israel's security in the future, Edom itself must be made desolate.

It is difficult to say how far the oracles derive from Ezekiel himself. They use a considerable number of stock-phrases, and may be, largely at any rate, due to disciples.

2. set your face Cf. 6.2, SEIR (Edom): see on 25.12-14.

3. desolate 'The keynote of the oracle is *desolation*, which reaches its climax in 14-15' (Muilenburg).

5. The Edomites had clearly done service to the Babylonians in connection with the fall of Jerusalem (Obad. 10-15; Lam. 4.21f.; Ps. 137.7). But the history of enmity between the two peoples was of long standing (II Sam. 8.13f.; I Kings 11.14-22; Amos 1.11f.) and was even carried back to patriarchal times (Gen. 27.41-45; Num. 20.14ff.). With THE TIME OF THEIR FINAL PUNISHMENT cf. 21.29.

6. Edom will be treated according to the *lex talionis*; because it shed BLOOD, by cutting down fugitives and handing survivors over to the Babylonians (Obad. 14), its BLOOD must now be shed (Ziegler). The clause I WILL PREPARE YOU FOR BLOOD, AND BLOOD SHALL PURSUE YOU is absent in LXX and should be omitted.

7-8. Omission of v. 7 and the first clause of v. 8 (AND I WILL FILL YOUR (MT his) MOUNTAINS WITH THE SLAIN) would avoid the awkward changes of person. ALL WHO COME AND GO: 'a Hebrew idiom whereby two opposites denote totality. The slaughter of the Edomites will be complete' (Fisch).

10. As well as her perpetual enmity against her sister nation and her actions against her in 586 BC (v. 5), Edom laid claim to the territory of both Israel and Judah (THESE TWO COUNTRIES).

Although the Lord was there Although Yahweh had exiled Israel, the land still belonged to him, and not to those who remained behind (33.24-29) or to the Edomites. It was still at his disposal, and was destined for the exiles on their return, 36.8; 48.35. Some (e.g. Bertholet) by a slight change read 'and the Lord heard', (cf. 13), but this seems unnecessary. The text of v. 11 has probably been expanded (LXX is shorter).

12-13. Revilings That is, blasphemies, because the mountains belonged to Yahweh. Since Israel was still Yahweh's people, arrogance towards her was arrogance towards him.

14-15. Read: 'Thus says the Lord God: Since you rejoiced over my land because it was desolate, so will I deal with you;

you shall be desolate, Mount Seir and Edom together, and know that I am the Lord'.

Davidson notes that while Nebuchadnezzar was the 'servant' of God, Edom received no commission from him against his people.

TRANSFORMATION

36.1-38

The chapter falls into two sections, vv. 1-15, the transformation of the land of Israel, and vv. 16-38, the transformation of the people of Israel.

THE TRANSFORMATION OF THE LAND

36.1-15

Chapter 35 is addressed to the mountains of Edom, 36.1-15 to the mountains of Israel, from which the Edomites are to be dispossessed and to which the transformed Israel is to return. But 36.1-15 is also the counterpart of ch. 6, where the mountains of Israel have devastation prophesied for them because of the idolatrous worship there practised. Thus the chapter at the same time points forward to the restored and purified worship of chs. 40-48.

The text has been expanded, but there is no agreement as to the original. In vv. 1-7 it may have been no more than 1 and 2, 3b and 4a (from BECAUSE, YEA, BECAUSE THEY MADE YOU DESOLATE to THE RAVINES AND THE VALLEYS), and 7b (from I SWEAR THAT THE NATIONS . . .): so largely Hölscher, followed by Cooke.

2. the enemy Edom, Moab, Philistia and Tyre had all laid claim to part of desolate Israel (ch. 25; 26.2); they are THE REST OF THE NATIONS of vv. 3-5 and 7; but Edom and her land-grabbing (cf. 35.10, 12) are particularly in mind.

The ancient heights have become our possession Read with

LXX (cf. 35.9): 'A waste for ever! It has become our possession.'

3. made you desolate, and crushed you As the Versions show, the meaning is very uncertain. Ziegler renders: 'panted and snapped round about you.' AND YOU BECAME THE TALK, etc.: 'you have been slandered and abused by people' (Cooke).

5. jealousy ' "Jealousy" is injured self-consciousness; it is the reaction of Jehovah's sense of himself against the injurious conduct of Edom and the nations in relation to him or that which is his, cf. *my* land' (Davidson). In 23.25 Yahweh's jealousy makes him punish Israel (cf. 5.13); in 38.19ff. he acts in his jealousy in order to magnify and sanctify himself and make himself known; and in 39.25ff. jealousy for his holy name makes him restore Israel.

7. A strong oath.

8-15. The judgment of the nations surrounding Israel is followed by the restoration of the land itself. With the various signs of fruitfulness and fertility (cf. 47.1-12; Isa. 30.23-25; Hos. 2.21-23, etc.) we may contrast the darkness etc. which were the traditional accompaniments of the Day of Yahweh. That Day is now past, and the age of salvation is about to break.

8. For they will soon come home Exiled Israel is about to re-enter her land. In 4.6 the exile was to last forty years.

10. Israel, all of it As well as Judah, the former northern kingdom, exiled in 722, is to be restored, cf. 37.15ff. For the increase of population, also in 37.26, cf. Isa. 54.1-3; Zech. 2.2ff.

13-15. The land is compared to a wild beast that eats men,

cf. Num. 13.32. The prophet probably has the disasters of
722 and 586 in view. Zimmerli says that the oracle is
addressed to a fear that the same thing might happen after
the return. 'Yahweh's word indicates a future in which danger
from the land will be done away with.'

THE TRANSFORMATION OF THE PEOPLE

36.16-38

The passage is one of the most important in the book, for
it is one of the clearest statements of Ezekiel's theological
principles and his philosophy of history, cf. ch. 20.

Israel defiled her land by bloodshed and idolatry (vv. 17f.;
cf. ch. 22). Yahweh therefore drove her into exile (vv. 18-19).
'Thus the exile was necessary for the vindication of Jehovah's
holiness as reflected in the sanctity of His land' (Skinner).
But the exile itself profaned Yahweh's holy name, because the
nations among whom Israel was scattered concluded that he
had not had the power to keep his people safe (v. 20). Therefore, out of regard for his name, and in no sense for Israel's
own sake, he re-establishes his name's holiness by restoring
his people—the restoration will demonstrate that he does
have power, and the nations will thereby realize that he is not
one god among many, but the sole God and a moral God
(vv. 21-24). But it must not be a non-moral restoration. Since
the cause of Israel's punishment was her sin, she must hence-
forth be a transformed Israel, an Israel that, in the prosperity
of the land to which she is restored, will look back on her old
self with loathing (vv. 25-31). The end of all this is recognition
by the heathen of Yahweh's power and lordship (v. 36).

17. The LAND was holy because it belonged to Yahweh. For
the sentiment, cf. Jer. 2.7. IN HER IMPURITY: cf. 18.6; Lev.

15.19ff. The term expresses very strong repugnance, and here refers to idolatry, as the following verse shows. With v. 18 cf. 16.36; 22.2; 33.25ff.

20. The nations among whom they were settled in exile concluded that Yahweh had been unable to save them, cf. Deut. 9.28. Thus again, and this time by no volition of their own, their idolatry was such that they brought their God's prestige into disrepute. 'Sin is not only evil in itself, but it compels God to do what men are bound to misunderstand. God's name is profaned not only when his people sin, but when they force him to punish them. Cf. 20.9; 22.16; 39.7' (Lofthouse). (It is not here a question of moral iniquity by Israel in exile such as might have shocked her pagan neighbours.)

22. It is not for your sake, O house of Israel, that I am about to act Cf. Isa. 43.22-28. The reason for Israel's restoration, which is the act referred to, had to be made perfectly clear: it was not for any merit of hers. 'This act of power will convince the nations that Jahveh is no mere tribal deity, but the only supreme and holy God. Underlying the argument are the great conceptions that the revelation of the true God is conveyed through the history of Israel, and that God's ultimate purpose is to reveal Himself to all the world. In the NT these ideas are carried still further; e.g. Eph. 1.3-10' (Cooke). 'Here too all gentle traits and warmer tones are lacking in Ezekiel. There is no talk of mercy, love, loyalty to the covenant, God's righteousness that makes for salvation' (Zimmerli).

25-29a. Inward purification. If Yahweh's name is to be seen as holy, his people too must be holy. The background to v. 25 is probably such purificatory rites as are mentioned in Num. 19. But the transformation (vv. 26f.) is radical. The heart is the seat of thought and willing, and a NEW HEART is equivalent

to a new nature, one no longer insensible to the divine leading
(OF STONE), but a heart OF FLESH, 'no longer ungrateful for so
many benefits received . . . but tender and obedient, turned
to him' (Spadafora). SPIRIT means principle of action, cf. Isa.
32.15; Zech. 4.6. With vv. 26f. cf. 11.19f., and also Jer.
31.31-34.

28. The reaffirmation of the promise to the patriarchs, e.g.
Gen. 12.2 (cf. 28.25; 37.25), and, since the last clause is the
covenant formula, the renewal of the covenant or a new
covenant (cf. Jer. 31.31-34, just referred to).

29a. And I will deliver you from all your uncleannesses 'The
nation's tendency to lapse into sin will be overcome by the
power of the new spirit' (Fisch).

29b-30. God's blessing will have as its outward sign abundant
material prosperity. SUMMON THE GRAIN: cf. Hos. 2.21ff. and
II Kings 8.1. THE DISGRACE OF FAMINE AMONG THE NATIONS:
cf. 34.29.

32a. The motive of the divine action is again stressed at what
was originally the end of this section.

33-36. An appendix adding two details to the picture already
given: (a) the rebuilding of the towns and villages destroyed
in 586, and (b) a further insight by the nations (THEY, v. 35)
into the power and faithfulness of Yahweh. The term EDEN
perhaps suggests that all this is the act of God rather than
of man.

37-38. A second appendix. LIKE THE FLOCK FOR SACRIFICES,
LIKE THE FLOCK AT JERUSALEM DURING HER APPOINTED
FEASTS: this was a natural simile for a priest like Ezekiel.
At the dedication of the temple, Solomon (according to I

Kings 8.63) offered a sacrifice of 22,000 oxen and 120,000 sheep, and at his passover Josiah (according to II Chron. 35.7) gave 30,000 lambs and kids, and 3,000 bullocks, in addition to those given by others. The figures are too high, but the number of animals sacrificed each year at the temple must have been very great. For the increase of population see v. 10; Isa. 49.19ff.; 54.1-3; Zech. 2.1ff. I WILL LET THE HOUSE OF ISRAEL ASK ME: cf. 14.3; 20.3, 31.

It will be noticed that Ezekiel is not perfectly consistent in his thought. Previously he spoke of Yahweh as dealing with individuals, and of individual responsibility (18.1-32; 34.17-22), but now it is of the nation as the unit, and of conversion by God's grace alone. The experience of the exile may have led him to take a more pessimistic view of human nature. While there is no evidence of this, the exiles in Babylon may have fallen back into idolatry as did those in Egypt (Jer. 44). So Ezekiel may have come to believe, like Jeremiah, that, if there were to be transformation, it could only come by the action of Yahweh in creating a new human nature. See also notes on ch. 18.

THE VALLEY OF DRY BONES

37.1-14

The starting-point of this, the best-known of Ezekiel's visions, is the saying of the exiles in v. 11: OUR BONES ARE DRIED UP, AND OUR HOPE IS LOST; WE ARE CLEAN CUT OFF. 'The expression, "my bone", means in Hebrew "my force" and often "myself" in the deepest sense. OUR BONES ARE DRIED UP signifies "we are enfeebled, worn away to the point of crumbling".[3] The verb 'cut off' is used of cutting off from life in Isa. 53.8, and from the hand of God in Ps. 88.5. The exiles thus considered themselves as good as dead, forsaken by Yahweh, and with no future to look forward to. But the phrase 'our bones' leads to Ezekiel's seeing in a visionary experience a great battlefield (SLAIN, v. 9) where the dead had been left unburied, and the bones were now bare. This is the nation of Israel. But Yahweh has the power to make these dead bones live, to revive his people (and restore them to their land, if vv. 12-14 are genuine, see below). The vision is therefore a parable of national rebirth (and not an announcement of the resurrection of the dead). It probably dates from the earlier part of the exile, before Ezekiel's prophecies of weal had begun to have any real effect.

1. THE VALLEY, cf. 3.22 (RSV margin). THE HAND OF THE LORD signifies ecstatic experience.

---

[3] Steinmann, referring for the first sentence to P. Dhorme, *Le sens métaphorique des noms de parties du corps en hébreu et en akkadien*, Paris, 1923, pp. 9-10.

2. MANY suggests the magnitude of the disaster that had over-taken the nation, as VERY DRY suggests the utter hopelessness of the exiles; cf. also FULL in 1.

3. The prophet's answer means 'humanly speaking, no'. But while Israel had as yet no doctrine of the resurrection of the dead, cf. Job 14.14 (Dan. 12.2-3 and Isa. 26.19 are both later than Ezekiel), Yahweh was known as a God who could call the dead back to life: I Kings 17.17-24; II Kings 4.32-37. Thus, THOU KNOWEST could also mean 'It is possible for thee'.

4. 'The prophet now suddenly changes from being the mouthpiece of human impotence to the mouthpiece full of divine potency' (Zimmerli).

5. 'The act of putting breath within them, being the main and final step of giving them life, is mentioned first as if it embraced all' (Davidson).

7-10. Note the vividness of the description. The RATTLING (v. 7) has been interpreted as an earthquake (so LXX), but is more probably the RATTLING as bone joined bone to form human frames.

9. The four winds The four quarters of the globe, cf. Dan. 8.8; etc. UPON: rather 'into', cf. Gen. 2.7.

11-14. The explanation of the vision. THE WHOLE HOUSE OF ISRAEL means Ephraim as well as Judah, cf. vv. 15, 22. Verses 12-14 are probably later, the addition of a disciple who had met the new idea of a resurrection from the dead. GRAVES have no part in vv. 1-11.

14. my Spirit As in 36.27, Yahweh's spirit, and not the breath of life.

I

THE TWO STICKS

37.15-28

Israel and Judah are to be reunited under one sovereign.
Yahweh also makes an everlasting covenant with them and
his sanctuary will be re-established among them. The way is
thus prepared for the vision of the new temple in chs. 40-48.

In spite of the division of the kingdom after Solomon and
the fall of the northern kingdom in 722, the idea of one Israel
was never lost sight of. Jeremiah also thinks of the reunion
of Israel and Judah, e.g. 3.18.

15-19 (20). *A symbolic action*

The prophet is to take two sticks, to inscribe the one FOR
JUDAH, AND THE CHILDREN OF ISRAEL ASSOCIATED WITH HIM,
and the other FOR JOSEPH, AND ALL THE HOUSE OF ISRAEL
ASSOCIATED WITH HIM. The parenthesis (THE STICK OF
EPHRAIM) is a gloss. He is then to join the two together. The
STICKS are probably rulers' staffs, sceptres. See the development of the idea in Zech. 11.7ff. ASSOCIATED: the southern
kingdom, Judah, included, as well as the tribe of Judah, parts
of Simeon and Benjamin (cf. II Chron. 11.10, 12). To begin
with Israel was the name of the northern tribes (II Sam.
19.41), but it also came to be used for the whole nation (I
Sam. 13.13). EPHRAIM, descended from Joseph's son of the
same name, was the most important tribe in the northern
kingdom, and here stands for it.

18. The prophet said nothing as he did the action, hence an
explanation is demanded.

20. Almost certainly a gloss.

21-28. *Some of the main elements in Ezekiel's hopes for the*

future. With vv. 21-23 cf. 36.23f. With v. 23 cf. 36.25. With
v. 24 cf. 34.23f. With v. 25 cf. 28.25; 36.28. With v. 26 cf.
34.25; 36.26f.; also 40.1-43.9.

28. Mention of THE NATIONS leads on to chs. 38-39. 'The
presence of his sanctuary in their midst is a pledge that the
covenant has been renewed, and because of it the nations will
see that Yahweh has sanctified his people and has set them
apart' (Muilenburg). 'To sanctify is not to protect, it is to
make his people his own and worthy of him, but this implies
protection' (Davidson).

GOG

38.1–39.20

Between the announcement in 37.26 that Yahweh is to set his sanctuary in the midst of the restored community and the detailed description of that sanctuary in 40ff. comes, unexpectedly, a section relating an invasion of Israel by heathen hordes led by Gog AFTER MANY DAYS, IN THE LATTER DAYS (38.8, 16), that is, a long time after the restoration. This final invasion will however be terribly repulsed by Yahweh, in order that he may vindicate his holiness, and the nations know that Israel was punished for her sins. Thereafter Israel will dwell in peace: AND I WILL NOT HIDE MY FACE ANY MORE FROM THEM (39.29).

38.17 runs: THUS SAYS THE LORD GOD: ARE YOU HE (*sc.* Gog) OF WHOM I SPOKE IN FORMER DAYS BY MY SERVANTS THE PROPHETS OF ISRAEL, WHO IN THOSE DAYS PROPHESIED FOR YEARS THAT I WOULD BRING YOU AGAINST THEM? At least two earlier bodies of prophecy are here taken up and actualized: first, Jer. 1.13f.; 4.6; 13.20, dealing with the foe from the north (Gog and his hordes come from THE NORTH, 38.6; 39.2; and cf. 38.9, 16 with Jer. 4.13) and, secondly, Isa. 14.24ff., where Assyria is to be trodden underfoot on the mountains of Israel —Gog comes against the mountains of Israel in 38.8; 39.2, and there falls, 39.4, 17. Isaiah also resumes a Zion tradition, in which God's enemies who attack Zion are dashed to pieces.[1] The exilic age had a keen interest in earlier prophecy and its fulfilment (cf. Zech. 1.4-6), and these prophecies from Isaiah and Jeremiah are here taken up and given a further reference.

[1] See G. von Rad, *Old Testament Theology* II, pp. 155-169, and A. R. Johnson, *Sacral Kingship in Ancient Israel*, Cardiff, 1955, pp. 77-93.

Other earlier motifs from the holy wars are also included in the chapters.

Who was Gog? And what is the land of Magog from which he comes? It is impossible to discuss the question in a small commentary like this. Gog has been taken to be:

(*a*) A single historical figure, such as Gagi, a chief who lived in the north of Assyria, the Lydian King Gyges (c. 605), Alexander the Great, Antiochus Eupator, etc.

(*b*) Collectively, the Scythians, the Cimmerians or the Babylonians. (It has been noted [see on ch. 25] that Ezekiel has no oracle against the Babylonians: this could be it, under a cryptogram.)

(*c*) A Babylonian god Gaga, mentioned in Enuma Elish III.11.

(*d*) Connected with the Sumerian 'gug', darkness.

A leader Gog may have been connected with the 'foe from the north' in prophecies and traditions now lost. At all events, he here represents the almost demonic leader of the final assault of the heathen on God's people—'the anti-god who represents the Nebuchadnezzar of the Books of Daniel and Judith, the "beast" of Revelation' (Steinmann). In Christian tradition the 'many days' of chs. 38-39 became the thousand years of Christ's reign before the last attack on the Church, Rev. 20.2-9. With 39.2, 4, 17-20 cf. Rev. 16.16, 19, 17f.

The chapters contain repetitions and contradictions, and may be a combination of parallel versions. Recent criticism (e.g. Fohrer, Howie, Zimmerli) is less ready to deny absolutely the genuineness of chs. 38-39, and finds a kernel of the prophet's own which has been expanded.

INTRODUCTION

38.1-2

2. On MESECH AND TUBAL see on 27.13. THE LAND OF MAGOG :
almost certainly delete.

GOG AND HIS HOST

38.3-9

4. I will turn you about (cf. 39.2) **and put hooks in your
jaws** (cf. 29.4). If the text is genuine, it must mean that Yahweh
is to compel Gog to march against Israel. But the words are
better omitted.

5. See on 27.10. But PERSIA, CUSH AND PUT, the lands mentioned, do not suit a foe from THE NORTH. The verse should
be omitted.

6. Gomer Mentioned in Gen. 10.2; I Chron. 1.5, along with
Magog. They are probably Cimmerians living by the Black
Sea in Cappadocia. BETH-TOGARMAH : see on 27.14.

7. For BE A GUARD FOR THEM read rather : 'Be at my disposal.'

8. the land that is restored from war The land that is
restored from desolation.

9. like a storm Cf. Isa. 10.3; Dan. 11.40. LIKE A CLOUD : cf.
Jer. 4.13. (Gog's troops are horsemen, vv. 4, 15.)

GOG'S PLOT

38.10-13

In vv. 4-9 Yahweh brings up Gog, in vv. 10-13 the move is Gog's own, to plunder. There is, however, no necessary inconsistency, for see Isa. 10.5-15, where Yahweh commands the king of Assyria to take spoil, while the latter boasts, 'By the strength of my hand I have done it.' Cf. also Jer. 25.9-12.

11. The undefined objective is specified in 14-16. 36.35 speaks of the cities as walled, but Zech. 2.4 speaks of cities without walls. NO BARS OR GATES: cf. Jer. 49.31.

12. At the centre of the earth At the navel of the earth, see on 5.5. Israel's central position in the world 'is mentioned to stress the viciousness of Gog's plan. He dwelt in the far north, a great distance from the Land of Israel; so the people of the latter could have had no aggressive designs upon him' (Fisch).

13. Sheba, etc., see on 27.12, 20, 22. 'The traders follow the army to buy the spoil from them and trade further with it, cf. I Macc. 3.41' (Ziegler). 'Their primary motive is the economic one, frequently at the base of conquest whatever its rationalization or justification' (Howie).

THE BATTLE

38.14-16

Neither Fohrer nor Zimmerli regards the passage, which describes Gog's attack and the destruction of his hordes, as original.

15. Cf. vv. 4, 6.

16. Cf. v. 9. 'Jehovah shows his great deeds in the sight of the nations, and thus they recognize his Godhead, cf. v. 23' (Davidson). He vindicates his holiness through Gog, as 'the object on whom his great operations of power are manifested' (*ibid.*).

THE DESTRUCTION OF GOG

38.17-23

17. See introduction to chs. 38-39 above. Read with the Versions 'You and he' and omit FOR YEARS. IN FORMER DAYS: in the eighth and seventh centuries. They are the 'former prophets' of Zech. 1.4.

18. my wrath will be aroused Lit. 'my fury shall come up in my nostril.'

19. Earthquakes accompany the appearance of Yahweh when he comes in judgment, I Kings 19.11; Amos 8.8; Micah 1.4; Joel 3.16; Nahum 1.5; Hab. 3.6f.; Zech. 14.5.

20. A panic sent by Yahweh used to come upon Israel's enemies in the old holy wars. With the fourfold division of the animal world cf. Gen. 9.2. For the phraseology cf. Gen. 1.25-26; 8.17. THE CLIFFS: elsewhere only in S. of S. 2.14, where it is parallel to 'rock'.

21b. Cf. Judg. 7.22; I Sam. 14.20; Zech. 14.13.

22. With pestilence and bloodshed Cf. 5.16f. RAINS AND HAILSTONES: cf. Ex. 9.13-35; Josh. 10.11. FIRE AND BRIM-

STONE, cf. Gen. 19.24; Isa. 34.9; Job 18.15. With v. 23 cf.
28.22. The destruction of Gog will show the nations that
Yahweh is all powerful.

THE DEATH OF GOG

39.1-5

Ch. 39 is closely connected with ch. 38. It gives a fuller
and more vivid account of the destruction of Gog and his
hordes.

Zimmerli regards this section as original.

1-2. Cf. 38.2-3a.

3. The foe from the north in Jeremiah is armed with bows
and arrows (Jer. 4.29; 6.23), as are also the Assyrians in Isa.
5.28.

4. It shamed the dead if they were not buried, and so became
a prey to birds and animals (cf. 6.5-7; I Sam. 17.44; I Kings
21.23; Jer. 7.33). Until they were, the soul had no rest. With
the fate of Gog and his hordes cf. that of the dragon in 29.5.
Verse 4 is taken up again in vv. 17-20.

6-8. A later addition. SECURELY: without any apprehension.
Not only Gog and his army, but also the lands from which
they are drawn, are to be destroyed. THE COASTLANDS are
those of the Black Sea. Gog's destruction brings recognition
of Yahweh's power both in Israel and among the Gentiles.

THE BURNING OF THE WEAPONS

39.9-10

seven years That is, 'many years', cf. SEVEN MONTHS in v.
1*

12. MAKE FIRES OF THEM: use them as fuel. This shows the immense multitudes that had gathered against Israel. It is to be noted that in the state of security assured by God, the weapons themselves serve no useful purpose, and are not gathered and stored for a future war.

THE BURIAL OF GOG

39.11-16

A later expansion.

11. For A PLACE FOR BURIAL read, 'a place of renown as burial place'. THE VALLEY OF THE TRAVELLERS EAST OF THE SEA: THE SEA is the Dead Sea. THE VALLEY OF THE TRAVELLERS represents the Hebrew text. Many read with Coptic 'the valley of Abarim', a valley in the mountains east of Jordan which included Mount Nebo, the burial place of Moses—see Num. 21.11; 33.47f.; Deut. 32.49. But there is no certainty. IT WILL BLOCK THE TRAVELLERS: again the meaning is uncertain. HAMON-GOG means the multitude of Gog.

12-13. As in v. 9, SEVEN indicates the immensity of the numbers of the slain. Bloodshed defiled Yahweh's land (cf. 36.18), and contact with the dead brought pollution (Num. 19.11ff.). ALL THE PEOPLE OF THE LAND: the whole population, again emphasizing the huge numbers. IT WILL REDOUND TO THEIR HONOUR: meaning uncertain. Davidson says: 'or [their] *glory* (lit. a name), viz. that they have seen their last enemy destroyed by their God. The triumph is theirs, being his, Ps. 149.9.'

14-15. A further regulation, reflecting the horror of the post-exilic age at ceremonial defilement. After the SEVEN MONTHS are over, a special body is to be appointed to keep going THROUGH THE LAND and SEARCH for any that remain unburied. When they find a bone, they are to mark the place, so that a burial party may take it away for burial.

16a. A gloss. HAMONAH: the root is that of 'multitude'.

A SACRIFICIAL FEAST

39.17-20

The verses are probably original, and a continuation of v. 4. Instead of being buried (11-16), the corpses are eaten by birds and beasts. In Isa. 34.5-8 the destruction of Edom is represented as a gruesome sacrifice, cf. also Jer. 46.10; 48.15; 50.26f.; and Rev. 19.17f., 21. 'To an Israelite, the sacrifice here described is a grim parody of the true sacrifice, since the "guests" drink the blood, a rite absolutely forbidden in Israel' (Lofthouse). Yahweh's 'guests' are the birds and beasts of prey.

18. the princes of the earth Gog is not now mentioned, and the leaders of the Gentiles seem rather to be envisaged. For the post-exilic attitude of ruthlessness towards the Gentiles, so different from that of Deutero-Isaiah, see Zech. 14.12-15. OF RAMS, OF LAMBS, . . . FATLINGS OF BASHAN: if the words are original, 'the bodies to be devoured are spoken of as though they were the choicest sacrificial victims' (Cooke). Bashan, east of Jordan, was noted for its pasture and its cattle (Deut. 32.14; Amos 4.1; Ps. 22.12).

20. my table Yahweh is the giver of the feast. RIDERS is not suitable; read 'beasts for riding'.

A SUMMARY

39.21-29

The verses have no connection with the Gog apocalypse.
Verses 21-24 summarize Ezekiel's teaching: because of the
judgment, all the Gentile nations will realize that it was not
for lack of power on Yahweh's part that Israel was taken into
exile or slain, but as a punishment for their sins. Verses 25-29
bring nothing new, cf. 20.41; 28.25; 36.22f.

27. For MANY NATIONS read 'the nations'.

IV

THE FUTURE TEMPLE AND COMMUNITY

40.1–48.35

The last nine chapters of the book describe the new temple to be established in Jerusalem, its sacrificial worship and personnel, the duties and privileges of the prince, the apportionment of the land, and some other matters affecting the life of the restored community. They form the climax of all that has gone before. This vision is very closely linked up with two earlier visions: (*a*) that of the profanation of the temple (chs. 8–11), which culminates in the departure of the glory of Yahweh from the temple and city, and (*b*) that of the glory which appeared to the prophet beside the Chebar (1–3.15). In 43.1-9 the glory returns to the temple to await the return of the exiles, and the regulations given in 40–48 are designed to preserve the holiness of the temple and community, and to preclude future profanation such as had been the cause of the exile. For, although Israel now has a new heart and a new spirit, there can be, in addition to possible moral lapses, sins of inadvertence and offences against ritual purity.

The chapters display a curious blend of the supernatural and the severely practical. Ezekiel takes up the idea, found also in Isaiah and Micah, of the physical elevation of Mount Zion above the other mountains. He also speaks of the river that is to issue from the temple and fertilize the country round about and sweeten the Dead Sea. At the same time we find precise legal regulations, and the exact measurements of

269

an architect. This makes an almost unique literary genre. It
may also help towards answering the question whether the
section is a blueprint for the temple as it was to be restored
when the time came. No doubt the writer (or writers) had
Solomon's temple in mind. But much more probably the
chapters sketch an ideal temple for a (purged and) ideal
Israel. Hence the combination of natural and supernatural.

The section is full of difficulties—much is obscure, there
are contradictions not only of the Pentateuchal laws but
apparently of things said in 1-39, the order is obviously disturbed, and terms are used which do not occur elsewhere. It
is also universally agreed that the chapters are not a unity,
and that the larger part of the material is much later than
Ezekiel.

THE NEW TEMPLE

40.1-43.11

INTRODUCTION

40.1-5

In ecstasy (THE HAND OF THE LORD WAS UPON ME, see on 1.3), Ezekiel is transported from Babylonia to Palestine and set on a high mountain, probably Zion, idealized as in Isa. 2.2; Micah 4.1; Zech. 14.10; cf. Matt. 4.8; Rev. 21.10. He comes from the north and sees on the mountain A STRUCTURE LIKE A CITY opposite him (so LXX for MT on the south). The temple and its environs are meant. There he is met by a heavenly figure whose appearance was like bronze, i.e. a radiant figure, but less splendid than the one in 8.2, whose appearance was like fire, cf. Zech. 1.9ff.; Dan. 10.18. This being, who is to be the prophet's guide, holds a cord of flax, for measuring large dimensions (47.3; Zech. 2.1), and a reed about nine feet long for shorter ones. Ezekiel is told to pay close heed to all that he is about to be shown, for he has to give an account of it to his people.

1. In the twenty-fifth year That is 572 BC. AT THE BEGINNING OF THE YEAR: Lev. 25.9 suggests that the year is the ecclesiastical year which began in the autumn. New Year's Day was 10 Tishri. The civil year began in spring.

5. The verse is probably not original, and the meaning of the clause IN THE MAN'S HAND . . . HANDBREADTH IN LENGTH is uncertain.

THE OUTER EAST GATE

40.6-16

The temple lay east and west, and the eastern gate was its main entrance. 'There is an amazing resemblance between this gate and the Solomonic gate at Megiddo, even to the extent that many of the measurements are almost identical.'[1] Yahweh was to return to the temple through it (43.4).

6. The temple area was higher than the surrounding land, therefore the GATEWAY had steps up to it, in number seven, according to LXX. Cf. vv. 22, 26 for the north and the south gateways. The gateway, which means the whole structure, had a threshold, that is, a space between the top step and the entrance into the vestibule of the gate, one reed, i.e. nine feet, long, the thickness of the outer wall, v. 5.

7. Within the passageway of the gate were six SIDE ROOMS, THREE ON EITHER SIDE (v. 10), ONE REED LONG AND ONE REED BROAD (cf. v. 12). These were guard rooms for the Levitical guard to control crowds at festivals, I Kings 14.28; cf. 44.11. They had no doors, but only a BARRIER, v. 12. The masonry between the side rooms, called in vv. 10 and 16 the JAMB, was five cubits in length. At the far end of the passageway of the gate was another threshold leading to the vestibule of the gate which opened on to the outer court of the Temple.

10. See on 7.

11-12. For THE BREADTH OF THE GATEWAY, THIRTEEN CUBITS, which contradicts v. 15, which gives fifty cubits as the breadth

[1] Howie, *The Date and Composition of Ezekiel*, p. 45.

of the gateway, we should probably read 'the passageway of
the gate', the passage down the gateway at its full breadth
between the jambs.

12. a barrier before the side rooms Perhaps a low parapet
one cubit broad before each end projecting into the passageway, on which the Levites could stand to control the crowd.
Each side room was SIX CUBITS (i.e. nine feet) square (cf. v. 7).

13. Twenty-five cubits was the overall width of the gateway
—'i.e. 1 cub. (thickness of outer wall)+6 (guard-room)+11
(passage)+6+1=25' (Cooke). (The length is given in v. 15 as
fifty cubits.) The side chambers had doors at the back opening on to the outer court. Verse 14 is extremely corrupt.
RSV, following the suggestion of LXX, thinks of a vestibule
leading into the outer court, twenty cubits wide.

16. The meaning is that the back walls of the side chambers
and the vestibule had windows let into them to lighten the
passageway. The form these had is not clear. WINDOWS
NARROWING INWARDS (Heb. 'closed'): cf. 41.16, 26 and I
Kings 6.4. On the JAMBS were palm trees, stone orthostats
with reliefs of palm trees, a common motif, used also in
Solomon's temple, I Kings 6.29-35.

THE OUTER COURT

40.17-19

Inside the outer wall is the OUTER COURT, the place where
the people assembled for worship. Abutting from the wall is
A PAVEMENT which runs round the court. Verse 18 means that
the pavement was as wide as the length of the gates, i.e. fifty
cubits (v. 15). It is called the LOWER PAVEMENT to distinguish
it from the higher pavement in the inner court, cf. 41.8; II

Chron. 7.3. (Each successive elevation represents an increasing degree of holiness.) It is not said how the THIRTY CHAMBERS, which seem to have been its only buildings, were disposed. They were for the use of the well-off laity, cf. Jer. 35.2, who might eat sacrificial family meals in them. The four corners of the wall held kitchens (46.21-24).

19. Measuring from the INNER FRONT OF THE EAST (LOWER) GATE TO THE OUTER FRONT OF THE INNER COURT, the outer court, which ran round the inner court, was one hundred cubits. The east gate was eight steps lower than the gate of the inner court, v. 31.

THE NORTH AND SOUTH GATES OF THE OUTER COURT

40.20-27

There was no west gate, since the temple, which faced east, had no rear entrance.

The north and south gates had the same measurements as the east gate (cf. vv. 6-16). In v. 20 read with LXX 'Then he led me to the north, and behold, a gateway that looked, etc.' In 22, read 'its windows, and the windows of its vestibule'. The gates were one hundred cubits distant from one another, and both had opposite them a gate leading into the inner court.

THE INNER COURT

40.28-47

The inner court was reserved exclusively for the priests.

28-37. *The gates of the inner court*

The south (28-31), east (32-34) and north (35-37) gates of
the inner court are identical with and have the same measurements as the corresponding outer gates, that is fifty by twenty-
five cubits. They have, however, eight steps (vv. 31, 34, 37)
instead of seven (vv. 22, 26) leading up to the vestibule. (Verse
30 is unintelligible.) The vestibules abutted on the outer court,
and were thus at the opposite end of the gates from those of
the gates of the outer court.

38-43. *Tables for sacrifice*

The verses are secondary. The text of 38 is uncertain, but
RSV may well be correct. It is not stated which of the gateways is meant, but on the basis of 46.1-2, many think of the
east gate. The intestines and legs of burnt offerings—'the
parts naturally rendered unclean' (Cooke)—had to be washed
before they were brought to the altar, Lev. 1.9.

39. There were four TABLES in the vestibule, TWO ON EITHER
SIDE, for the slaughter of the animals ('Possibly the words "to
slay thereon" are used generally, not of the actual slaughtering, but of the manipulation of the flesh of the victims'
[Davidson]). The BURNT OFFERING was completely burnt up
on the altar. In the case of the other offerings, part of the
flesh was eaten by the offerers and by the priests. For the
various offerings see Lev. 1-7. Verse 40a is obscure, but
seems to mean that outside this east gate were four more
tables, two to the north and two to the south, used, as suggested by v. 41, which is probably a gloss, for slaughtering.
Verse 42 speaks of FOUR more TABLES OF HEWN STONE,
smaller in size than those of vv. 39-41, on which the instruments used for sacrifice were kept. Verse 43 is also obscure.
The first part probably means a rim a handbreadth high round
the edges of the tables to stop instruments from falling off.
In the second part the LXX is often adopted: 'over the

tables above was an awning to protect from rain and
heat.'

44-47. *Two chambers on the north and south*

44. The prophet is now brought INTO THE INNER COURT, where
he sees TWO CHAMBERS which are reserved for the priests who
minister at the altar. This service is more nearly defined in
44.11 as slaying the burnt offering and offering sacrifice for
the people. The priests had also to provide the incense, oil
and lamps.

These higher priests who serve the altar are designated as
Zadokites. Ezekiel makes a distinction between the Levites
in general and the Zadokites (43.19; 44.5–45.5). Zadok was
a priest in the time of David (II Sam. 15.24; I Kings 1.8), and
was made high priest by Solomon in place of Abiathar (I
Kings 2.35). He was descended from the family of Eleazar,
the son of Aaron, I Chron. 24.1-6. Many regard v. 46, which
anticipates 43.19; 44.15-16 (see notes there), as secondary.

47. The inner court is a square. AND THE ALTAR WAS IN FRONT
OF THE TEMPLE: this altar is described in 43.13-17.

THE VESTIBULE OF THE TEMPLE

40.48-49

We now come to the temple itself, and the verses describe
its vestibule on its east front. The PILLARS BESIDE THE JAMBS
—either flanking the jambs or in front of them—correspond
to the pillars Jachin and Boaz of Solomon's temple (I Kings

7.15-22). Josiah stood by one of them when he made his covenant, II Kings 23.3.[2]

Thus, the inner court was higher than the outer court, and the temple itself higher than the inner court.

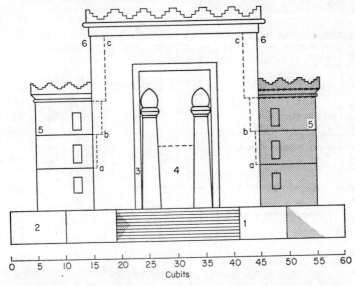

1. Ten steps, 40.49 2. Platform, 41.8 3. Pillars (the 'jambs' are at the side of them), 40.49 4. Entrance (the dotted line represents the entrance to the most holy place), 41.3 5. Walls of the three–storeyed side–chambers (the dotted lines a–b–c represent the offsets in the walls), 41.6 6. Level of window along side of temple, 41.16

THE NEW TEMPLE

[2] For further information on the pillars, see R. B. Y. Scott, 'The Pillars of Jachin and Boaz', *JBL* 58, 1939, pp. 143-9; H. G. May, 'The Two Pillars before the Temple of Solomon', *BASOR* 88, 1942, pp. 19-27.

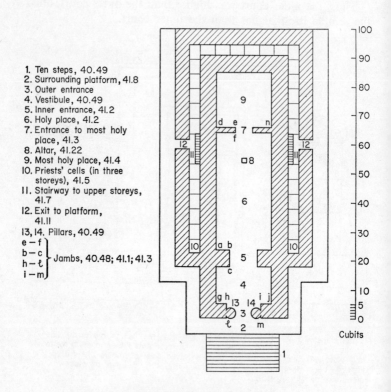

1. Ten steps, 40.49
2. Surrounding platform, 41.8
3. Outer entrance
4. Vestibule, 40.49
5. Inner entrance, 41.2
6. Holy place, 41.2
7. Entrance to most holy place, 41.3
8. Altar, 41.22
9. Most holy place, 41.4
10. Priests' cells (in three storeys), 41.5
11. Stairway to upper storeys, 41.7
12. Exit to platform, 41.11
13, 14. Pillars, 40.49

e − f
b − c
h − ℓ   } Jambs, 40.48; 41.1; 41.3
i − m

THE NEW TEMPLE

I am grateful for permission to reproduce this diagram and the preceding one from W. F. Lofthouse's commentary on *Ezekiel* in the Century Bible series, published by T. C. and E. C. Jack, Edinburgh, 1907, pp. 300f.

THE TEMPLE ITSELF

41.1-26

THE DIMENSIONS OF THE TEMPLE

41.1-4

(Much is obscure in ch. 41.)

Following the pattern of ancient Near Eastern sanctuaries, the temple had three parts, the vestibule ('*ūlām*), which has just been described, the nave (*hēkāl*), and the most holy place (*dᵉbīr*).[3] This type of building originated in Phoenicia or Syria, and it was from Phoenicia that Solomon got workers for the construction of his temple (I Kings 5.18).

The prophet is now brought to the *hēkāl*, the holy place, the main room of the temple. The guide measures the jambs projecting on either side of the entrance.

2. The sides of the door are THE SIDEWALLS OF THE ENTRANCE, FIVE CUBITS ON EITHER SIDE. The nave itself was a rectangle forty cubits long by twenty broad, i.e. about seventy by thirty-five feet. These measurements are the same as those of Solomon's temple, I Kings 6.2, 17. Nothing is said of the height. In I Kings 6.2 Solomon's was thirty cubits high (twenty-five cubits in LXX).

3. the inner room The *dᵉbīr* (from Arabic *dbr*, back), THE MOST HOLY PLACE. The angel alone enters it, for though Ezekiel was a priest and therefore had access to the nave, only

---

[3] On the subject see G. E. Wright, 'The Significance of the Temple in the Ancient Near East: Part III. The Temple in Palestine-Syria', *BA* VII (1944), pp. 65-77.

the high priest might enter the most holy place, and that only
once a year, on the Day of Atonement, Lev. 16. The entrance
to the most holy place was four cubits narrower than that of
the nave, signifying increasing holiness. The place itself is
square, of the same dimensions as the holy of holies in Solomon's temple, I Kings 6.20. In the latter the holy of holies was
higher than the nave, but Ezekiel says nothing of this.

THE SIDE CHAMBERS

41.5-11

The text is very difficult and often quite unclear. Space
allows of only a few comments. The general sense is that the
wall of the temple, i.e. of the nave and the most holy place,
was flanked, like that of Solomon's, on all sides except the
east by a three-storied building, four cubits wide, which in
turn was surrounded by a wall of five cubits (cf. v. 9). Neither
the number nor the purpose of these side rooms is clear.
Verse 6 suggests that there were THIRTY IN EACH STORY, which
would make them very small; their use may have been to
store temple furnishings or gifts. 6b and 7 are obscure, but
RSV gives the sense. The outer wall of the temple narrowed
as it went up, being six cubits broad at the bottom, five cubits
at the floor of the second story, and four at the third, cf.
Solomon's temple, I Kings 6.5f. These OFFSETS or rebate-
ments supported the beams of the side chambers, to avoid
holes being let into the wall. 'This structural formation is to
keep the side chambers from infringing on the greater sanctity
of the walls of the nave and inner room' (May). The offsets
made the rooms of the second story one cubit larger than
those of the first, and those of the third one cubit larger than
those of the second. In 7b RSV suggests that there was a
stairway leading up, but ladders are more probable.

8-11. The temple stood on a RAISED PLATFORM (cf. John 19.13) six cubits higher than the level of the inner court. Round about this in turn there seems to have been on the north, south and west sides, a yard. On the north and south sides there was access from the platform to the side chambers. But the verses are very obscure.

12. The building that was facing the temple yard on the west side This may only have been an open court, since it would be difficult to roof such a large building without pillars. Its use is not stated, but many think it may have been the stalls for the horses dedicated to the sun and removed by Josiah, II Kings 23.11. It may be the same as the building called the '*parbar*' in I Chron. 26.18.

OVERALL MEASUREMENT OF THE TEMPLE

41.13-15a

Four measurements are given:

13a. Measuring from east to west, the temple ($h\bar{e}k\bar{a}l + d^eb\bar{i}r$) is 100 cubits long: jamb 5 (40.48)+vestibule 12 (40.49) + jamb 6 (41.1) + nave 40 (41.2) + jamb 2 (41.3) + most holy place 20 (41.4) + wall 6 (41.5) + breadth of side chambers 4 (41.5) + outer wall 5 (41.9) = 100.

13b. From east to west, from west temple wall to west outside wall, 100 cubits: the yard behind the temple 20 + the wall 5 (v. 12) + the building 70 (v. 12) + outer wall 6 (40.5) = 100.

14. From north to south, the breadth of the east front of the house and the yard 100 cubits: yard 20 + 20 (41.10) + pave-

ment 5 + 5 (41.11) + outer walls of the side chambers 5 + 5
(41.9) + side chambers 4 + 4 (41.9) + temple walls 6 + 6
(41.5) + interior breadth of temple 20 (41.4) = 100.

15. The length of the building and its walls, 100 cubits—the
walls 5 + 5 (41.12) and the inside of the building 90 (v. 10).

The temple thus formed a perfect square.

DETAILS OF THE TEMPLE INTERIOR

41.15b-26

The text is almost hopelessly corrupt in parts, and the
passage may be secondary.

15b-16a. A possible rendering is: 'The nave, the inner part
(i.e. the most holy place), and its outer vestibule were panelled,
and the splayed windows (cf. 41.16) and the door frames
round all three of them, over against the threshold, were of
shāḥīp (i.e. black wood).' The rest of it may mean that
the panelling stretched FROM THE FLOOR TO THE WINDOWS,
and that THE WINDOWS WERE COVERED. The holy of holies in
Solomon's temple was in darkness.

17-20. These were decorations on the walls, covering them
from floor to roof in the form of CHERUBIM AND PALM TREES.
These were also in Solomon's temple (I Kings 6.29), and were
a common decorative motif of panelling and furniture inlay,
often being of gold (I Kings 6.28) or of ivory, as excavations
at Samaria have revealed where, as well as palm trees, sphinx
fragments, winged figures in human form, mythological and
other motifs were found.[4] In contrast to the beings with four

[4] See J. W. & G. M. Crawford, *Samaria-Sebaste II: Early Ivories
from Samaria*, London, 1957.

faces in 1.6 and ch. 10, the cherubim here have TWO FACES.
The Hebrew of v. 21 is untranslatable. It apparently refers
to the entrance of the nave. RSV follows LXX. This TABLE
WHICH IS BEFORE THE LORD is the table for the shewbread or
bread of the Presence, Ex. 25.23-30; Lev. 24.5-9. Such an
altar has also been found in Canaanite temples and Assyrian
monuments. The reason why it is called 'something resembling
an altar' is that, though it had the shape of an altar, it was in
fact a table. In I Kings 6.20 it is made of cedar, in Ex. 25.23f.
it is of acacia wood overlaid with pure gold. The shewbread,
twelve unleavened loaves, made from the finest flour, were
placed in two piles upon the table each sabbath. Originally
conceived as food for the deity, it came to be thought of as a
concrete expression of the fact that Yahweh was the source of
every material blessing. 'As the "continual bread" (Num. 4.7),
it became the standing expression of the nation's gratitude
to the Giver of all for the bounties of His Providence.'[5]

23-25a. The doors of the temple and the holy of holies were
EACH A DOUBLE DOOR. SWINGING: here again Ezekiel has
Solomon's temple in mind, I Kings 6.31-35.

25. The doors were decorated like the walls. And THERE WAS
A CANOPY OF WOOD IN FRONT OF THE VESTIBULE OUTSIDE: the
text here, and in v. 26, is uncertain.

THE PRIESTS' CHAMBERS

42.1-14

The text is again in great disorder, and the meaning is
often uncertain.

[5] A. R. S. Kennedy, Art. 'Shewbread', *HDB* IV, p. 497.

1. The prophet is brought from the vestibule of the temple into the INNER COURT to cells (CHAMBERS), one block of which faced THE TEMPLE YARD and the other THE BUILDING ON THE NORTH. They are thus north and south of the temple. As vv. 13f. make clear, these were for the use of the priests.

2. Only THE BUILDING ON THE NORTH is fully described. It was one hundred cubits long and fifty broad.

3. The TWENTY CUBITS are probably the space between the temple and the cells referred to in 41.10. GALLERY AGAINST GALLERY IN THREE STOREYS: uncertain. Galling thinks it means that the cells were in three rows on the slope leading from the outer court to the yard.

4. Perhaps read: 'And before the chambers there was a passage ten cubits broad and a (boundary) wall of one cubit, and their doors were on the north.'

5. The cells on the third story were smaller than those on the storeys below, because of the gallery which ran in front of them.

7. The situation and purpose of the wall are hard to determine.

8. The smaller block of chambers lying towards THE OUTER COURT was FIFTY CUBITS LONG. The block of chambers alongside the yard facing the temple was double that length.

9. Below these chambers BELOW, because the outer court was on a lower level than the temple platform on which the cells stood. The entrance was at the east end of the shorter block.

10-12. These verses describe the cells on the south side of the temple. The text is in confusion, but the building had the same plan as the one on the north side.

13-14. The use to which the cells were to be put. The priests are to EAT THE MOST HOLY OFFERINGS there. These are the three classes of offerings immediately spoken of, cf. 44.28-30. The PRIESTS WHO APPROACH THE LORD are the Zadokites, cf. 40.46; 44.15ff. 'These most holy things are only to be kept, and consumed, by holy persons in a holy place' (Lofthouse). The rooms also served as sacristies—when the priests had finished their service in the holy place, they were to deposit their 'holy' garments there before going out into the outer courtyard, cf. 44.19.

OVERALL MEASUREMENTS OF
THE TEMPLE AREA

42.15-20

When the angel finished measuring the INTERIOR OF THE TEMPLE AREA (15), which here means the whole complex of buildings within the walls, he brought the prophet back to the point from which they had started, the east gate, 40.6, and MEASURED THE TEMPLE AREA ROUND ABOUT. This area is a perfect square, about 850 feet on each side.

20. The HOLY is the temple area, the COMMON the land outside it, used for secular purposes. These two words, HOLY and COMMON, embody the purpose of all the architectural details and cultic regulations of chs. 40-48. They can be set against the background of the Deuteronomic reform and seen as an extension of it. The latter had given effect to the monotheism proclaimed by the prophets. But it was not enough to make the sanctuary in Jerusalem the one holy place. Its holiness, and with it the holiness of Yahweh, had to be safeguarded, cf. 43.7. Hence the principle of gradation seen in 40-42. First, the holy temple area is walled off from the secular world outside. Then, within it, secular men may come only so far—they may not go beyond the outer court—while the most holy place, where was the presence of Yahweh, might only be entered once a year, and that by the 'holiest' of men, the high priest. Stringent regulations were also laid down to ensure the ritual holiness of the ministering priests. To us there is something formal and even artificial about the whole thing, and it seems in contradiction with the 'new heart and the new spirit'. We must however, remember that it represented the dominant ideas of the time, and also, that before Ezekiel became a prophet he was a priest, and he never to any degree lost his priestly outlook.

THE RETURN OF THE GLORY OF YAHWEH

43.1-5

Now that all the temple area is ready, the glory of Yahweh may return. But the vision in 43.1-5 connects much more directly with that of the departure of the glory in 10.2-5, 18-19 and 11.22-23 than with what here immediately precedes it. The glory returns by the east door, through which it had departed before the temple and city were given over to fire, (10.19). Verses 2ff. stress the connection with the earlier visions—THE SOUND OF Yahweh's COMING WAS LIKE THE SOUND OF MANY WATERS, cf. 1.24; 3.12f.: Ezekiel falls UPON HIS FACE and is raised by THE SPIRIT, cf. 1.28–2.2

5. Brought me into the inner court 'He cannot enter the temple itself, because it is full of the brightness which radiates from the presence of God. The presence of God means destruction for men, cf. Ex. 19.21; 33.20; Isa. 6.5' (Ziegler).

THE GLORY . . . FILLED THE TEMPLE, as at the consecration of the first temple, I Kings 8.11.

THE ROYAL PROCLAMATION

43.6-9

As generally, the vision is followed by an audition.

6. one speaking The speaker is Yahweh, THE MAN is the guiding angel. 'The royal proclamation heard by the prophet directly echoes the oracle uttered by Solomon at the time of the dedication of the first temple (I Kings 8.12-13). It proves that Ezekiel was not able to adhere to the idea of a purely spiritual presence of Yahweh. He needs "a throne, a pedestal, a dwelling place" in the midst of the children of Israel. Yahweh certainly moved to the banks of the river Chebar and his dwelling place is in heaven, but he requires an earthly palace or, rather, men need to give it him in order there to receive the communication of his holiness' (Steinmann).

This idea of the future temple as God's dwelling-place with his holy people is a favourite one of Ezekiel's. The most holy place, the $d^{e}bîr$, is thought of as Yahweh's throne-room and his footstool. These were common concepts in the ancient East. For the Temple as a throne, see Jer. 3.17; 17.12; as footstool, Pss. 99.5, 9; 132.7; Lam. 2.1. Elsewhere Yahweh's throne is in heaven (I Kings 8.27; Isa. 66.1).

There is, however, a precondition for Yahweh's abiding presence with his people—the temple must be safeguarded from all profanation. There must be no more HARLOTRY. By this may be meant idolatry in general (cf. v. 8 and chs. 16, 23) or, more specifically, sacral prostitution carried on in the temple, II Kings 23.7. Further, the dead bodies of kings were to be removed. The Deuteronomic reform had conferred a new status on the temple. It now became the one legitimate place of worship for the kingdom. Hitherto it had been simply a chapel royal, separated from Solomon's palace only by a wall (cf. I Kings 7.8), and kings had been buried in the palace garden, II Kings 21.18, 26. Another royal burial place was the city of David, the hill on which the temple stood (I Kings 2.10; 11.43 etc.). Earlier times did not see any profanation in this, but Ezekiel is of the same mind as the Priestly writer, for whom any contact with the dead means uncleanness, cf. Num. 19.14-16. Verse 8, which is most probably an explanatory gloss, refers to the proximity of royal palace and temple. THRESHOLDS and DOORPOSTS may refer to tombs constructed to look like houses, but more probably to the royal palace.

A COMMAND TO THE PROPHET

43.10-11

The verses are probably in the wrong place: we should expect them after 42.20 as the conclusion of the description of the temple. They have also been expanded. If the words, THAT THEY MAY BE ASHAMED OF THEIR INIQUITIES are original, they should be taken as meaning 'if they are ashamed', as in the next verse. But they should probably be omitted in both places.

K

THE NEW LAWS FOR WORSHIP
43.12–46.24

12. The superscription of the new section on cultic laws.

THE ALTAR OF BURNT OFFERING
43.13-17

In 40.47 it was said that the altar was in the forecourt of the Temple. Originally this description of it may have stood at that point.

The altar is constructed of three square blocks, each having sides two cubits shorter than the block below it, but increasing in thickness. Its foundation or base (v. 13: lit. bosom of the earth), which is apparently let into the surrounding pavement so that its top is level with it, is one cubit high (so LXX) and one cubit broad, and round it a border (RIM) measuring A SPAN, HALF A CUBIT (17), to serve as a channel to carry away the blood.

14. the height of the altar The first block is a square of sixteen cubits, two cubits high, and one cubit recessed from the base. The middle block is fourteen by fourteen cubits, four cubits high, and again one cubit recessed.

15-16. On it stands the ALTAR HEARTH, twelve by twelve cubits and four cubits high, with HORNS at each corner one cubit in height. Thus, the total height of the altar was just over twenty feet. Each successive block signifies increasing holiness. It had steps on the east side. (In v. 17 the measurements of the first (lowest) blocks, sixteen by sixteen cubits, have almost certainly fallen out.)

13. The cubit is a cubit and a handbreadth Cf. 40.5: a 'long cubit'.

Albright believes that the altar represents Mesopotamian cosmic ideas. The 'bosom of the earth' (see on v. 13) is Akkadian (Galling however connects it with an Assyrian word meaning 'iron collar' and thinks of it as the outer band round the altar's base), while the word generally rendered HEARTH is again Akkadian, with 'the dual sense of "underworld" and "mountain of the gods", the cosmic mountain on which the gods were born and reared'.[1] The altar has clear connections with the Babylonian *ziggurat*. 'Ezechiel may have been thinking of the altar in the first temple, for he had himself seen it, but the shape of the new altar and the names given to its parts are of Babylonian inspiration, as in the symbolism which results. There is no evidence whatever that the altar built after the Return was modelled on the description given by the prophet.'[2]

The material of the altar is not given. According to Ex. 20.24-26, an altar could be of earth or of unhewn stone. Solomon's altar was of bronze: I Kings 8.64; II Kings 16.14; cf. II Chron. 4.1; the post-exilic altar was of unhewn stone: I Macc. 4.47.

15. Horns were a part of the altar, and are often mentioned in Exodus in connection with the altar of burnt-offering, e.g. Ex. 27.2. Horned altars have been found in excavations not only of Israelite and Canaanite cities, but also of Minoan ones. The original significance of the horns, a projection at each of the four corners of the upper surface, is unknown, but they probably represented in some way the strength of the deity.

17. Steps to an altar were originally forbidden in Israel, Ex.

[1] *Archaeology and the Religion of Israel*, 3rd edn., Baltimore, 1953, pp. 150-2.
[2] R. de Vaux, *Ancient Israel, its Life and Institutions*, ET, London, 1961, p. 412.

20.26, but the increasing size of altars led to their use as in
the world round about, cf. Baalbek, Petra, Ras Shamra.

THE CONSECRATION OF THE ALTAR

43.18-27

The passage has been edited, and has close affinities with
the Priestly writings, e.g. Ex. 28.36f.; 30.28; 40.10.

The idea underlying the consecration of the altar is 'the
inherent sinfulness of material things' which must be 'ex-
piated and removed' (Cooke). The act is the consecration of
the whole temple as well as of the altar itself. The speaker is
the angel. On the YOU in the passage, Cooke says: 'Ezekiel
appears to be the person addressed, but really it is Moses,
according to the convention adopted by the priestly legislators, who were engaged in committing to writing the rules
and customs which they administered or wished to introduce, cp. the commands given to 'Moses' in Ex. 29.36; 37;
30.26-29, and the execution of them in Lev. 8.11.'

18-19. The altar has two uses, the offering of burnt sacrifices
and the application of the BLOOD of sacrifice. The Zadokites
(see on 40.44). were to take a bullock as a sin offering. The
SIN OFFERING (see Lev. 4.27-35; Num. 15.27-29) is by far the
commonest rite in P, though, apart from Ezekiel, who lays
great stress upon expiatory rites, there are only two references
to it in the earlier literature (Micah 6.7; II Kings 12.16). It
effects cleansing for offences against cultic regulations, especially those committed inadvertently. Here it purifies the altar
from the contamination of the material and brings it within
the sphere of the 'holy'; 'the "sin" has thus nothing to do with
moral misdeeds' (Lofthouse).

20. A description of the rite of cleansing: some of the
bullock's blood is smeared on the horns of the altar with the

finger (Ex. 29.12; Lev. 4.7 etc.), on the four corners of the middle and lower blocks, and UPON THE RIM ROUND ABOUT. The effect of this is both to remove 'sin' (CLEANSE) and to expiate it (MAKE ATONEMENT FOR IT); it 'elevates the altar from a secular to a sacred status fit for its sacrificial purpose' (Rashi).

21-26. The consecration lasts for seven days.

21. On the first day the bullock is completely burnt somewhere outside the sacred precincts—THE APPOINTED PLACE is unknown, but Nehemiah (3.31) refers to the Gate of the Appointed Place (AV keeps the Hebrew word Miphkad, the word used here in Ezekiel; RSV translates Muster Gate), leading into the temple area from the east. This corresponds to the 'outside the camp' of Ex. 29.14; Lev. 4.12, 21; 8.17, etc.

22. The rite is repeated on the second day with a he-goat, and this is done on the succeeding days also (v. 25).

23. The altar is now cleansed from sin; a burnt offering of a bullock and a ram is therefore to be made: this continues daily for the space of the SEVEN DAYS (v. 25).

24. sprinkle salt upon them This is the only reference to salt in connection with the burnt offering. It was prescribed for the cereal offering in Lev. 2.13. The rabbis explained salt as a symbol of the covenant between Yahweh and Israel.

26-27. After SEVEN DAYS of such offerings (cf. the seven days of the consecration of the altar by Aaron, Ex. 29.36f.), the altar is consecrated; thereafter regular sacrifice may start. With the peace-offering, only the fat parts were burnt on the altar, and the flesh was eaten by the worshippers. 'This sacrificial act was always a social occasion . . . [It], more than any other, came into the category of a communion sacrifice—the participants knew Yahweh to be invisibly present as the guest of honour.'[3]

[3] G. von Rad, *Old Testament Theology* I, p. 257.

REGULATIONS FOR THE CULTIC PERSONNEL

44.1–45.17

A PREROGATIVE OF THE PRINCE

44.1-3

The angelic guide brings the prophet back from the inner court (43.5) to the east gate, which was shut and was to remain shut: now that Yahweh had entered in through it, no human foot might tread it. The prince, however, and he alone, may sit in the new vestibule of it when he eats a sacrificial meal. He is not, however, on this occasion to come in through the door, but to enter the outer court by some other gate and then come to the vestibule from the court.

In Ezekiel's scheme of things the prince, unlike his royal predecessors, had no priestly rights in the temple. But the privileges here accorded him may be a relic of sacral kingship in Israel.

The idea of the closed gate has a Babylonian counterpart —the holy east gate of the temple of Marduk was only opened for the images of the gods at their procession in the Marduk festival. Other reasons suggested for its closure are that it was a symbol that Yahweh would never again leave the temple (cf. 43.7), or, less probably, that the east gate could never again be used for such practices as the sun-worship described in ch. 8.

EXCLUSION OF FOREIGNERS

44.4-9

'The detailed and solemn introduction (4-5) shows that the

theme of the word which follows was particularly important for Ezekiel. Because of this he chose to clothe it in the form of an appearance in ecstasy' (Fohrer).

The prophet is brought from outside the east gate of the temple by the northern inner gateway, cf. 43.5. According to 46.1, the eastern inner gateway was shut on weekdays.

7. In 43.7f. Israel had been charged with desecrating the temple by harlotry and allowing kings to be buried in it. Here the rebellious house is charged with a different sort of ABOMINATION, the admission of FOREIGNERS. Since these were uncircumcised, the temple had been profaned. Ezekiel is thinking of temple-slaves who performed more menial duties, e.g. the Gibeonites, Josh. 9.23, 27, the Carites, II Kings 11.4-8, or the later Nethinim (men *given* to the sanctuary), Ezra 2.43-54; Neh. 7.46-56.

my food Kaufmann calls expressions such as this 'petrified linguistic survivals which by biblical times had lost their original significance. . . . That the classical prophets felt free to use these phrases is the best testimony to their innocence. Had the people at large believed that sacrifice was food for the deity, the prophets and legislators—who surely did not hold this view—would hardly have used such expressions which could only have lent support to what they must consider a gross error.'[4]

The exclusion of foreigners became all the stricter as time went on. Haggai (2.14), Ezra (4.3) and Nehemiah (13.7-9, 30) excluded those who had not been in exile and the Samaritans, who claimed Jewish blood, and in Herod's temple the outer court had a barrier beyond which no Gentile might pass on pain of death. As part of the same process, circumcision, as the mark of the covenant, was more strongly stressed in the post-exilic period.

[4] Y. Kaufmann, *The Religion of Israel*, p. 111.

THE LEVITES

44.10-14

The duties of the foreigners are to be taken over by the Levites. These had been the priests of the country sanctuaries before the reform of Josiah. Ezekiel, quite against the facts, regards the worship they had offered as idolatrous (10, 12). Deuteronomy, which did recognize them, made provision that such Levites might worship in the temple and receive a portion of the dues (Deut. 18.6-8). This however had not happened, perhaps because of the exclusiveness of the Jerusalem Zadokite priesthood (II Kings 23.9).

11. Now, with Ezekiel, 'what had come about *de facto* was now to be valid *de jure*' (Bertholet), or, as Wellhausen puts it, Ezekiel 'drapes the logic of facts with a mantle of morality'[5] —the Levites were no longer to be priests in full status, as they had been before the exile, but were to be no more than watchmen at THE GATES (see on 40.7) and MINISTERS in the temple, their ministry being to SLAY the sacrificial animals, to assist (ATTEND) the people in their ritual duties, and to work in the kitchens (46.24).

13. Only such Levites as were descended from Zadok—i.e. the Jerusalem priesthood—might serve as priests (COME NEAR TO ME).

Ezekiel thus occupies a position between that of Deuteronomy and that of the Priestly Code. He followed ancient usage in regarding the Levites as legitimate priests, but regards their loss of status after Josiah's reform as punishment for their 'idolatry'—i.e. ministering at shrines other than the temple. However, he proposes menial employment for them

[5] *Prolegomena to the History of Israel*, ET, Edinburgh, 1885 (reprinted New York, 1962), p. 124.

in the temple. P adopts Ezekiel's innovation, but regards the distinction in status between Zadokites and Levites as one which had existed from the beginning.

Later, the Levites' status improved, and they functioned as temple singers.

The section is therefore of great importance for the development of the priesthood in Israel.

REGULATIONS FOR THE ZADOKITES

44.15-31

17-18. The priestly vestments. When the priests enter THE INNER COURT, they are to WEAR LINEN GARMENTS, cf. Ex. 28.42, 39.27-29; Lev. 6.10; 16.4, 23. The same were prescribed for Egyptian and Syrian priests. Wool is prohibited, perhaps as causing sweat (18). Since holiness was thought of almost as something material, cf. Hag. 2.12, and might therefore attach to the priests's clothing, and so endanger laymen who came into contact with it (such are the implications of COMMUNICATE HOLINESS, v. 19), the priests must put off their official garments in the cells (42.14).

20-31. A series of regulations, not all or any of which necessarily came from Ezekiel himself.

20. Cf. Lev. 21.5, 10. Egyptian priests shaved their heads. It has been thought that the prohibition against allowing the hair to grow long was to make it impossible for priests to take certain vows (cf. Num. 6.5), since they would not be able to perform their office when under a vow.

21. They are not to DRINK WINE in the INNER COURT, cf. Lev. 10.9, also Hos. 4.11. Wine was the typical product of Canaan,

K*

and in abstaining from it the Rechabites protested against
Israel's adoption of the Canaanite civilization (Jer. 35).

22. Lev. 21.7 13ff. is less stringent, though there a distinction, as yet unknown to Ezekiel, is made between the high
priest and ordinary priests. Later, all Israelites were forbidden
intermarriage with foreigners, Ezra 9.12; Neh. 10.30; 13.23-30.

23. A main activity of the priesthood was to direct the people
on ceremonial matters of cleanness and uncleanness, cf. 22.26;
Lev. 10.10; Deut. 33.10; Mal. 2.7.

24. They have also certain judicial functions. Deuteronomy
had already laid down that in certain difficult cases, the
decision should be referred to a court in Jerusalem, part of
whom were Levitical priests, Deut. 17.8-13. Cf. also II Chron.
19.5-11. They are also to be an example to the people in
observing the laws concerning the festivals and the Sabbath,
cf. 22.26.

25-27. Contact with the dead brought ritual uncleanness,
therefore they were not to go near any dead body. Certain
exceptions are made, however, as in Lev. 21.1-3. The wife is
not included in them, the reason being that she was not a
blood relation. Verses 26f. are probably a secondary gloss
dependent on Lev. 15.13, 28.

**26. After he is defiled, he shall count for himself seven days,
and then he shall be clean** The meaning is not certain. RSV
accords with P (Num. 19.11, 13, 14; 31.19). But Kimchi
explains the regulation as meaning that after a priest has
become clean at the end of seven days, he has to wait another
seven days until he enters the sanctuary. HE SHALL COUNT:
AV follows MT in reading 'they shall reckon'. Kimchi says
that 'they' are his fellow priests, who are to prevent him from

entering the sanctuary if he himself forgets the special regulation for priests.

28-30. Maintenance of the priests.

28. They shall have no inheritance Since Yahweh provides for them, they need no earthly inheritance (cf. Deut. 10.9; 18.2; Josh. 13.14, 33; 18.7). As provision they are assigned THE CEREAL OFFERING (cf. 45.24; 46.5, 7, 11, 14; Lev. 2.3; 7.9f.), THE SIN OFFERING and the trespass or GUILT OFFERING (cf. Lev. 6.17; 7.1ff.; Num. 18.9f.), EVERY DEVOTED THING (cf. Lev. 27.28; Num. 18.19), THE FIRST FRUITS (see below), the various oblations (cf. Lev. 27.28; Num. 18.14), THE FIRST OF the COARSE MEAL (cf. Num. 15.20f.).

29. every devoted thing 'All kinds of property consecrated to God which could not be redeemed and had to be given to the priests' (Fisch).

30. the first of all the first fruits Rather 'the best . . .', cf. 20.40. First fruits are commanded to be offered in Ex. 34.26a=23.19 (E). They are specified in Deut. 18.4; 26.1-11, and are to be given to priests and Levites. Num. 18.25-32 also makes this provision for the Levites, but they are not mentioned here.

31. Cf. 4.14; Lev. 22.8. This prohibition applies to all Israelites, laymen as well as priests (Ex. 22.31; Deut. 14.21). The verse is secondary.

THE ALLOTMENT OF THE LAND: THE OBLATION
FOR YAHWEH

45.1-8

The passage allots the land. (See map on p. 314.) Territory is

to be set apart for the temple, the maintenance of the priests,
the Levites, and the prince. The verses are, however, out of
place here. In subject matter they go with 47.13–48.35, and
are paralleled in 48.8-15. It is uncertain whether the passage
owes anything to Ezekiel.

The restoration of Israel demands a re-allocation of the
land.

1. While the whole land is Yahweh's, the territory here mentioned is specially set aside for him, A HOLY DISTRICT, which,
as 48.8, 23 show, lies between Benjamin and Judah. It is to
be twenty-five thousand cubits long by twenty thousand cubits
broad. (No word for 'cubits' stands in the Heb., but the
parallel passage 48.8ff. implies cubits. LXX gives twenty
thousand for MT ten thousand. MT would exclude the
Levites' land.)

4. This verse should follow 1: this land is for the priests, for
their houses and perhaps (since A HOLY PLACE FOR THE
SANCTUARY is corrupt) for pasture lands and for the cattle.

2. Of this priestly territory an area five hundred cubits square
is set apart from the temple. This is surrounded by a strip of
land fifty cubits wide to be an OPEN SPACE. (Nothing is said
of this in 42.20, which speaks of a wall separating the holy
from the profane. Both passages cannot come from the same
hand.)

3, 5. The final clause of v. 3 is uncertain, but the emergent
picture is this. The whole area mentioned in v. 1 is divided
into halves, each twenty thousand by ten thousand cubits.
The southern part belongs to the Zadokite priests, (although
provision has already been made for them, 44.28-30), the
northern to the Levites, cf. 48.10-14. In the middle of the
southern half stands the sanctuary.

6. An additional twenty-five thousand by five thousand cubits parallel to the priests' portion belong to THE WHOLE HOUSE OF ISRAEL, the state.

7. The prince is then assigned land on either side of the area assigned to Levites, priests and the state, equal to it in extent (twenty-five thousand cubits), and bounded on the east and west by the Jordan and the Mediterranean respectively. For CORRESPONDING IN LENGTH. . . PORTIONS, read 'parallel to one of the (tribal) portions' (Cooke), implying that the land has already been divided among the tribes, as is described in 47.13–48.7.

8. This generous provision is to prevent oppression on the part of the prince. THEY SHALL LET THE HOUSE OF ISRAEL HAVE THE LAND . . . means that the princes will let the people have the rest of the land and not encroach upon it, cf. 46.18.

THE SECULAR DUTIES OF THE PRINCE

45.9-12

9. Enough No more of your oppressions! To EXECUTE JUSTICE AND RIGHTEOUSNESS was a regular demand of the earlier prophets, cf. Amos 5.7; Isa. 1.17, while Micah in particular complained of violence and oppression on the part of the wealthy and powerful (Micah 2.2, 9; cf. Isa. 5.8; Jer. 22.13-17). EVICTIONS, a word occurring only here, means treatment such as Ahab's treatment of Naboth (I Kings 21), cf. Isa. 5.8. With Ezekiel's picture of the ideal future ruler cf. Jer. 21.11f.; 22.1-5.

10-12. just balances There had been much dishonesty in business, cf. Hos. 12.8; Amos 8.5; Micah 6.10f. The demand for just weights and measures appears throughout the OT, cf. Lev. 19.35-36 (H); Deut. 25.13-16; Prov. 11.1; 16.11. 'These definitions of old measures are given to avoid the capricious alterations of the kings in time past' (Lofthouse). 'The homer is assumed as the standard both for liquid and dry measures. The ephah was a tenth of a homer, dry measure; and the bath a tenth of the homer, liquid measure, Isa. 5.10' (Davidson). The ephah was equivalent to a bushel, the bath to about nine gallons.

12. Five shekels shall be five shekels The meaning is that the shekel is to be exact. There was to be no trimming of metal from it, as was common before the use of milling. The mina was the standard, the shekel weighed one fiftieth of a mina, and the gerah, the smallest weight, a thousandth of a mina.

THE OFFERINGS FOR SACRIFICE

45.13-15

Those addressed are the people, but those to whom the offering is to be made are not clear. Most commentators understand the prince, but some (e.g. Cooke) think of the priests.

14. The regulation for oil (is) a tenth of a bath from each cor; ten baths make one cor.

15. The meaning is ONE SHEEP out of every TWO HUNDRED. FROM THE FAMILIES OF ISRAEL probably means 'as offering for the families of Israel'. The offerings mentioned in vv. 13-15 are to be used for the cereal offering etc.—for these see on 44.29.

THE PRINCE'S SACRIFICIAL DUTIES

45.16-17

If the dues in 13-15 were in fact paid to the priests, others of a similar kind were to be provided by THE PEOPLE . . . TO THE PRINCE, from which he must furnish what was needed for the offerings listed in v. 17. 'The list differs from that in v. 15, and conforms to P's rule for the daily, weekly, monthly and festival sacrifices, Ex. 29.41; Lev. 23.37; Num. 28.3-8, 9; 29.39' (Cooke). DRINK OFFERINGS: libations (cf. 20.28; Gen. 35.14; Num. 15.5).

THE FESTIVAL CALENDAR

45.18-25

18-20. Sacrifice to purify the sanctuary is to be made twice a year, ON THE FIRST DAY OF THE FIRST MONTH (Nisan, March-April, New Year), and on the first day of the seventh month (Tishri, September-October, the beginning of the second half of the year). (In v. 20 read with LXX 'in the seventh month on the first day of the month'.) In Lev. 16; 23.27-32 (P); Num. 29.7-11 (P); Ex. 30.10 there is only one such day of expiation and it takes place on the tenth day of the seventh month. For a young bullock as sin offering, cf. Ex. 29.36 (P); Lev. 16.3, 5. Verse 19 is generally taken as a secondary expansion. LEDGE: cf. 43.20.

20. Any one who has sinned through error or ignorance For sins committed unwittingly or through ignorance, cf. Num. 15.22-31. 'In spite of all precautions there may be error or misunderstanding; Ezekiel does not mention wilful sins. But the atonement is made, not directly for such error, but for the ceremonial impurity thus caused to the temple (an idea not found in Lev. 16): cf. 44.27' (Lofthouse).

21-25. Passover and the Harvest Festival. Ezekiel's regulations stand midway between those of D and those of P. 'In Ezekiel the festivals lose all their old character, partly surviving in Deut. 16, of agricultural rejoicings, and Whitsuntide ("Weeks") drops out altogether, though it occurs in both Ex. 23.16; Deut. 16.10; and the Priests' Code. In each case the stated offerings differ from the parallel offerings in the Priests' code; sometimes one, sometimes the other is more costly. Like the Priests' code, but unlike the earlier legislation, Ezekiel fixes his festivals by the days of the month; on the other hand, he is never in direct contradiction to Deuteronomy, and he assigns as the length of his festivals, not eight days (as the Priests' code), but seven (as Deuteronomy: cf. also I Kings 8.66; II Chron. 7.9; Neh. 8.18)' (Lofthouse). Ezekiel's instructions 'are at variance with those recorded in Numbers and elsewhere, proving that the cultic practice of a dynamic faith changes with time'.[6]

21. In the first month This means the festival of Passover. A sin offering at Passover is a new feature in Ezekiel.

24. Josephus says a HIN is a sixth of a bath. Ezekiel makes no mention of the Passover lamb.

25. In the seventh month This means the festival of Tabernacles. THE SAME PROVISION, i.e. as for Passover.

The Harvest Festival was 'the feast *par excellence* of the year, concluding the round of festivals (Isa. 29.1)' (Davidson), cf. Judg. 21.19ff.; I Kings 8.2; 12.32ff. It is called the feast of the Ingathering in Ex. 23.16; 34.22. It celebrated the vintage, but Ezekiel says nothing of the booths.

[6] Howie, *Ezekiel, Daniel*, p. 84.

THE PRINCE'S OFFERING FOR SABBATH
AND NEW MOON

46.1-8

1-3. The outer east gate is always to be kept shut, since Yahweh had entered the temple through it, 44.1f.; the inner gate is to be opened on the sabbath and the new moon, the latter of which was the first day of the month. The prince enters from the outer court into the vestibule of the inner gate, passes through the length of the gate and takes his stand at its exit at the door-post, from which point he can see what takes place at the altar in the inner court, though he may not enter that court itself. THE PRIESTS SHALL OFFER HIS BURNT OFFERING: This is a circumscription of the prince's rights of access as compared with earlier usage (cf. I Kings 8.22; II Kings 16.12, 18; 23.3). The people also offer their worship at the entrance of the inner gate.

4-5. On the sabbath the prince's burnt offering is SIX LAMBS AND A RAM, the six lambs corresponding to the six working days of the week, the ram to the seventh. P (Num. 28.9) demands two lambs only, as well as the CEREAL OFFERING. The latter is an ephah of flour with the ram, whatever the prince cares to give with the lambs, and a libation of a hin of oil.

6-7. Ezekiel's regulations for the prince's new moon offerings also differ from those of P, which prescribe two bullocks, seven lambs and a ram, with differences too in the cereal offering (Num. 28.11-15). The new moon festival was ancient, reaching back into nomadic days (cf. I Sam. 20.5; II Kings 4.23; Hos. 2.11; Amos 8.5; Isa. 1.13, in all of which except the first it is mentioned in conjunction with the sabbath). The earlier law codes ignore the new moon festival.

ARRANGEMENTS FOR ENTERING AND LEAVING
THE TEMPLE

46.9-10

The temple area was relatively small, and at the APPOINTED FEASTS, the three great festivals of Passover, Weeks and Tabernacles (45.18-25), which all were bound to attend (as distinct from the festivals of the sabbath and new moon), great concourses of pilgrims gathered in Jerusalem, e.g. Ezra 10.1. So regulations were required to prevent confusion.

10. When they go in, the prince shall go in with them; and when they go out, he shall go out. THEY are the ordinary pilgrims, THE PEOPLE OF THE LAND (v. 9). The meaning seems to be that the prince has no special time of access private to himself. He is to worship at the same time as the rest and with them, a further limitation of any royal pretensions. Kimchi, however, (cited by Fisch), says that it accords with the honour and dignity of a ruler to be with his people.

SUNDRY REGULATIONS FOR OFFERINGS

46.11-15

11. The CEREAL OFFERING at the pilgrimage festivals (FEASTS) is the same as that at the sabbath and new moon (APPOINTED SEASONS), cf. vv. 5, 7. ONE is not the prince, but the ordinary worshipper.

12. When the prince makes a private FREEWILL OFFERING on a weekday, the east gate is to be opened, then closed immediately he leaves. This contradicts v. 2, and seems (in contrast with v. 10) to imply a privilege for the prince. The freewill offering was one made in addition to the obligatory offerings, out of benevolence, thankfulness, etc. See Lev. 7.16; 22.18-23; Num. 15.3; Deut. 12.6; 16.10; 23.23; Amos 4.5.

13-15. *The daily sacrifice*

13. He shall provide This makes the prince responsible for providing the daily sacrifice also. Daily sacrifice had been offered in both of the former kingdoms (I Kings 18.29, 36; II Kings 16.15). Ezekiel and P again differ (P Ex. 29.38-42; Num. 28.3-8). Ezekiel speaks only of a morning offering, but P prescribes an evening one as well. P: tenth of an ephah of fine flour, a fourth of a hin of oil, and a libation of a fourth of a hin of wine.

THE PROPERTY OF THE PRINCE

46.16-18

This is an addition to what is said about the prince's land in 45.7-8.

'As in other agrarian societies, the greatest evils occurred in connection with land ownership. Most people could have economic independence only if they owned land. Ezekiel's constitution for the restored commonwealth, therefore, gives land-ownership special protection.'[7]

When the prince makes a gift of a portion of his land to his sons, it remains their permanent property and passes on to their heirs, cf. II Chron. 21.1-3. But when he does the same to his officials, they may only enjoy it till the YEAR OF LIBERTY, when it reverts to the prince.

17. year of liberty Lev. 25.10 speaks of the year of jubilee,

[7] I. Mattuck, *The Thought of the Prophets*, p. 93.

the fiftieth year, 'when each of you shall return to his property'. This may be what is thought of here. Others, however, believe it to be the sabbatical year, every seventh year, cf. Jer. 34.14; Ex. 21.2; Deut. 15.12, also Lev. 25.2-7. Cooke is probably right when he prefers the former: 'a fifty years' tenure is more probable than one of seven years.'

18. In Israel all land belonged to Yahweh, as in Scots and English law all land belongs to the crown. Cf. 45.8.

KITCHENS FOR THE SACRIFICES

46.19-24

This section belongs to the vision, as the HE of v. 19 (the angel) makes clear. If its position is original, and this is doubtful, Ezekiel is brought from the front of the temple (44.4) by the northern door (42.9) to the northern block of priests' cells, where the priests were to eat the most sacred offerings (42.13). Somewhere to the west of them was a place where the priests were to boil the guilt offering and the sin offering and bake the cereal offering. These were offerings to be eaten by the priests exclusively, and were not to be brought into the outer court where they might communicate holiness to the laity, see on 44.19.

21-24. In the outer court there were similar kitchens where the Levites cooked the offerings of which the people could partake—note again the characteristic distinction between priesthood and laity: the priests' sacrifices and those of the people represent different degrees of holiness, and must therefore not be brought into contact. The verses are not from Ezekiel.

THE LAND

47.1-48.35

Now that the temple, enshrining the glory of God, and symbolizing his presence with his restored people Israel, is complete, blessing spreads out from this focal point all over the land.

WATERS ISSUING FROM THE TEMPLE

47.1-12

'The new age is a new creation and properly has its paradise, with its sacred river and trees' (May). The background of the passage is the mythological motif of the river of God with its life-giving streams. Gen. 2.10 speaks of the river which flowed out of Paradise and became the four world rivers, and Ps. 46.4 of 'the river whose streams make glad the city of God'. Zechariah (later than Ezekiel) says: 'On that day living waters shall flow out from Jerusalem, half of them to the eastern sea (i.e. the Dead Sea) and half of them to the western' (i.e. the Mediterranean), (Zech. 14.8). In Joel the stream comes from the temple (3.18), and in Rev. 22.1 the river issues from the throne of God and of the Lamb, cf. also John 4.14; 7.37f. With Ezekiel the stream, which will be supplied with its water from the great deep (cf. 17.8; 19.10), issues FROM BELOW THE THRESHOLD OF THE TEMPLE and flows eastward, flowing down on the south side of the temple, on the south of the altar.

2. was coming out Trickled. As the following verses show, the stream is to increase in volume.

5. river A torrent.

6-12. *The significance of the vision*

7. The wadi from Jerusalem down to the Dead Sea area had been treeless. But now it is to have many trees, cf. v. 12.

8. toward the eastern region The desert country east of Jerusalem. The desert is the 'Arabah, the depression which contains the Jordan and the Dead Sea and terminates in the gulf of Elath (the part south of the Dead Sea is still called Wadi el 'Arabah). THE SEA is the Dead Sea. It has 'deep saline deposits along the shores at various points, and probably also at the bottom of the sea' (Cooke).

9-10. The text is confused, but the meaning plain. No fish can live in the Dead Sea, but the stream (RIVER) will change all this and fishermen will stand on its once desolate shore fishing. 'The diction [of v. 9] recalls that of Gen. 1, perhaps in an earlier form, and suggests something of the new creation ideology that is involved' (May). EN-GEDI ('the spring of the goat') is about half way down the west side of the Dead Sea, the modern Tel-ej-Jurn. EN-EGLAIM ('the spring of the calf') is probably the modern Ain Feshkhah, two miles south of Qumran where the Dead Sea Scrolls were found. The end of v. 10 means that the fish will be of many kinds, as in the Mediterranean. 'Again we have the message of the gospel as we had it in ch. 37. It is the glory of God that he can achieve the impossible, giving life to the dead.'[1]

11. SWAMPS AND MARSHES are to be retained in order that there may still remain a supply of SALT.

12. The trees, too, have mythological connections, cf. the

[1] E. L. Allen in *The Interpreter's Bible* 6, p. 238.

tree of life, Gen. 2.9. THEIR LEAVES WILL NOT WITHER: cf. Ps. 1.3. HEALING, medicinal purposes. All this new life is ultimately due to God's renewed presence in the sanctuary.

'As yet the Israelite had no conception of a transcendent sphere of existence for men in the fellowship of God, such as we name heaven. Man's final abode even in his perfect state was considered to be still on the earth. God came down and dwelt with men; men were not translated to abide with God. But God's presence with men on earth gave to earth the attributes of heaven. Yet man's needs remained, and God's presence was the source of all things necessary to supply them' (Davidson).

Water is a purifier. When we first met the temple, it was polluted (chs. 8-11). The vision of the new temple closes with the health-giving waters that issue from it. God is now the well-spring of Israel's whole life. And since THE WATER is 'living' (John 4.10), Israel is to be God's holy people in perpetuity.

THE BOUNDARIES OF THE NEW HOLY LAND

47.13-21

This section was anticipated in 45.1-8.

The land, which here is the land west of Jordan (v. 18), is to be equally divided among the twelve tribes. JOSEPH, or more precisely his two sons, Ephraim and Manasseh (cf. 48.4f.) are to receive TWO PORTIONS, since for Levi (the priesthood) provision had already been made (45.1-8). The number thus remains at twelve.

The boundaries of the land are symbolic of the outlook and practice of post-exilic Judaism. Since foreign influences were regarded as a main cause of the exile, steps were taken to minimize them for the future. Renewed stress was laid on things particularly Jewish, for example circumcision and the food-laws, the latter of which makes social contact between Jew and Gentile difficult. Ezekiel himself excluded foreigners from the sanctuary (44.9). The borders too—a mountain-mass, a river, a river-valley, the desert and the sea—together with the abandonment of all territorial claims or aspirations east of Jordan, suggest a people living its own life in isolation. All dreams of political grandeur are over, and Israel is now a church rather than a state.

P also gives a description of the boundaries (Num. 34.1-15, cf. Josh. 15.1-4, the southern boundary). They are in general agreement, except that P settles two and a half tribes east of Jordan. Both ignore the older idea that Israel's territory should stretch from the Nile to the Euphrates (Gen. 15.18; Ex. 23.31; Deut. 1.7 etc.).

14a. Each tribe is to possess the same amount of territory. The granting of the land to the patriarchs (e.g. Gen. 12.7 and repeated) is confirmed by oath (see on 20.5 and cf. Gen. 22.16f.).

15-17. The northern boundary runs from the Mediterranean (THE GREAT SEA) eastward TO THE ENTRANCE OF HAMATH and the boundary of Hauran. The identification of the places is not certain. Hamath, now Hama, on the Orontes, indicates the depression between Lebanon and Hermon. It marked the limit of David's and Solomon's kingdom, and is mentioned as the ideal boundary, cf. Num. 34.8; Josh. 13.5, etc. HETHLON may be north of the mouth of the Nahr el-Kâsimîjeh, just north of Tyre. HAZAR-ENON, at the western end, may be the modern Banias, at the source of the Jordan. HAURAN is approximately Bashan. Verse 17 mentions the districts which now lie outside Israel. It should read, 'The (north) boundary shall run from the sea to Hazar-enon, the territory of

Damascus lying northward beside the territory of Hamath.
This is the northern boundary.'

18. The eastern boundary is the Jordan, starting FROM
HAZAR-ENON, WHICH IS BETWEEN HAURAN AND DAMASCUS, then
along the Jordan between Gilead (east of Jordan) and the
Israelite territory (west of Jordan), to the Dead Sea (THE
EASTERN SEA), AS FAR AS TAMAR. Tamar is somewhere south-
west of the Dead Sea. The land east of Jordan, Gilead, is thus
excluded, though it was earlier possessed by the Israelites.
(The boundary list in Num. 34.1-12 also excludes Trans-
jordania.)

19. The southern boundary (cf. 48.28) runs FROM TAMAR AS
FAR AS THE WATERS OF MERIBATH-KADESH, THENCE ALONG THE
BROOK OF EGYPT TO THE GREAT SEA. For Meribath-Kadesh,
see Num. 20.1-13. It is the district round Ain Kadeis. The
Brook of Egypt is the present Wadi-el-Arish.

20. The western boundary is the Mediterranean from the
Brook of Egypt to a point opposite Hamath, see on 15. Cf.
also I Kings 8.65 for the same extent, north and south, of
Solomon's kingdom.

21-23. Foreigners who have settled permanently in Israel and
borne sons are to be treated as native Israelites for the purpose of land allocation. This is in line with the provisions in
H and P (Lev. 16.29; 17.15; 24.22; 25.45; Num. 15.29f. etc.,
cf. also Isa. 56.3-7). These would presumably be, as LXX
suggests, proselytes, that is, resident aliens who had embraced
Judaism. Their inclusion would serve to augment the population, cf. 36.37f. It may be noted that, in contrast with Second
Isaiah, there is no thought here of Israel as missionary. Non-
Jews who accept Judaism are welcomed, but nothing more.
This is typical of Judaism to this day.

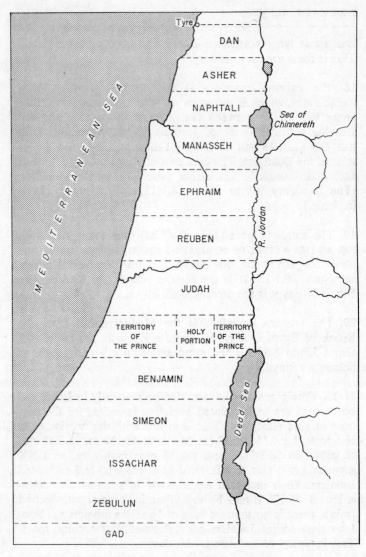

THE REDISTRIBUTED LAND

ALLOCATION OF LAND TO THE TWELVE TRIBES

48.1-7, 23-29

An equal area is to be allotted to all the tribes, and since
Jerusalem is not in the exact centre of the land, seven tribes
are placed to the north of it, and five to the south. Judah and
Benjamin are given the places of importance on either side
of the portion set apart (see vv. 8, 22), Judah on the north of
it, Benjamin on the south. Verse 1 is not clear, but it re-states
the northern border as given in the previous chapter, and says
that the most northerly tribe is Dan. EXTENDING FROM THE
EAST SIDE TO THE WEST means that Dan—and all the rest of
the tribes—occupy the whole area from east to west. Dan's
location follows historical facts, for Dan was always regarded
as the northern boundary of Israel, cf. II Sam. 3.10. Then
follow, from north to south, Asher, Naphtali, Manasseh,
Ephraim, Reuben and Judah. South of the portion set apart,
again reading from north to south, are (22ff.) Benjamin,
Simeon, Issachar, Zebulun and Gad.

The sons of Leah and Rachel are placed nearest the holy
area, four on either side. Manasseh and Ephraim reckon as
Joseph, since Levi has no portion, cf. 47.13. The sons of the
concubines, Dan and Naphtali (Bilhah) and Asher and Gad
(Zilpah), are set furthest away from the holy area—as
though the most privileged positions were determined by rela-
tive purity of blood. In Num. 2 (P) there is a somewhat similar
grouping of the tribes round the Tent.

THE PORTION SET APART

48.8-22

With this section cf. 45.1-8, which treated the subject more
briefly. It is probably a later addition.

The portion set apart lies between the territories of Judah (on the north) and Benjamin (on the south), and includes the territory of the priests and of the Levites, the city and the land belonging to it, and also the prince's domain. Its area is twenty-five thousand cubits from north to south, and from east to west the same length as each of the tribal territories, that is, it stretched from the Mediterranean to the Jordan.

9. In the centre is the portion set apart for Yahweh. Its length from east to west is twenty-five thousand cubits. MT gives the distance from north to south as ten thousand cubits. But this can only refer to either the priests' domain (v. 10) or the Levites' (v. 13), and we should read either twenty-five thousand cubits with LXX, to harmonize with v. 8—this would give a square including the city—or twenty thousand cubits with LXX of 45.1, which would take in the priests' and Levites' territories, but not the city and its land.

10-12. The central part is the priests' portion, with the temple area in the middle of it. It measures twenty-five thousand cubits on the north and south and ten thousand on the west and east. This is reserved for the Zadokite priests, see 44.15. For the charge made against the Levites, see on 44.10.

13-14. To the north of this and equal in area is the territory of the Levites. This land is inalienable. 'Since it is holy, to sell it would mean degradation to ordinary uses, i.e. profanation' (Lofthouse). It is described as THIS CHOICE PORTION OF THE LAND. The regulations about alienation in Lev. 25.32-34 are less stringent.

15-20. The area to the south of the priests' portion, five thousand cubits from north to south, and twenty-five thousand cubits from east to west (about seven miles by one and a half miles), is for Jerusalem and its territory. This means that the city is no longer to contain the temple. Since the temple retains its original hallowed site on Mount Moriah, the city has to be moved to the south of its original location. FOR ORDINARY USE FOR THE CITY: land not consecrated to Yahweh, and therefore available for secular uses. The measurements for the city (16) and for the OPEN LAND (17), a free space on all four sides of it, (cf. the open space around the temple in 45.2), are in cubits. The city is thus about one and a half miles square.

18. The portions of land east and west of the city, each of about four square miles, are to supply the city with food. Omit AND IT SHALL BE ALONGSIDE OF THE HOLY PORTION (dittography).

20. The area of the whole portion set apart, including the city, is TWENTY-FIVE THOUSAND CUBITS SQUARE.

21-22. The prince's portion. The text is confused, but the meaning is that all the land to the east of this square, reaching to the Jordan, and to the west of it, reaching to the Mediterranean, belongs to the prince. This land is bounded on the north by the portion of Judah, and on the south by that of Benjamin. The reason why the prince is given so large a possession is not prestige, for he has a singularly unimportant role in the new community, but that he has to provide the sacrifices, cf. 45.17.

THE CITY'S GATES AND ITS NEW NAME

48.30-35

'Like the tribal divisions, so the plan of the city is purely theoretical: the four sides are equal in length; each of the twelve gates is called after one of the tribes; the name is changed. In other words, the city represents an ideal of orderly arrangement, of security and protection, of a common centre for the whole nation, and of a religious character imparted by Jahveh's Presence. Ezekiel's teaching in ch. 18 and 37.15-22 had not been in vain: we can trace the effects of it here on the mind of a later generation, and, still later, upon the Christian ideal, Rev. 21.12, 13' (Cooke).

30-34. On the north and south sides, going from west to east, are the gates of the six sons of Leah. In order that Levi may come in, Joseph is now represented by himself, and not, as in the allocation of the land to the tribes, by his two sons (47.13). The gates on the east are the two Rachel tribes, Joseph and Benjamin, and Dan, the son of Rachel's handmaid, while on the west are the other three concubine tribes, Gad and Asher (Leah) and Naphtali (Rachel).

35. The circumference of the city is about five miles, cf. vv. 16f. The city is to have a new name: THE LORD IS THERE. As Cooke points out, 'the ideal *city* of the future becomes Jahveh's dwelling-place. This goes further than 43.1-9, which described Jahveh's return to the ideal *temple*; but Ezekiel's own teaching promised that Jahveh would dwell above and in the midst of His people for ever, 37.26-28'. Thus, in a sense, in the restored community the profane as well as the sacred is holy to Yahweh (cf. Zech. 14.20), for Ezekiel has insisted that the new city stands on non-holy soil. Another apparent paradox is that of continuity and discontinuity. The tribes link up with the nation's ancient past, but the old Canaanite name of Jerusalem (and, by implication, all heathen influences) are abolished, and a new name given.

Speaking of the book's curious final paradox, Steinmann says: 'On the one hand, Ezekiel wishes to blot out the old Jerusalem from the land and abolish its history. He accepts the entire destruction of past, and in this he already acts like Jesus and seems to prepare the way for the future prophecy of destruction made in the Gospel. On the other hand, because of his theocratic dreams, Ezekiel was to become the prophetic type of the Judaism which later was to use all its resources to oppose Christianity at its birth.

'In a word, Ezekiel was rich enough and contradictory enough to prepare at one and the same time for the coming of Judaism and the coming of a Christianity which, while showing every respect for Jerusalem, was to suppress its hegemony in religion.'